# Islam
## Opposing Viewpoints®

Other Books of Related Interest in the Opposing Viewpoints Series:

# Islam
## Opposing Viewpoints®

David Bender & Bruno Leone, *Series Editors*

Paul A. Winters, *Book Editor*

OPPOSING
VIEWPOINTS
SERIES®

Greenhaven Press, Inc., San Diego, CA

Greenhaven Press, Inc.
PO Box 289009
San Diego, CA 92198-9009

Cover photo: Rocky Thies

Library of Congress Cataloging-in-Publication Data

Islam : opposing viewpoints / Paul A. Winters, book editor.
    p.    cm. — (Opposing viewpoints series)
  Includes bibliographical references (p.   ) and index.
  Summary: Presents opposing viewpoints on the role of religion in Islamic countries.
  ISBN 1-56510-248-7 (lib. : acid-free paper) —
ISBN 1-56510-247-9 (pbk. : acid-free paper).
  1. Islam and politics [1. Islam.] I. Winters, Paul A.,  1965–
II. Series: Opposing viewpoints series (Unnumbered)
BP173.7.I854   1995
320.5'5'0917671—dc20                          94-41044
                                                CIP
                                                 AC

"Congress shall make no law . . . abridging the freedom of speech, or of the press."

First Amendment to the U.S. Constitution

The basic foundation of our democracy is the First Amendment guarantee of freedom of expression. The Opposing Viewpoints Series is dedicated to the concept of this basic freedom and the idea that it is more important to practice it than to enshrine it.

# Contents

## Chapter 4: Does Political Islam Promote Terrorism?

## Chapter 5: Is the Islamic World a Threat to the West?

## Chapter 6: Is Islam Uniting the Islamic World?

# Why Consider Opposing Viewpoints?

*"The only way in which a human being can make some approach to knowing the whole of a subject is by hearing what can be said about it by persons of every variety of opinion and studying all modes in which it can be looked at by every character of mind. No wise man ever acquired his wisdom in any mode but this."*

John Stuart Mill

In our media-intensive culture it is not difficult to find differing opinions. Thousands of newspapers and magazines and dozens of radio and television talk shows resound with differing points of view. The difficulty lies in deciding which opinion to agree with and which "experts" seem the most credible. The more inundated we become with differing opinions and claims, the more essential it is to hone critical reading and thinking skills to evaluate these ideas. Opposing Viewpoints books address this problem directly by presenting stimulating debates that can be used to enhance and teach these skills. The varied opinions contained in each book examine many different aspects of a single issue. While examining these conveniently edited opposing views, readers can develop critical thinking skills such as the ability to compare and contrast authors' credibility, facts, argumentation styles, use of persuasive techniques, and other stylistic tools. In short, the Opposing Viewpoints Series is an ideal way to attain the higher-level thinking and reading skills so essential in a culture of diverse and contradictory opinions.

In addition to providing a tool for critical thinking, Opposing Viewpoints books challenge readers to question their own strongly held opinions and assumptions. Most people form their opinions on the basis of upbringing, peer pressure, and personal, cultural, or professional bias. By reading carefully balanced opposing views, readers must directly confront new ideas as well as the opinions of those with whom they disagree. This is not to simplistically argue that everyone who reads opposing views will—or should—change his or her opinion. Instead, the series enhances readers' depth of understanding of their own views by encouraging confrontation with opposing ideas. Careful examination of others' views can lead to the readers' understanding of the logical inconsistencies in their own opinions, perspective on why they hold an opinion, and the consideration of the possibility that their opinion requires further evaluation.

## Evaluating Other Opinions

To ensure that this type of examination occurs, Opposing Viewpoints books present all types of opinions. Prominent spokespeople on different sides of each issue as well as well-known professionals from many disciplines challenge the reader. An additional goal of the series is to provide a forum for other, less known, or even unpopular viewpoints. The opinion of an ordinary person who has had to make the decision to cut off life support from a terminally ill relative, for example, may be just as valuable and provide just as much insight as a medical ethicist's professional opinion. The editors have two additional purposes in including these less known views. One, the editors encourage readers to respect others' opinions—even when not enhanced by professional credibility. It is only by reading or listening to and objectively evaluating others' ideas that one can determine whether they are worthy of consideration. Two, the inclusion of such viewpoints encourages the important critical thinking skill of objectively evaluating an author's credentials and bias. This evaluation will illuminate an author's reasons for taking a particular stance on an issue and will aid in readers' evaluation of the author's ideas.

As series editors of the Opposing Viewpoints Series, it is our hope that these books will give readers a deeper understanding of the issues debated and an appreciation of the complexity of even seemingly simple issues when good and honest people disagree. This awareness is particularly important in a democratic society such as ours in which people enter into public debate to determine the common good. Those with whom one disagrees should not be regarded as enemies but rather as people whose views deserve careful examination and may shed light on one's own.

Thomas Jefferson once said that "difference of opinion leads to inquiry, and inquiry to truth." Jefferson, a broadly educated man, argued that "if a nation expects to be ignorant and free . . . it expects what never was and never will be." As individuals and as a nation, it is imperative that we consider the opinions of others and examine them with skill and discernment. The Opposing Viewpoints Series is intended to help readers achieve this goal.

David L. Bender & Bruno Leone,
Series Editors

# Introduction

*"On both sides the interaction between Islam and the West is seen as a clash of civilizations."*

Samuel P. Huntington

Islam is the second largest and the fastest growing of the three major monotheistic religions. One-fifth of the world's population are Muslims, and Muslims constitute the majority in states in North Africa, the Middle East, and Central Asia. The phenomenon called political Islam, or Islamic fundamentalism, emerged in the late 1970s as a revival of religion in political and social life and has grown to challenge long-standing governments in the region into the 1990s. In Iran, an Islamic government has ruled since 1979. In Afghanistan, Muslim *mujahedeen* defeated the Soviet army in 1989 and later toppled the secular government. In Algeria in 1991–92, the Islamic Salvation Front (FIS) was poised to win democratic elections and form a new government when a military coup ended the election process and outlawed the FIS. Since then, armed factions of the fragmented FIS have carried out acts of terrorism against the military government and foreign targets. In Egypt, Islamic groups have waged a campaign of terrorism against Egyptian citizens and foreign tourists in an attempt to destabilize the government of Hosni Mubarak. The Egyptian government has ruled under a state of emergency since 1992 and has conducted summary military trials against the Islamic groups. Samuel P. Huntington, director of the Olin Institute for Strategic Studies at Harvard University, has argued that, collectively, these events represent a political movement that will ultimately produce a cultural (and possibly a military) clash between Islam and the West.

Mark Juergensmeyer, author of *The New Cold War?* agrees that "taken together, [these events] are not just a congeries of particular cases but a worldwide phenomenon." Enhancing the perception of a growing and spreading phenomenon, many writers and reporters apply the label "Islamic fundamentalism" to the various movements. Though the movements invariably espouse strict adherence to Islamic law, or *sharia* (making the term "fundamentalist" somewhat fitting), many Muslims and Western scholars reject the label because the movements do not share a single, "fundamental" set of beliefs. Iran's Islamic government, for instance, is based on Shia beliefs and practices, but only 10 percent of Muslims are Shias. Further, many Muslims reject the "fundamentalist" label because it has a negative connotation, associated with fanaticism and violence. They contend that portraying militant groups as fundamen-

12

talist has created the false impression that Islam is a violent religion. In fact, they argue, Islam stresses justice and peace. Many Muslims do not identify with the movements and do not approve of their goals and tactics. Others point out that the factions that are the most violent, and therefore the most visible, represent only a small minority of the Muslim population. "Political Islam" is the term preferred by many to describe these movements, denoting their religiously based effort to transform the political life of Muslim societies. It is seen by some as a movement to increase the role of religion in Muslim societies and by others as a militant revolutionary movement aimed at overthrowing governments and uniting the Muslim world under religious law.

"Islam is a religious belief that covers all aspects of life and denies the validity of any philosophical separation between 'church' and state," note Charles E. Butterworth and I. William Zartman, professors at the University of Maryland and Johns Hopkins University, respectively. This fusion of religion and politics stands in direct contrast to the separation of church and state valued in Western governments. And it is this diametric opposition of values, combined with the inequality in military and economic power between the West and the rest of the world, that is the basis of Huntington's hypothesized clash of civilizations. The West, "now at an extraordinary peak of power in relation to other civilizations" following its cold war victory, according to Huntington, faces an Islamic culture it sees as economically underdeveloped, politically unstable, and historically a military enemy. On the other hand, "Western efforts to propagate such ideas [as liberalism, democracy, free markets, and separation of church and state] produce a reaction against" the West, Huntington argues, a reaction embodied in the political Islamic movements. According to Juergensmeyer, the rejection of Western secularism by the Islamic movements is "fundamental—often hostile and violent." With their basic opposition to the West, he warns, the Islamic movements "hold the potential of making common cause against the secular West, in what might evolve into a new Cold War."

In exploring the causes of political Islam's predicted conflict with the West, Bernard Lewis, author of *Islam and the West*, writes, "Ultimately, the struggle of the fundamentalists is against two enemies, secularism and modernity." Islamic fundamentalist groups give form to the popular resentment toward the transformation of Muslim societies by Western technological and communications advancements, explains Lewis, and struggle to limit the influence of Western culture. Western television, for instance, broadcast worldwide by satellite, "infects Islam with 'cheap alien culture' and spreads 'the family-devastating disease of the West,'" according to Iran's Ayatollah Mohammed Ali Araki, quoted by *Wall Street Journal* reporter Peter Waldman. Such fundamental opposition to Western influence, in Lewis's opinion, signifies a movement that is capable of uniting the Islamic world against the West. "This is no less than a clash of civilizations," he concludes.

Others in the West and in the Islamic world do not think a clash is inevitable. Leon T. Hadar, author of *Quagmire: America in the Middle East*, contends that the predicted clash of civilizations is a Western-made "conspiracy theory" that ties together unrelated events and portrays them as a monolithic threat. "This specter is symbolized by the . . . Muslim fundamentalist, a Khomeini-like creature armed with a radical ideology . . . intent on launching a jihad against Western civilization," he says. Daniel Pipes, editor of *Middle East Quarterly*, argues that the various Islamic movements are too disparate in their beliefs and goals to become a unified political force in opposition to the West. In fact, according to Pipes, the majority of Muslim governments find their interests coinciding with those of the West. In determining the future relations between Muslim countries and the West, he contends, "the key issue is whether Muslims will modernize." If they oppose the adoption of democracy, free markets, and technological advancements, he believes, the poverty and autocracy of the Muslim countries will deepen, and their relations with the West will consequentially worsen, possibly to the point of military tensions. "But if Muslims do modernize, things will turn out differently," says Pipes.

According to Michael M.J. Fischer, author of *Debating Muslims*, Muslim societies are already modernizing, in their own way, and "the Muslim world is now more than ever part of the West." Demonizing Islamic civilization as antimodern or anti-Western is pointless, in his opinion, because "the modern world is reworking even so-called fundamentalist movements in the Islamic world." In fact, according to Fischer, Islamic groups are adopting Western technology and modernism in their attempts to remodel Muslim societies on religious principles. These movements have successfully opposed the West's secular cultural influence and are challenging the belief that the West should propagate liberal, secular values in non-Western societies, in Fischer's analysis. Mohammed Sid-Ahmed, an Egyptian newspaper columnist, author, and politician, also rejects the West's equating of modernity with secularism. Islam can adopt modernity "without necessarily having to adopt the Western 'secular' model," according to Sid-Ahmed.

Predictions about the future relations between Islam and the West, ranging from a new cold war or clash of civilizations to increasing integration into a modernized world, center on the compatability of values between the two cultures. *Islam: Opposing Viewpoints* presents debates on the nature of political Islam and its significance for the West in the following chapters: What Is the Goal of Political Islam? What Is the Status of Women Under Islam? Can Democracy Coexist with Islam? Does Political Islam Promote Terrorism? Is the Islamic World a Threat to the West? Is Islam Uniting the Islamic World? This anthology offers diverse opinions, from Western and Muslim sources, on the values of political Islam and their influence in both the Muslim world and the West.

# What Is the Goal of Political Islam?

**Islam**

# Chapter Preface

In 1989, in the face of civil unrest protesting economic stagnation and a single-party monopoly on power, Algerians enacted a new, democratic constitution and scheduled their first-ever multiparty elections. As the democratic process got under way, the Islamic Salvation Front (FIS) quickly emerged as a leading party, drawing support from a network of neighborhood mosques and charitable religious organizations. With the FIS poised to win a majority in the January 1992 national elections, Algeria's military disrupted the democratic process, outlawed the FIS, and took over the government. Since that time, Algeria has been mired in violence between the military regime and armed Islamic groups—violence that has also targeted civilians, foreigners, and journalists. Jailed FIS leaders declared a *jihad* (religiously sanctioned struggle) against the regime in November 1994, threatening a full-scale civil war.

Shortly after the 1992 military coup, John P. Entelis, a professor at Fordham University, and Lisa J. Arone, a student at the University of Toronto, characterized the FIS as "a populist party . . . and not the fundamentalist threat that the regime has tried to portray it as." They were among those who believed the FIS was committed to democracy in Algeria and who believed the FIS should be given the chance to govern.

The Islamic Front's transformation from leading political party to armed insurgency calling for *jihad* caused others to question the nature and goals of the Islamic movement in Algeria. After witnessing three years of escalating violence committed by factions of the Islamic movement, a growing number of observers now doubt the FIS's democratic intentions. Among the doubters, Karima Bennoune, a lawyer and Arab-American activist, expressed her reservations: "If Algerian fundamentalists have carried out this level of violence, . . . one can but imagine the possible level of brutality to be enacted if these forces were to come to power."

The choice Algerians face, according to reporter Caryle Murphy, is between the "present police state" and a possible "religious dictatorship." Others insist Islamic rule would not preclude the formation of a democratic society. The viewpoints in the following chapter present alternative portrayals of the goals of political Islamic movements.

*"Militant Islamic movements . . . create an ideology of redemption wherewith all societal problems can be resolved through religion."*

# Militant Political Islam Seeks to Establish an Islamic Republic

Mary-Jane Deeb

In the following viewpoint, Mary-Jane Deeb argues that militant Islamic movements, such as the Islamic Salvation Front in Algeria, emerge under unstable political, economic, and cultural conditions. These Islamic movements gain popular support by promising a salvation from unstable conditions through a return to religion, according to Deeb. She characterizes militant Islamic movements as being ready to use violent means to establish "an Islamic republic that would transcend national borders." Deeb is director of the Omani Program of the School of International Service at American University in Washington, D.C., and the author of *Libya's Foreign Policy in North Africa*.

As you read, consider the following questions:

1. What are the five conditions for the rise of militant Islam, according to Deeb?
2. According to Max Weber, quoted by Deeb, when does the idea of redemption attain a specific significance?
3. In the author's view, how are militant Islamic movements different from previous Islamic movements?

From Mary-Jane Deeb, "Militant Islam and the Politics of Redemption," *The Annals of the Academy of Political and Social Science*, 524, November 1992, pp. 52-65, copyright ©1992 by The Academy of Political and Social Science. Reprinted by permission of Sage Publications, Inc.

Militant Islam has emerged in the 1980s and 1990s as a major political force to be contended with in the Middle East. It is characterized by its readiness to use violence and by the challenge it constitutes to existing political institutions. Although ideologically it may not differ greatly from the earlier and somewhat more moderate Islamic movements, it is more aggressive in propounding and attempting to implement its ideas. The overwhelming success of the Islamic Salvation Front (FIS) in December 1991 in the first free elections since independence in Algeria highlights the significance of this new trend. Iran has been a Shiite Islamic republic for more than a decade, and in the Sudan the first military-Islamic government in the modern history of the Middle East came to power in 1989 by means of a coup that overthrew a democratically elected government.

This viewpoint looks at the conditions under which five Arab militant Islamic movements have emerged as a political force and at the concepts they have used to mobilize public support and to create a mass base of support for themselves in order to challenge leaders or governments in power. The basic thesis is that militant Islamic movements emerge under certain specific conditions that enable them to capture a broad audience and they capitalize on those conditions to create an ideology of redemption wherewith all societal problems can be resolved through religion.

## Conditions for the Rise of Militant Islam

Militant Islam has emerged under five broad conditions: the first is political stagnation and the weakening of central authority. This could be due to a loss of legitimacy with a change of leadership, as in the case of Tunisia; the failure of the ruling party to fulfill its promises or to live up to the expectations of the people, as in Algeria; the regional and international isolation of the Libyan leadership; an inability to control the political events or prevent the breakdown of law and order, as in Lebanon; or the inability [until 1993] of the Palestine Liberation Organization (PLO) leaders to achieve any significant gain for Palestinians despite the enormous costs of the *intifada* for the Arab population of the West Bank and Gaza.

The second condition for the emergence of Islamic militancy has been economic stagnation and decline and/or a growing gap between the haves and the have-nots. In all five cases—in Algeria, Tunisia, Libya, Lebanon, and the West Bank and Gaza—life became harder, unemployment increased, as did inflation, while major shortages in commodities and housing occurred and even accessibility to good health care was severely reduced. Higher education was no longer a guarantee of employment, and even the number of jobs abroad declined as did remittances to families dependent on them for survival. In Lebanon the misery was compounded by a war that impoverished large sections of the population and destroyed houses and places of work. Militant Islamic movements emerged in the 1980s as a direct outcome of the war.

## The Vote for the Islamic Party in Algeria

"To vote for the Islamic Salvation Front [FIS] is to vote for God; to vote against the FIS is to vote against Islam." It is with elementary slogans such as this one that the fundamentalists won the admiration of a largely illiterate, profoundly religious Algerian population. The result was a shock for the West: In the first round of Algeria's legislative elections in December 1991, the FIS, recognized as a party only since March 1989, obtained an overwhelming victory and was reasonably hoping to win an absolute majority in the second round originally scheduled for mid-January 1992. [The elections were voided after a new government, backed by the army, took power in early January.] How could this have happened? From an analysis of the voting, it seems easy to explain: In a country brought to the brink by economic crisis and poor government by the National Liberation Front, it was not difficult for the extremists to bring together under the flag of Islam all those who wished to have done with that kind of Algeria.

Massimo Dini, *World Press Review*, March 1992.

The third condition under which militant Islamic movements have thrived has been a deteriorating security situation that could be caused by external or internal factors or both. In Tunisia, Israelis attacked PLO headquarters twice, and Libya supported a very serious armed attack on Gafsa; Libya was bombed by the United States in 1986 and suffered a major military defeat by Chad in 1987; Algerian-Moroccan relations were tense throughout the 1980s over the Western Sahara; insecurity was prevalent in Gaza and on the West Bank, exacerbated by the *intifada* and the Israeli reaction to it. In Lebanon the civil war threatened everyone in the country, and the air raids by Israel culminating in the 1982 invasion of Lebanon were the ultimate security threat.

### The Invasion of Western Secularism

What was perceived as an even greater threat to the Muslim populations of the Middle East was the insidious invasion of the region by Western culture and values. Every night, Maghrebi television broadcast shows from Europe depicting a way of living that was different but fast becoming the model of the good life for North Africans. Western and Jewish culture were the dominant cultures in Israel, where Arab and Islamic cultures were disparaged. In Lebanon, the dominant culture by the mid-1970s in Beirut had become Western, with shops carrying the latest in fashion, music, books, and newspapers from the West; the restaurants, cafes, and nightclubs being similar to those on the other side of the Mediterranean; and the most prestigious academic institutions being American or French.

In every case, finally, the governments in power were perceived as encouraging this cultural change and as being themselves secular or paying only lip service to Islam. In Algeria, Libya, and Tunisia, the governments were seen as attempting to separate religion from politics and as harassing and persecuting Islamic organizations and their leaders. The PLO's leadership was always secular, with Christian and Muslim leaders sharing power and formulating policy for the rest of the movement. In Lebanon, the president was Christian, and the Muslim leaders came from traditional bourgeois and notable families who were westernized and secular.

It is under those conditions that strong militant Islamic movements emerged throughout the southern Mediterranean claiming to be able to save Muslims from the political, economic, social, and cultural problems they were facing in their bewildering and fast-changing societies.

## The Politics of Redemption

There is nothing new in such movements. Max Weber, in "The Economic Ethic of the World Religions," noted:

> The conception of the idea of redemption as such is very old, if one understands by it a liberation from distress, hunger, drought, sickness, and ultimately from suffering and death. Yet redemption attained a specific significance only where it expressed a systematic and rationalized "image of the world" and represented a stand in the face of the world.

The militant Islamic movements that emerged in the region in the 1980s and 1990s offered to save Muslims from those very conditions that had enabled them to mobilize public opinion in the first place. They did not portray themselves as revolutionaries trying to create a new society but rather as saviors trying to save the old society from self-destruction. This may explain why they look back to a golden age to which they wish to return, rather than forward to a new age that they want to create. In the final analysis, the two processes may be the same, and the retrospective movement may be as revolutionary as the forward-looking one, but, at the outset at least, the conception of what each is trying to achieve is different.

Although Islam became the religion of the state under the new Algerian Constitution after independence [in 1962], the *shari'a*, or Islamic law, was not made an integral part of the legal system of the state, nor were Muslim jurists allowed to play an independent role in legislative matters on the national level. Instead, a minister of religious affairs was appointed by the Algerian leaders to head a bureaucratic organization that had the final authority to appoint or dismiss clergymen, review Friday sermons, administer religious endowments, control religious publications, and set up Islamic institutions of higher learning.

In 1964, an Islamic militant group, al-Qiyam (Values), with links to the Algerian Muslim Brothers, emerged and became a precursor of the Islamic fundamentalists of the 1980s. It called for a more visible role for Muslim practices in society and opposed Western cultural manifestations in clothing and entertainment in Algeria. One of its leaders, Muhammad Khider, was a founding member of the National Liberation Front (FLN) [Algeria's ruling party since independence], who had broken away from the party and set up the nucleus of an opposition to President Ahmed Ben Bella and later to President Houari Boumedienne. The movement was eventually suppressed by the Boumedienne regime, and Khider was assassinated in 1967.

By the end of the 1970s, Ahl al-Da'wa (People of the Call), an autonomous Islamic movement with strong links to the original al-Qiyam movement, began to voice the dissatisfaction of many Algerians with state policies and with the direction they were taking the country. But it was only after the death of Boumedienne in 1978 and the emergence of an Islamic republic in Iran the following year that the movement became organized and active.

## Islamic Protests

In the early 1980s, the members of al-Da'wa took over mosques that had been under government control for two decades, and when government security forces attempted to stop the takeover—in Laghouat, in 1981, for instance—bloody clashes erupted and resulted in a number of casualties. University campuses witnessed pitched battles between Muslim fundamentalists and left-wing students. These confrontations culminated in the death of a student on the Ben Aknoun campus of the University of Algiers in November 1982.

This event led to the government of Chadli Bendjedid, whose policy toward al-Da'wa activities had hitherto been rather tolerant, to clamp down. During the rest of the 1980s, the Algerian state began a systematic campaign to undermine the movement by arresting its leaders, conducting police raids on the homes of suspected members, and branding them in the mass media as "criminals" and "agitators." Three of the leaders arrested were

21

clergymen and founding members of the FIS.

In October 1988, riots broke out in the Bab al-Oued sector of Algiers over government austerity measures to cut state subsidies on some basic commodities. The riots spread quickly to the rest of the capital, to Oran, Constantine, Annaba, Blida, Tiarret, and Sinya, and beyond to Tizi-Ouzou in the Berber Kabylie region. Demonstrators were protesting the high unemployment, the shortage of basic consumer goods, and the unavailability of affordable housing in the cities. The armed forces brought in to quell the riots were unable to restore law and order for ten days, at the end of which more than 150 people were reported dead, over 1000 injured, and an estimated 3000 arrested.

Although the riots were not initiated by Islamic militants, these militants tried to exploit the disturbances to mobilize support for their views. Two days after the riots broke out, several thousand young Muslim fundamentalists demonstrated in the Belcourt District of Algiers, while the army attempted to keep them away from demonstrations in other sectors of the city. When the riots were over, President Bendjedid met with Muslim fundamentalist leaders. They condemned acts of violence and sabotage and submitted a number of proposals for economic and social reforms including a demand that Islam constitute the basis of all such reforms.

## Algerian Elections

In February 1989, a new constitution was approved in Algeria. Among other things, it permitted the creation of "associations of a political character." In March 1989, the first Algerian Islamic political party, the FIS, was proclaimed in Kouba, a suburb of Algiers, and was officially legalized in September 1989. It had a consultative council, or *shura*, made up of fourteen members, some of whom were very important Islamic leaders in Algeria. In June 1990, the first test of strength took place between the FLN and the FIS in local elections for the 1539 municipal councils and the 48 provincial assemblies. The Islamicists won 54 percent of the vote as compared to the FLN's 28 percent, giving them control of 850 municipalities, including those of major urban centers such as Algiers, Constantine, and Oran. On 25 May 1991, on the eve of general legislative elections, the FIS called for an indefinite and nationwide strike and announced rallies and marches all over the country. The strike was called to protest the government's gerrymandering tactics to give rural districts a greater electoral representation, which would favor the ruling party. They also demanded that presidential elections be held simultaneously with the legislative elections.

After days of disturbances, the Algerian government took new measures to deal with these disturbances: it ordered the reestablishment of all public services and the arrest of those who were obstructing government officials from performing their duties. Clashes between demonstrators and the gendarmerie turned violent, and the security forces used firearms. Finally, on 5 June 1991, President Bendjedid ordered a state of siege for four months to restore public order. All gatherings, demonstrations, and marches were banned. A curfew was imposed between 11 p.m. and 3:30 a.m. in the provinces of Algiers, Blida, Tipasa, and Boumerdes, and the military began patrolling the capital in tanks. Legislative elections were postponed, and the government resigned.

After jailing both the leader of the FIS and his deputy and breaking off further negotiations with the Islamicists, the government set the date for legislative elections. On 26 December 1991, elections were held, and the FIS won a landslide victory, capturing 188 seats out of the National Assembly's 430, with 176 seats to be contested in a runoff election three weeks later. The FLN came in third, with only 15 seats. Bendjedid resigned on 11 January 1992, leaving the door open to a confrontation between the army and the FIS. The army created a High Security Council, which canceled the runoff elections and effectively blocked the FIS from coming to power.

Ideologically, the Algerian Muslim fundamentalists are among the most radical in North Africa. They advocate a complete restructuring of society "in an attempt to realize the City of God on Earth," according to John P. Entelis. They have pushed for the application of Islamic law, *shari'a*, to replace the code of civil law of Algeria and for reforms based on Islamic principles such as a stricter dress code for women, more religious broadcasts on radio and television, and banning the consumption of alcohol in public places. . . .

## Establishing an Islamic Republic

Militant Islamic movements in the Arab world have emerged in the 1980s, but all derive from earlier movements that either were suppressed or agreed to play by the rules of the governments in power. Most of the Sunnite militant groups were influenced by, or were offshoots of, organizations having links with the Muslim Brotherhood of Hasan al-Banna in Egypt, which emerged in 1928. The Shiite movements, on the other hand, have their roots in Iran or in the Iraqi holy cities of Shiism like Najaf and Karbala.

Ideologically, they are not very different from their predecessors. What differentiates them is their commitment to achieving their goals not in the distant future but in the present. They are much better organized than earlier movements; they are better financed, as they raise money from their members and from external sources and governments; and they have younger, better-educated, and more active leaders. Most are very secretive about their organizational structures and have separate wings with different names that perform different functions. All have a paramilitary arm for terrorist activities.

Militant Islamic movements are also much more outspoken than their predecessors in their criticisms of governments and leaders in power. They use the difficult economic conditions under which their fellow citizens live to support their allegations of corruption, mismanagement, and kowtowing to the West. They argue that those leaders have failed and that it is time for change, an idea appealing even to those who do not support them.

These movements are militant because they refuse to compromise with the powers that be. They all argue that there can be no compromise with the forces of evil. They are, however, pragmatic and ready, as in Algeria, to maneuver tactically to achieve their goals. The ultimate goal is an Islamic republic that would transcend national borders, but until that time they want to establish Islamic republics within national borders that would assist similar movements elsewhere. Another characteristic of these movements, therefore, is the close links they maintain with each other and the support they give one another.

Because of their unwillingness to compromise, their criticisms of governments in power, their use of force and violence, and their expressed goal of overthrowing ruling elites, they have all been suppressed and their leaders and followers imprisoned. Many have had harsh prison sentences, have suffered torture in captivity, and have been sent or have fled into exile. They have therefore been able to glean a great deal of support as the underdog organization that has stood up to the powerful and corrupt.

*"Islamists in essence espouse the nationalists'
program, translate it into religious terms, and
promise to achieve it the moment they gain power."*

# Political Islam
# Opposes Secular
# Nationalist Regimes

Ghassan Salamé

In the following viewpoint, Ghassan Salamé argues that Islamic movements in the Middle East have arisen as an alternative to secular, nationalist governments that failed to achieve the goals they set for themselves: political legitimacy based on Western-type nationalism, political development, economic prosperity, national security, and independence from the West. According to Salamé, Islamic movements seek to gradually establish, through democratic means, the same nationalist program fused with the religious identity of the population of the Islamic world. Salamé is a professor of international relations at the Institut d'études politiques in Paris.

As you read, consider the following questions:

1. What are the three embarrassments that current governments in the Islamic world face, according to Salamé?
2. Among what groups of people do today's Islamic movements draw the most support, according to the author?

From Ghassan Salamé, "Islam and the West." Reproduced (with permission) from *Foreign Policy* 90 (Spring 1993). Copyright 1993 by the Carnegie Endowment for International Peace.

Now that the Cold War is over, many Western strategists have identified a new enemy of the West: Islam. But among those strategists knowledge of Islam is minimal. What is the challenge? How powerful is it? Do Western policies help or hurt? How those questions are answered will determine to a significant degree the international agenda for the rest of this decade.

The political program of the Islamists, who are often inaccurately called "Islamic fundamentalists," seeks to restore a heavily idealized old order of things. It is driven in part by an alienation from the present world system, in which they consider the Muslim world's position as unjustly marginal in light of Islam's past glories. Their chief criticism of the nationalist powers that have ruled the Muslim countries since independence is that nationalism, though designed to repel Western military and political domination, did not dare to challenge Western concepts and modes of government and reinstate the Islamic tradition (al-turath). Islamists would like to be viewed as the true anti-imperialist force, pushing the struggle a step further by resisting not only the West's political hegemony but also its intrusive ideas like liberalism, socialism, and secularism.

## The Failures of Current Regimes

Opposed to the Islamist program, governments of the Muslim world face a triple embarrassment. First, because they rarely challenged the Western world view, they have failed to develop alternative legitimating factors other than an obsession with political independence and cultural authenticity. Second, the regimes have been unable to convince their peoples of any outstanding successes in the tasks they proclaimed for themselves: the "liberation of Palestine," pan-Arab or pan-Islamic reunification, political participation, and social and economic prosperity. Third, they are relying, more and more, on foreign support to stay in power and to fend off their domestic opposition or their neighbors' aggressions. That dependence on the West was demonstrated most spectacularly in the American-led campaign to retrieve Kuwait from Iraqi annexation. It was also confirmed by the West's relief, too openly expressed, at the military's interruption of the electoral process in Algeria [in 1991–1992], which threatened to bring pro-Islamist forces to power.

Hence, most current regimes suffer intrinsic weaknesses against the emerging Islamist challenge. The Islamists gain popular appeal by endeavoring to accomplish the very program nationalist regimes had devised but were unable to achieve—be it because of the regimes' widespread corruption, their squandering of oil revenues, their reliance on the West, their more recent submission to International Monetary Fund strictures, or their persistent lack of interest in tradition.

Islamists in essence espouse the nationalists' program, translate it into religious terms, and promise to achieve it the moment they gain power. Islamists thus embody an ambiguous mixture of continuity in policy and radical shift in elite identity. Algerian Islamist leader Abassi Madani, himself a former militant of the National Liberation Front (FLN in French), which has ruled the country since independence [in 1962], insists that the Islamic Salvation Front (FIS) program is a return to the FLN's "authentic" foundations during the war of liberation from 1954–1962. Elsewhere, Islamist groups attract thousands of militants who had political experience in nationalist, Baathist, Nasserist, or Mossadeghist parties and who have been disappointed by those parties' inability to keep their promises. One Lebanese thinker, Munah al-Solh, noted twenty years ago that Arab elites were basically nationalist while Arab masses were religious. The formula may be simplistic, but it is fairly accurate. In some sense, the Islamic revival is a kind of elite adjustment to the popular preference.

## Fundamentalism Opposes the West

The dominant secular politics of the Middle East in the 1950s, 1960s, and 1970s began to give way to a new wave of fundamentalism in the 1980s and 1990s. . . . The 1967 [Six Day War] defeat suffered by Arab states at the hands of Israel, armed and supported financially by the United States, contributed to public disillusionment with secularized Arab regimes. Local leaders trusted by the West were no longer trustworthy for the people. Noteworthy was the assassination of Anwar Sadat in 1981 and the fall of the Shah of Iran in 1979. The Middle East grew more restive when the days of employment and comparative security under socialism gave way to *infitah*, or an opening of countries to the free market and Western capitalism; when poverty and inflation increased; when bread riots erupted; when national pride was hurt and humiliated; when Palestinians were thrown out of their lands and homes; and when the superpower, America, vetoed many United Nations resolutions granting Palestinians their legitimate right to return to their homes and achieve their self-determination, while doling out billions of dollars every year to Israel and strengthening its occupation of Palestinian lands.

Abbas Hamdani, *Mediterranean Quarterly*, Fall 1993.

Because "the FIS is the son of the FLN," as the Algerian sociologist Mohammed Harbi has put it, it would be a grave error to believe that today's Islamist groups originated in those traditional sectors of Muslim societies that opposed post-independence modernization policies. Sociological surveys in countries such as Algeria, Egypt, and Lebanon indicate that Islamist activists tend to come from university campuses rather than from among illiterates. One striking finding is the Islamists' strength in university science departments as compared to literary or legal studies. Science students feel that their rejection of Western-style modernity stems from a basic understanding of where modernity can lead them. They are very critical of the traditional religious establishment, which they deem too passive or too subservient to the government. Religious intellectuals (ulama), in fact, are on the government payroll in most countries. Thus, in the case of post-revolution Iran, the Ayatollah Ruhollah Khomeini imposed his own disciples and partisans on the traditional Shiite "clergy."

Not surprisingly, Islamist militants generally received a lukewarm reception from the traditional religious establishment of their countries. In Egypt, ulama at Al-Azhar (a religious university that recently celebrated a millennium of existence) are generally on the government's side. In Saudi Arabia, most of them support Saud family rule and operate as the regime's spokesmen and advocates. And in Algeria, most of the religious establishment did not participate in the FIS attempt to take power.

## The Third Wave of Islamists

Today's Islamists actually represent the third generation of militants inspired by religion. The first was part and parcel of the national liberation movement against foreign domination, and in places like the Maghreb and Iran sometimes represented the largest trend within that movement. When Hassan al-Banna founded the Muslim Brotherhood in 1928, it was conceived as part of the Egyptian national struggle against the British colonialists and came to represent some 3 million militants in the wake of the 1952 Free Officers coup. In Iraq, religious and nationalist supporters of the "1920 revolution" against the imposition of British rule were indistinguishable. The Algerian FLN was as Islamic as it was nationalistic in its struggle against French colonialism.

After independence, nationalists achieved a monopoly over the state. In most Middle Eastern countries, nationalist and secularist military officers took over the state apparatus and ostracized the religious elements of the anti-Western struggle. Muslim Brothers were killed in Egypt, Iraq, and Syria; Egypt's Gamal Abdel Nasser had the leader of the Brotherhood executed in Cairo, and the Baath party was extremely tough on religious movements in Iraq and Syria. Mustafa Kemal (Atatürk) of Turkey, the Shah of Iran, and Habib Bourguiba of Tunisia embarked on clearly Western-inspired policies, notably in matters of women's rights, public observance of the Ramadan fast, and even personal dress. The second generation of Islamic militants was thus composed of "martyrs"—those killed, jailed, or exiled by their one-time comrades.

Governments now face a third generation of militants, fostered by the spread of mass education and disenchantment with the current regimes. The new wave is drawn mostly from well-educated cadres who had some access to a Western-style education but who did not easily find a job. They have seen that Islamism now has a chance to repeal the nationalist monopoly on power, as was demonstrated in Iran and Sudan, and as was nearly won in Algeria. Generally speaking, they are more patient than their predecessors about attaining political power; they intend to pressure governments to gradually implement the Islamist program before directly challenging a regime's rule. For example, Islamists in 1980 forced an amendment to the Egyptian constitution introducing *sharia*, Islamic law, as the main source of legislation, and engineered the *sharia's* actual imposition in Mauritania in 1983 and in Pakistan in 1985. They pressured Algeria's FLN to amend the family code in 1984 and forced changes in Sudan's penal code while General Gaafar al-Nimeiry was still in power. Governments have tended to offer concessions to reduce the Islamist thirst for power. However, the concessions do not prevent Islamist groups from attempting to control professional unions (such as those of engineers, lawyers, physicians, and professors) or from creating "Islamist areas" where government control is phased out and replaced by direct management of public order and provision of social services by the Islamist militants themselves. Those areas include certain neighborhoods in Cairo [Egypt], some governorates in Upper Egypt, the city of Hama in Syria before its destruction by the army, the southern outskirts of Beirut [Lebanon], most of the Gaza Strip, and now some of southern Iraq's marshlands.

## A Shortsighted Focus on Violence

It is thus shortsighted to concentrate exclusively on the most spectacular Islamist-inspired events, such as the [1979] revolution in Iran, the [1981] assassination of Anwar el-Sadat, the [1989] coup d'etat in Sudan, and the results of the [1991–1992] Algerian elections. It is just as important to note the points Islamists are scoring almost everywhere in pushing governments to adopt Islamist measures and to tolerate their hold over professional unions, university campuses, and inner-city neighborhoods. Whatever the outcome of Islamist attempts to dominate governments, the re-Islamization of societies is proceeding. That fact is becoming an obsessive worry of non-Muslim minorities and of secular members of the intelligentsia, though not necessarily of the man on the street. Most governments seem

29

unable to stop the movement, when they do not inadvertently accelerate it through indiscriminate punishments.

The movement has gained in particular when natural disasters have struck, such as the earthquakes in Tipasa, Algeria, in 1989 and in Egypt in 1992 and the 1990 floods in southern Tunisia. Islamists then have been quick to show their efficiency in bringing relief and compassion to the victims, while ineffective governments show the overall waning of state authority in the Third World, with or without an Islamist challenge. Aside from those crises, Islamists are offering help to many: distributing photocopies of expensive textbooks on campuses, making available free medical treatment, defending and serving squatters on the outskirts of cities, cleaning streets, extending protection to *trabendists* (smugglers), and providing all kinds of social services. Meanwhile, governments—stuck with impotent and corrupt bureaucracies, financial austerity programs, and heavy demographic challenges—can hardly respond.

## Diversification of the Islamic Movement

Even while growing, the third wave of Islamism is being diversified. It would be a serious mistake to lump Islamist groups together as a monolith: Some Islamist groups backed Iraq during the Persian Gulf war; others supported the coalition or issued contradictory statements. Some seek the kind of honorable behavior and large appeal they know are necessary to attain power, while others operate in small, secretive, violence-prone groups known as *gamaat*.

In Egypt, for example, most analysts (and the government in normal times) make a clear distinction between the well-established Muslim Brotherhood, which has won most of the recent professional union elections, and the *gamaat* that attack or kill government officials (as in the October 1990 assassination of the speaker of parliament), secularist thinkers, and, more recently, Western tourists. The distinction between those groups, though justified, does not necessarily mean that they are a nuisance to each other. The extremists' methods, paradoxically, enhance the moderate Islamists' respectability. In the professional union elections, extremist Islamists do not hesitate to help moderate Islamists win a majority of seats. Their combined pressure pushes the government to Islamize some policies, in order to accommodate the moderates and hit at the extremists. Arrests of members of the mainstream Egyptian Muslim Brotherhood suggest that the distinction between the two groups is becoming less clear. Governments face a Catch-22 dilemma: If they lump Islamists together, they tend to help the most extremist; if they distinguish between them, they have to placate the moderates with new concessions. . . .

Today, regimes face a problem similar to the one many European governments experienced immediately after World War II: how to deal with large communist parties, representing 20 to 30 per cent of the electorate, when those parties were not ready to commit themselves to the basic principles of democratic, peaceful alternation of governments. Governments in France and Italy chose to let the communists be represented in parliaments and city councils but kept them away from the executive for decades until communist parties were waning from the political scene in the early 1980s.

If today's Muslim governments followed a similar path, they would allow Islamist groups to register supporters and elect members of parliament to present their views, represent their ties and constituents, and take over municipal or provincial governments. Doing so might expose the Islamists' inability to govern or devise economic and social policies that are radically different from (let alone superior to) those of the governments in place.

The governments do not accept that argument. They regard such an opening to the Islamists as too risky. Islamist groups might well register more than 20 or 30 per cent of the vote in a fair and free contest. Such support was demonstrated in Algeria's December 26, 1991, elections. The electorate, unused to free elections and unaware of what is at stake, could prove to be volatile and unpredictable. In a burst of populist enthusiasm, it could put the Islamists in power, especially if winning a plurality is sufficient to govern. Moreover, while West European countries had a Marshall Plan pumping more than $100 billion (in today's dollars) into their coffers and benefited from legitimate, charismatic figures like Charles de Gaulle, Alcide De Gasperi, and Konrad Adenauer, who could face down the communist challenge, the secular leaders in today's Muslim world are hardly inspiring, and no Marshall Plan is available to them. Those who do sit on oil riches tend to use them to strengthen their (and their neighbors') authoritarian rule rather than to democratize.

"*A modern nation-state cannot be built upon ideas that emerged in the Arabian desert more than 1,300 years ago.*"

# Political Islam Opposes Intellectual Freedom

Salman Rushdie

Salman Rushdie is the India-born author of the novel *The Satanic Verses*. In February 1989, Ayatollah Khomeini of Iran declared the novel blasphemous and issued a decree calling for Rushdie's death. Rushdie has been in hiding since that time. In the following viewpoint, he lists several incidents from 1993 in which secular thinkers and authors in Islamic countries have been attacked or killed. Rushdie argues that there is a concerted effort by Islamic fundamentalists to silence these secular voices of dissent. The West should support these secularists, according to Rushdie, because they represent the best hope for the development of modern nation-states in the Islamic world.

As you read, consider the following questions:

1. According to Rushdie, how are Islamic fundamentalists being allowed to set the agenda?
2. What do you think the author means by the "inevitable hybrid nature" of modern Muslim societies?
3. What are the weapons used against secular dissidents, according to Rushdie?

The following news stories are all taken from the first half of 1993.

In Pakistan, a poet, Akhtar Hameed Khan, 78, is quoted as having said that while he admires Mohammed his real inspiration has been Buddha. He denies saying this but nevertheless is accused of blasphemy by mullahs. In 1992, he was arrested for allegedly insulting the Prophet's descendants by writing a poem about animals that, the fundamentalists asserted, contained hidden allegorical meanings. He managed to beat that charge but now once again his life is in danger.

In Sharjah, one of the United Arab Emirates, an Indian theater group in 1992 performed a play titled *Corpse-Eating Ants*, which was held to be blasphemous. The actors, who were sentenced to six-year jail sentences for blasphemy, appealed and some went free, but the sentence of one was increased to ten years and an appeals court has upheld the six-year term of another.

## Secularists Killed in Islamic Countries

In Istanbul, one of Turkey's most respected secular journalists, Ugur Mumcu, is gunned down in the street. Turkish fundamentalists take responsibility for the attack, and the [Turkish] government says it has evidence linking the murderers to Iran. The Interior Minister says that at least three previous killings had been carried out by a group called Islamic Movement whose members have been trained in assassination techniques "at an official Iranian facility between Teheran and Qom."

In Egypt, the assassins who in 1992 murdered the distinguished secular thinker Farag Fouda currently [as of July 1993] are being tried. However, extremist bombings and killings continue. On Thursday, July 8, 1993, seven followers of Sheik Omar Abdel Rahman were hanged for attacks on foreign tourists and conspiring to overthrow the government of President Hosni Mubarak.

In Algeria, the writer Tahar Djaout is one of six secularists murdered in a killing spree in several cities by what security forces call "Muslim terrorists."

In Saudi Arabia, distinguished intellectuals form the country's first human rights group. Within days many are fired from their posts, arrested and jailed.

In Egypt, a noted law professor is charged with apostasy because of his critique of strict Islamic law. Fundamentalists ask the courts to dissolve his marriage, since it is illegal for a Muslim to be married to an apostate. Otherwise, his wife would be stoned to death as an adulteress.

In Turkey, thirty-six secularist writers and artists gathered for a conference in the town of Sivas are burned to death in their hotel by a mob of Islamic fundamentalists that accuses them of being atheists and therefore deserving of being burned alive.

And in the Sudan . . . and in Iran . . . but enough, perhaps.

The United States has become all too painfully familiar with the nature of the holy—rather, unholy—terrorists of Islam. The crater beneath the World Trade Center and the uncovering of a plot to set off more gigantic bombs and to assassinate leading political figures have shown Americans how brutal these extremists can be. These and other cases of international Islamic terrorism have shocked the world community, whereas the incidents of domestic terrorism I have listed here are relatively little known.

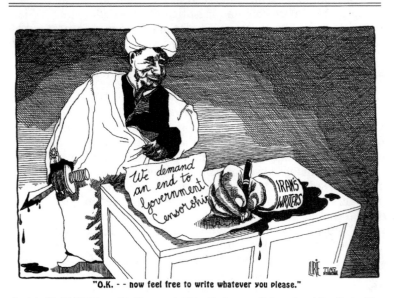

"O.K. - - now feel free to write whatever you please."

Lurie's World ©1994 worldwide copyright by Cartoonews International Syndicate, New York City, USA. Used with permission.

I suggest that this imbalance in our attention represents a kind of victory for fanaticism. If the worst, most reactionary, most medieval strain in the Muslim world is treated as the authentic culture, so that the mullahs get all the headlines while progressive, modernizing voices are treated as minor and marginal and "Westoxicated"—as small news—then the fundamentalists are being allowed to set the agenda.

The truth is that there is a great struggle for the soul of the Muslim world and, as the fundamentalists grow in power and ruthlessness, those courageous men and women who are willing to engage them in a battle of ideas and moral values are rapidly becoming as important for us to know about, to understand and support as the dissident voices in the old Soviet Union used to be.

The Soviet terror state, too, denigrated its opponents as being overly Westernized and as enemies of the people; it, too, took men from their wives in the middle of the night, as the poet Osip Mandelstam was taken from Nadezhda. We do not blame Mandelstam for his own destruction; we do not blame him for attacking Stalin, but rather, and rightly, we blame Stalin for his Stalin-ness.

In the same spirit, let us not fall into the trap of blaming the Sharjah theater folk for their rather macabre ants and Turkish writers for "provoking" the mob that murdered them. Rather, we should understand that secularism is now the fanatics' most important target.

## The Threat of Secularism

Why? Because secularism demands a total separation between church and state in the Muslim world: Philosophers such as the Egyptian Fouad Zakariya argue that free Muslim societies can exist only where this principle is adhered to.

And because secularism rejects utterly the idea that any late twentieth-century society can be thought of as "pure," and argues that the attempt to purify the modern Muslim world of its inevitable hybrid nature will lead to equally inevitable tyrannies.

And because secularism seeks to understand the Muslim verities as events within history, not outside it.

And because secularism seeks to end the repression against women that is instituted wherever the radical Islamists come into power.

And, most of all, because secularists know that a modern nation-state cannot be built upon ideas that emerged in the Arabian desert more than 1,300 years ago.

The weapons used against the dissidents of the Muslim world are everywhere the same. The accusations are always of "blasphemy," "apostasy," "heresy," "un-Islamic activities." These "crimes" are held to "insult Islamic sanctities." The people's wrath, thus aroused, becomes impossible to resist. The accused become persons whose "blood is unclean," and therefore deserves to be spilled.

The British writer Marina Warner once pointed out that the objects associated with witchcraft—a pointed hat, a broomstick, a cauldron, a cat—would have been found in most women's possession during the great witch hunts. If these were proofs of witchcraft, then all women were potentially guilty; it was only necessary for accusing fingers to point at one and cry, "Witch!" Americans, remembering the McCarthyite witch hunts, will readily understand how destructive the process can still be.

And what is happening in the Muslim world today must be seen as a witch hunt of exceptional proportions, a witch hunt being carried out in many nations and often with murderous results.

So the next time you come across a news story like the ones I've reported here, perhaps an article tucked away near the bottom of an inside page in the newspaper, remember that the persecution it describes is not an isolated act. It is part of a deliberate, lethal program, whose purpose is to criminalize, denigrate, and even to assassinate the Muslim world's best, most honorable voices: its voices of dissent. And remember that those dissidents need your support. More than anything, they need your attention.

*"We'll have a state where we apply Islam, where honesty and justice will reign. . . . It's a moral contract, not an electoral program."*

# Political Islam Is a Grassroots Renaissance Movement in Algeria

Rabia Bekkar, interviewed by Hannah Davis

In 1989, the National Liberation Front (FLN), which had ruled Algeria since 1962 as the only legal party, legalized opposition parties and scheduled elections. In the following viewpoint, Rabia Bekkar, interviewed by Hannah Davis, describes the development of the Islamic Salvation Front (FIS) from an Islamic-oriented charitable organization to a political party. She argues that the FIS became popular not only because it inspired religious devotion to its cause, but because it provided occupations for unemployed young people and needed services for cities that the FLN government could not provide. Bekkar is an urban sociologist at the Institut Parisien de Recherche: Architecture Urbanistique et Société.

As you read, consider the following questions:

1. What was the role of the mosque before the Islamic front emerged, according to Bekkar?
2. Where did the FIS get money to run municipal projects and programs, according to Bekkar?
3. According to the author, was the FIS a democratic party?

Excerpted from "Taking Up Space in Tlemcen: The Islamist Occupation of Urban Algeria," an interview with Rabia Bekkar by Hannah Davis, *Middle East Report*, no. 179 (pp. 11-15), November/December 1992. Reprinted by permission of MERIP/*Middle East Report*, 1500 Massachusetts Ave. NW, #119, Washington, DC 20005.

Rabia Bekkar is an urban sociologist who has spent more than 12 years doing research in Tlemcen, Algeria. She first came into contact with the Islamist movement in the form of neighborhood charitable associations. When the Islamic Salvation Front (FIS) became a legal entity in 1989, these associations became the support network of the new party. Bekkar was in Tlemcen during the 1990 municipal election campaign that led to the victory of the FIS, and when she returned in 1991 she met with newly elected FIS officials. Although the FIS is now banned and its leaders imprisoned, Algerian Islamist activism remains a significant phenomenon. Rabia Bekkar's observations provide a rare local perspective on the Islamist movement.

*Davis: Can you describe Tlemcen?*

Bekkar: Tlemcen is a city of 170,000 in northern Algeria, not far from the border with Morocco. It lies against a mountain, part of it on the mountainside and part of it on the plain. Looking down on the city from above, you can see that it's fragmented, with ensembles of urban fabric that are completely different.

Tlemcen has a *medina*, an old city. Around it is the colonial city with wide avenues, beautiful villas. On the periphery of the city is an expanse of housing projects. One of these, Sidi Said, is where I'm doing my research. Then there's a part of the city that is self-constructed, juridically "illicit," which clings to the slope of the mountain. The people squatted on the land and built their own houses in this enormous quarter. I did my doctoral research in Boudghène, the largest of the self-constructed neighborhoods, with over 30,000 inhabitants.

*Does each of these quarters have a particular population?*

The only place in which there is a mixing of social strata is in the *medina*, which mainly consists of working-class people but includes some who are more well-to-do. The villas are occupied by the traditional bourgeoisie, which is rather strong in Tlemcen, and also by the new bourgeoisie, including high state functionaries. The housing projects are mainly inhabited by the middle strata, including technicians, engineers, doctors and so on.

*What about the self-constructed neighborhoods like Boudghène?*

Boudghène is inhabited by three kinds of people. There are old immigrants from the Sahara, nomads who lost their land. There are people who left the *medina* when it became crowded due to the rural exodus. And there are the rejects of the city, people with no place to live, no way to get into the circle of housing allocation. It is not entirely true to say that this quarter is inhabited by the most disadvantaged. The first generation is largely made up of laborers, construction workers, the unemployed, but these families had children who sometimes succeeded. They became teachers, functionaries.

*What are the problems facing the people of Tlemcen?*

More or less the same as in the rest of Algeria. There is an enormous backlog in housing construction. At the same time, the rate of population growth is among the highest in the world. In the villas, you might find only two people living in an enormous home. But in the *medina*, you find twelve, fifteen, twenty people in one room.

The other problem is unemployment, in spite of a very strong industrial sector in Tlemcen—several large electronics and textiles factories, and other, smaller industries. Tlemcen is in what used to be an agricultural region, and since the beginning of the rural exodus people have been arriving from the countryside, trying to find work. Unemployment essentially affects youth. The factories gave jobs to the first generation after independence. But these people will not retire tomorrow. So there is saturation without the creation of new jobs.

## Separation of Men and Women

*The crowding at home—fifteen people in a room—must put pressure on public space.*

This depends on whether you're talking about boys or girls. The girl is educated to be turned towards the interior. But the boy, from the earliest age, is pushed outside. By the time they reach adolescence, young men think of their life as taking place entirely outside. Public space, it's theirs.

*What is there for them to do?*

There are youth centers and cultural centers built as part of the FLN [National Liberation Front] programs. But these places are so institutionalized. The young people feel suffocated; they can't relax. There have been a few attempts to create mixed tea salons. You find places with signs reading "second floor for families." Around the university there are a few cafes that will admit young women as well as men, but in the center of the city there is no mixed cafe. It's unthinkable. . . .

*Are public spaces the domain of men?*

Young men call themselves *hittiste*—those who hold up the walls. When you walk through the city, there are entire quarters full of them: settled in, leaning back against the wall. The impression is of some kind of event, as though something is happening or is about to happen. Once I asked my brother what he does when he spends the day outside. He told me he goes to his regular cafe, meets his friends, drinks a cup of coffee. He leaves the cafe and takes a stroll in the city. He returns to the cafe, drinks a cup of coffee with other friends, then he walks until noon.

So you can see the vacuum, the emptiness, the readiness for any force at all that could attract them.

*The Islamist movement apparently managed to harness some of this energy. How?*

The first thing that happened was the emergence of many so-called charitable neighborhood associations in vulnerable quarters like Boudghène—places where there are chronic problems.

Before the Islamists emerged, the mosque served as a kind of community headquarters, rather like the village council. The mosque was active, but in a social rather than a political sense. Neighborhood conflicts and disputes were resolved; a family with economic problems could get help.

In the self-constructed quarters there is an enormous amount of mutual aid. It starts with the construction of a house—the whole neighborhood helps. This network of mutual aid laid the groundwork for these associations. In Boudghène, the first thing the association did was work on building and embellishing the mosque. They financed this by collecting funds door-to-door.

*What kind of people were active in the associations?*

University students, unemployed people and ex-delinquents. These were the three groups in Sidi Said and in Boudghène. The members were entirely from the quarter, the office was in the quarter, the leader was from the quarter. The central organization came afterwards. There was a progression: from the mosque playing the role of regulating social conflicts, to a semi-organized system of neighborhood committees, to a national organization after the legal incorporation of the FIS in 1989. The local groups were easy to pull in. All the FIS had to do was to incorporate them politically, ideologically. They were already doing the work. Before 1989 there was already this base.

*So after they fixed up the mosque, what next?*

Their work expanded after the FIS won the municipal elections of 1990. In Sidi Said, for example, the associations began to clean up the housing project. You have to imagine what it's like in these neighborhoods. It's desolate. You go out, you come back with fifteen kilos of mud on your shoes. Public space is abandoned. The Islamist groups started planting trees and rose bushes, creating a green space. They painted stores, facades of buildings. They marked out a soccer field, put up the goal posts and cleaned the field every day. In these housing projects household garbage is just thrown outside where children play. Through the municipality, they brought in big garbage bins with lids. A truck comes, empties the bin and takes away the garbage.

In Sidi Said there was a university student on the neighborhood committee. Whenever he saw a child about to destroy a plant, or whatever, he went over and said to him, "No, that's a plant. It lives like a human being. God doesn't want you to hurt it." They sensitized children to the plants, but in relationship to religion.

## The Islamists Occupy the Mosques

*How did things change at the mosque itself?*

Before the elections the Islamists occupied only the mosques in the peripheral quarters of the city. These were really just prayer rooms turned into mosques. The main mosques are under the state. The imam is named by the state, and the weekly sermon is sent in by the Ministry of Religious Affairs. The Islamists didn't try to occupy the large mosques. But in the peripheral quarters, the mosque, its upkeep and embellishment, was financed by contribution. There, people made the mosque, with contributions and shared work. It was *their* space. And the Islamists quickly put in one of their own imams.

*The imam in the peripheral quarters wasn't named by the state?*

Well, like any other shortage—food shortage, housing shortage—there was an "imam shortage." The state couldn't keep up with urban growth and with the proliferation of mosques. They couldn't find enough people to appoint as imams. So the Islamists occupied that space. After the municipal elections, they spread out into all the mosques.

In June 1990, I happened to go to the city hall to see the FIS mayor. In came the technical director: the mayor had asked him for a map with all the mosques marked on it in red. The technical director said, "Why point out the mosques, as we have other urban problems!" And the mayor said, "I want first to know which quarters have mosques, how many mosques there are, and where they're situated." It was the key for them!

As for children, there were more and more young people, preschool kids of five or six years old, going to Quran school in the mosque.

*Was this new?*

The state couldn't put a Quran teacher everywhere. The Islamists found volunteer teachers who gave free courses. So more and more parents, while they prayed, had their children in Quran school. You can't imagine how happy the mothers were to find a place they could leave their children instead of having them play in the mud. There are no kindergartens, no child-care centers. Parents also liked the idea that their children were learning something before they started school. Of course, in the minds of the Islamists, it was good that children start to learn the Quran rather than watch Mickey Mouse on TV.

---

### The Birth of the Islamic Salvation Front

On February 19, 1989, a group of Islamic fundamentalists gathered in a half-built mosque in Algiers and made a decision which was to change the face of Algerian politics forever. The fundamentalists decided to come out of the shadows and form a political party, the Islamic Salvation Front (FIS).

By this time, the FIS already had a well-developed party network. It used the mosques to preach its litany of social justice and organized its own social welfare system to fill the void left by the state. Even before joining the political mainstream, the FIS had a broad constituency among the frustrated youth of the poor districts, who spent their days leaning against the walls of overpopulated apartment blocks, waiting for their moment to come.

Alfred Hermida, *Africa Report*, September/October 1994.

---

*What about adolescents?*

At certain hours, the Quran school becomes a kind of tutoring center for junior and high school students. The Islamists asked university students and high school teachers from the neighborhood to give courses in math, physics, languages—any subject— for pupils with problems. In these quarters, one of the major problems is failure in school. Free tutoring was great.

*Did the teachers and university students do this out of religious conviction?*

Most of them were Islamists, but not all. In Sidi Said, I met young people who had practically nothing to do with the Islamist movement but were either giving courses or taking courses, not out of ideological conviction. Others found themselves swept up in the movement.

The Islamists had an implicit project of trying to find activities for unemployed young people and delinquents. This included not only volunteer activities but projects that allowed them to make a little money. They set up a system of small shops, like newspaper kiosks, where they could sell newspapers, fruits and vegetables, groceries, perfume.

*How did they do this?*

In Sidi Said, there had been a site under construction for a "farmer's market." It was part of an FLN state project for neighborhood renovation. Then the FIS took over the municipality and they took over this space. The platform had been built, the foundations already laid. But the Islamists built little shops, and gave them to unemployed people. Of course, on the list were young people judged potentially favorable to the Islamist movement.

Symbolically, the Islamists occupied an empty space. These foundations had been built years ago but the supermarket never appeared. Then, in a very short period of time, they created shops, and commerce started: a concrete fact in public space, seen by the whole housing project.

*Did they try to give a religious resonance to this project?*

The opening ceremonies were held at the mosque, even though the municipality was running the project. They took great care that the ceremony was religious even if the project was secular. This took place in 1990—three months after the municipal election. When I left in 1991, people were still talking about it.

## The FIS Runs the Municipal Government

*How did the FIS manage to finance these projects? Did FIS municipalities get state money like other city governments?*

It seemed that the FLN had a strategy of reducing municipal budgets: "We'll cut the budget, things'll get even worse and the people who elected the FIS at the municipal level will see that they've done nothing." But the charitable associations stepped in and bailed out the FIS. At the municipal level, the FIS couldn't yet run things. They didn't have the means and they were inexperienced. But the charitable associations were in place; they had already done consciousness-raising in their neighborhoods. They made sure everyone knew that the FIS hadn't been given the budget to run a city.

*The charitable associations and the FIS were separate groups?*

In a given neighborhood you would find what was known as a "family" of FIS militants which was the base organization of the

FIS. These groups operated alongside the charitable associations, which were larger, more open, and included FIS militants as well as other local people. It was the FIS militants who ran for municipal office. The associations supported the FIS candidates.

*How did the municipality get money to function?*

As a municipal government the FIS couldn't receive any money officially from a private source or a foreign government. But the charitable associations could. There were several levels of funding. Locally, the associations continued door-to-door fund raising. The commercial bourgeoisie was a very important contributor. In Tlemcen there are mosques and charitable sites (shelters) that are entirely maintained by the local bourgeoisie. There were the *affairistes*—entrepreneurs who wanted to get rich quick. The FLN had blocked them with various laws controlling import-export, resale and speculation. There were the big industrialists who also felt suffocated by the regulation of commerce and investment. All these groups supported the FIS because the FIS had promised to suppress taxes and deregulate production. There was also external financing, from Saudi Arabia in particular. The FIS wasn't worried about money.

They always seemed to have money to carry out their projects. For example, in Tlemcen there used to be a colonial square in the middle of town. A part of the *medina* had been destroyed and a rectangular plaza installed, with the great mosque on one side, the city hall on the other, the *medina* to one side, and across from it the colonial city. This square was cut in two by a roadway. The FLN municipality destroyed the road to create one big square with the traffic going around the outside. In the middle they built a monument: a rock with fountains. Outside of Tlemcen there used to be waterfalls that are now dried up because of a dam. Maybe the rock was supposed to ease the nostalgia of the Tlemcenians for these waterfalls.

The FIS came and said, "What's this? It's no good! The space was better before!" In two days, they took out the rock and the fountains, rebuilt the road, put it all back the way it was before, but fixed up. How could a municipality with budget problems do this so quickly? They called on people to volunteer. But also there were two big private companies with modern equipment that did the work. One can deduce that the companies supported the FIS, since they did it for free.

## The Enthusiasm of the Islamists

*I'm struck by your description of the efficacy of the FIS.*

In meeting these young people, one *is* struck by their great discipline and by the organization of their local cells. At the same time, as a woman, as a democrat, I find it terrifying what an institution this well-organized can do. In the electoral campaign we saw this same efficiency and mobilization. They were everywhere.

*How do you explain that enthusiasm?*

Islamists came onto a completely empty field. You had a society that was morose, mired in a kind of lassitude, where people were completely burnt-out, in despair—and they suggested something.

In the electoral campaign, the FIS brought up questions of honesty, of justice. The FLN had a program: housing, work, education. But the FIS said: we won't promise you anything. We'll have a state where we apply Islam, where honesty and justice will reign. And if there's no corruption, there'll be money. If there's justice, there'll be an equitable distribution of housing, and so on. It's a moral contract, not an electoral program.

There was another important element. The FIS touched on the issues which are the most sensitive: concerns about women, about the degeneration of moral values. On their side were upright women, as guardians of moral order. They were cleaning up public space. On the other side were bars, alcohol, urban degradation. . . .

*What has happened in Tlemcen since the rupture in the electoral process in December 1991?*

I was in Tlemcen the day after the forced resignation of President Chadli Benjadid. We had the impression that political life had stopped for a moment. The next day, I went out to Sidi Said to see what people were saying, how people experienced the end of the electoral process. There was consternation. Many people had forgotten about the army, about the possibility of intervention. There had been the feeling that a breath of liberty was coming, and then—it collapsed.

There was incredible restraint on the part of the Islamists, which was much more important than what happened afterwards: the coup d'etat, military take-over, and then the punishing of the FIS.

Police and soldiers kept a close watch on the associations and the mosques. They tried to push them to extremism. Then there was violence, imprisonment. This is all classic.

Now the FIS is legally out of commission. There is a new party called the Islamic Solidarity Front—the acronym is still FIS. But its activity is under close surveillance.

The FIS discourse made it clear that they weren't going to be democratic. But to stop the process by nondemocratic methods gave the FIS the ideological and moral claim to say, "The FLN just doesn't want to let go of its power, its privilege."

Before the multiparty system was instituted and the FIS became a party in 1989, all their activities took place clandestinely. In 1989, an Islamist party emerged from underground. Now they're being pushed again into clandestinity, but their activities have not stopped.

*"[Islam] offers a sense of common allegiance. . . . The idea of the 'nation' has offered nothing in this regard."*

# Political Islam Furthers Development in Sudan

Hassan al-Turabi, interviewed by Nathan Gardels

Hassan al-Turabi is party chairman of Sudan's National Islamic Front, which has imposed one-party rule and seeks to re-impose Islamic law (*sharia*) on Sudan. In the following viewpoint, al-Turabi, interviewed by Nathan Gardels, argues that the revival of Islam is a response to the failure of secular nationalism and socialism—adopted by previous governments in the Middle East and Africa—to promote political and economic development. Al-Turabi contends that Islam is mobilizing the Sudanese people for development by imbuing the pursuit of development with spiritual significance. He also argues that under Islamic law, women's and minorities' rights are protected and penal codes are fair.

As you read, consider the following questions:

1. What does al-Turabi say is the difference between the Islamic awakening in Malaysia and in Iran?
2. Why has the loss of *sharia* led to absolutist government in Muslim countries, according to the author?
3. According to al-Turabi, is *sharia* observed the same way in all Islamic countries?

"The Islamic Awakening's Second Wave," an interview with Hassan al-Turabi by Nathan Gardels, *New Perspectives Quarterly*, Summer 1992. Reprinted with permission.

*Nathan Gardels: As the fervor of the Iranian revolution fades, you are said by many in the West to be the "new Khomeini," the new bearer of the flame of Islamic fundamentalism. What do you think of that perception?*

Hassan Al-Turabi: Well, people in the West are fond of personalizing the Islamic revival. No doubt, they will ultimately reduce it to a conspiracy to export Islamic revolution, of which I am the leading villain. But there is nothing of the sort.

I merely represent a new, mature wave of the Islamic awakening taking place today from Algeria and Jordan to Khartoum [Sudan] and Kuala Lumpur [Malaysia]. As first evidenced in the Iranian revolution, this awakening is comprehensive—it is not just about individual piety; it is not just intellectual and cultural, nor is it just political. It is all of these, a comprehensive reconstruction of society from top to bottom.

## The Failure of Western-Style Nationalism and the Islamic Awakening

This widespread Islamic revival has been given impetus by the vacuum left by a bankrupt nationalism, especially Arab nationalism, and African socialism. The post-colonial nationalist regimes had no agenda but to throw out the imperialists. Once they achieved their goal, they had nothing to offer the people. Then they turned to socialism as an alternative to the imperial West. Now, like everyone else, the Islamic world is disillusioned with socialism.

The Islamic awakening began to build in South Asia and the Arab world, as well as in Iran, in the 1950s—participating in some administrations in the 1970s. Perhaps due to the limitations of language and access to the sources of Islamic law, the expansion of Islamic consciousness came somewhat late to North Africa and then south of the Sahara. The Gulf war, which brought foreigners into the vicinity of our sacred religious centers in Saudi Arabia, gave an enormous boost to the movement in North Africa, not only among the general population but also among the elites.

The new and critical aspect of the recent Islamic awakening is that the elites in the army and government—the so-called "modern" sector—are themselves becoming Islamicized.

This has already happened in the Sudan, and is in the process of happening in Algeria. In 1985 the Sudanese army led by Defense Minister General Abdel Rahman Siwar el-Dahab intervened to stop Islamization. But his efforts led to an uprising by junior officers who supported Islamization. I have no doubt the same thing will happen in Algeria. The Islamization of the modern sector is the prevalent trend throughout the region.

*You include Malaysia in your web of Islamic awakening. But one has a very different impression of the Islamic current there than, for example, Iran. Islam in Malaysia is much more open, liberal and tolerant, whereas in Iran there is the totalitarian effort to impose* shari'a, *the Islamic code governing all aspects of life.*

Although these two countries have experienced the Islamic awakening, each has taken a different form. Much has depended on the nature of the challenge from the West. In Iran, the challenge was very sharp, so the Islamic movement became obsessed with the West. The U.S. identified so closely with the Shah's effort to introduce the post-Christian-West lifestyle—materialistic, sexually licentious, highly emancipated in terms of drinking alcohol—that Ayatollah Khomeini and his followers became fixated on confronting "the Great Satan."

Also, the movement in Iran was very unusual in that it was led by traditional Shi'ite scholars, the *mullahs*. Since they are a minority sect in Islam, they organized a separate, alternative leadership structure.

The hostility of the Shah's regime, like the hostility of the Roman Empire to the early Christians, gave rise to an analogous church structure. Unlike the rest of Islam, the Shi'ite individual can only relate to God through the *mullahs*.

In Malaysia, decoloniation came about rather gently. So the people there focused less on the common enemy than on common ideals. The awakening there has thus been more constructive than Iran's revolutionary reaction.

### Islam Offers a Sense of Allegiance

*What does Islamic rule offer Sudan that neither nationalism nor socialism did?*

Like all religions, of course, it provides people with a sense of identity and a direction in life, something shattered in Africa since colonialism. In the African context in particular, it offers a sense of common allegiance.

Islam provides a focus for unity and a minimum consensus in the face of the regionalism and tribalism which have been so devastatingly rampant in Africa. The idea of the "nation" has offered nothing in this regard. Everyone knows that African nations are only the legacy of colonialist cartographers.

Moreover, the Islamic code of *shari'a* provides the people with higher laws and values, which they obey out of belief and not because they are enforced by government.

In the wake of the collapse of materialist totalitarianism in the Soviet Union and Eastern Europe, the West has talked endlessly about the rebirth of "civil society," that sphere of activity beyond the reach of government. But only when Muslims lost the *shari'a* as their binding law under colonialism did they suffer the bitter experience of absolutist government.

Under *shari'a*, no ruler could suppress his own people. So the individual was protected and society was autonomous. People felt that the norms that governed the society were their norms because they were God's laws.

The colonialists did away with that, introducing a sense of alienation between people and government with their secular laws divorced from indigenous values and internal norms. That alienation remained as the legacy of colonial rule. Even if there were formal elections, people just elected their tribal relatives, or voted for those who would give them money. There was no representation.

In the absence of *shari'a* in poor, largely illiterate societies like Sudan, corruption ruled because there was also no accountability or moral checks on government. The public sector squandered its resources and brought the people nothing. Only when all subscribe to the moral code of Islam in public affairs can corruption be eliminated.

---

### Islamists Oppose Corrupt Governments

Islamists are bitter critics of government corruption and of rulers who look out for themselves and not for the welfare of the people.

They trace the root of this problem to 1916, when European powers decided to partition the eastern Arab world into entities— Syria, Lebanon, Palestine, Transjordan—that later became countries. The creation of artificial states to serve Western interests left Arabs weak, divided and under nondemocratic regimes without true legitimacy.

Islamists look to a time when the region will once again be integrated into some common system, perhaps a federation of states. As one Islamist said of the various countries, "If we woke up tomorrow and they were all gone, we would not shed one single tear."

Ronald R. Stockton, *The Washington Report on Middle East Affairs*, November/ December 1993.

---

Finally, and fundamentally, neither nationalism nor socialism could mobilize our societies to develop. Religion can be the most powerful impetus for development in social situations where profit and salary incentives are insufficient.

In societies that lack opportunity, people have no motivation to go to school or to seek knowledge. Islam provides that motivation because it mobilizes people to pursue divine ends. The appeal of God reaches their heart. The pursuit of knowledge becomes an act of worship.

When people are taught that agriculture is their *jihad*, their holy struggle, they will go for it in earnest. *Be good to God and develop agriculture.* That is the slogan that is transforming Sudan from near-famine to self-sufficiency in food.

To the rich West that may sound strange. But what role did Puritanism play in carving America out of the wilderness? What role did the Protestant ethic play in the development of the European economies? Religion is a motor of development.

## Islam and Rights

*To get a tangible sense of the brand of Islamic rule you promote, let me ask about four areas where Islamic fundamentalism has clashed with the West: the rights of women, the rights of non-Muslims, the penal code under* shari'a, *and the case of Salman Rushdie.*

First, women. It is true that a very powerful tradition developed in some Islamic countries that segregated women from men and deprived them of their rights of sharing equally and fairly in society.

With the new revival of Islam, women are gaining their rights because no one can challenge the Koran in the name of local custom or convention. In Sudan in particular, the Islamic movement campaigned for giving women their political rights. Now, women not only have equal educational chances, but are playing substantial roles in public life—some have gone to parliament. Women returned to the mosque, as well.

As a way to protect women, since they might constitute a temptation to men, there was a time when convention had it that they should stay home. But that is not what religion taught. Of course, accordingly, women must dress modestly, covering their heads and bodies in public. Men also have to dress decently. Both must act properly toward each other.

Forcible female circumcision, another customary practice in parts of the Sudan that often led to the death of women, has faded away due to the Islamic awakening. To the extent it is practiced at all today, it is practiced symbolically. Many in the West have identified this cruel custom with Islam. But it has nothing to do with Islam. It was, in fact, called "Pharaonic circumcision."

On the rights of minorities, under *shari'a* there is a guarantee for non-Muslims of freedom of religion and cult. Private life, including education and family, are immune from interference by Islamic state law. Under *shari'a*, if they happen to live together in one area, a minority is entitled to a large measure of administrative autonomy. Their relationship to the Muslim majority can be organized according to a covenant that spells out and regulates reciprocal duties and obligations, defining what is common and what is private.

50

Under such covenants in Islamic history, for example, alcohol was free to be consumed in the Jewish or Christian quarters while prohibited in Muslim quarters.

The *shari'a* itself is not one standard code observed worldwide in a monolithic way. It is applied in a decentralized way according to varying local conditions. Different Muslim communities have different schools of law. These Islamic principles of governance are being invoked to settle the war with the non-Muslims of southern Sudan.

*Shari'a* will be applied in the north, where the Muslims dominate, but in the south, where Christians and pagans make up the majority, the criminal provisions of *shari'a* will not apply.

---

### The Islamic Movement and Democracy

The Islamic movement has occurred in a context of the intellectual bankruptcy of slogans like Arab socialism. These slogans did assist in gaining national independence but they were empty of concrete detail of application. In the case of the Sudan, for example, a British administrator was replaced by a Sudanese administrator. The Islamic movement is also criticized for not being democratic. Within the movement there has been a question of the meaning of the term *dimuqratiyya* (democracy) as a foreign word in application to Islamic societies. The Western association of secularism and cutthroat competition for power with the term is objectionable, but also objectionable is the prominence of politics in the term. In Islam, politics is considered amoral, not immoral. The critics of the Islamic movement want to label it as antidemocratic when in fact it is essentially a grass-roots and populist phenomenon and highly democratic.

Remarks of Hasan Turabi (Hassan al-Turabi) summarized by Louis J. Cantori and Arthur Lowrie, *Middle East Policy*, vol. 1, no. 3, Summer 1992.

---

On the penal code, when Maj. Gen. Gaafar Mohammed Nimiery applied the *shari'a* penal code in a makeshift manner back in the 1980s as a political gesture to demonstrate his Islamic commitment, it brought worldwide condemnation of cruelty and abuse of human rights. As a result, many in the West think that, under the rule of *shari'a*, every act of theft will result in such punishments as the severing of hands or even execution.

That is not true. Between 1990 and 1992, there were only two such sentences because, under properly administered Islamic law, the degree of proof required is very high. And there are other considerations—the value of the stolen property, the absence of any extenuating circumstances like dire need, or repentance and restoration of property.

The whole idea is to associate severe punishment with major theft as a deterrent in order to morally educate the people. Petty theft is punished no more severely than in most of the world. In spite of the severity of punishment under Islam, the crime scene in the U.S., with all its violence, is a worse alternative.

Homicide law is even more flexible under *shari'a* than the English law, which was formerly enforced in Sudan. For example, even when the charge is intentional homicide, if there is conciliation between the parties or compensation paid, the perpetrator may actually be pardoned and go free. *Shari'a* also de-emphasizes prison sentences because such punishment is subversive of character and extends beyond the culprit to the innocent family members.

On Salman Rushdie, in Sudan, he could not be convicted of apostasy. Although Islam is very universal in its implications, it does accept territory as the basis of jurisdiction. Thus, the jurisdiction of an Islamic state does not extend beyond that state. Those living abroad are not subject to Islamic law, but to international treaty obligations between states.

Within Muslim states, it has been a traditional view that public apostasy is punishable by death, subject to trying to persuade the perpetrator to change his mind and recant. But, from the early days of Islam, apostasy completely coincided with treason, because warring societies were based on religion and someone who publicly abused his religion would objectively join the other party as a combatant.

Today in the Sudan such intellectual apostasy as Rushdie's is not punishable by death. It must involve active subversion of the constitutional order.

### The Situation in Sudan

*These responses all sound moderate, but isn't it a fact that opposition parties have been banned in the Sudan?*

The case of Sudan today is not, of course, the ultimate model of where the Islamic awakening should end up. The Sudan is an Islamic state-in-process and is going through many emergencies as a result of the war in the south. Security is at risk. Masses of people are streaming toward the urban centers searching for food and relief. Under such circumstances, one can't maintain the ordinary due process of law.

We have been through so many cycles of uprisings and coups in the past several years that the equation between freedom and order must, at the moment, have a balance tilted toward stability and order that it wouldn't have in times of peace. Such abnormality in the time of war is, so to speak, normal. After all, the Americans imprisoned nationals of Japanese descent during World War II.

In any event, the situation is improving. Tens of thousands are not detained, as in some neighboring countries. Only a few dozen. After the coup in 1989, the maximum detained was two hundred. But we look forward to a state where such exceptional procedures would end.

*In early April 1992, Amnesty International accused the Sudanese regime of torture. It said, "Prisoners have been shackled and suspended from their cell walls, sometimes upside down. Others have had their testicles crushed with pliers." Africa Watch has also charged torture. How do you respond?*

I do not speak for the government. The charges of torture might have been true, especially in the early days after the coup of June 1989. But not since. Certainly such episodes, or reports of them, instill fear of the Islamic awakening as the dreaded spread of Islamic "fundamentalism." But they are transitional features that arise from the tension of an old order dying and a new one being born.

The social change taking its course may be rough, but all changes are like that. And where there is suppression, as in Algeria, it will mean revolution instead of peaceful evolution. Peaceful change through persuasion and sincerity is the path dictated by Islam. But what if there is no alternative to revolution?

## The Relations of Sudan and Iran

*In the wake of Iranian President Hashemi Rafsanjani's 1992 visit to Sudan, you have been accused of exporting Islamic revolution in consort with Iran. Sudan has also been accused of becoming the new haven for terrorists.*

The Iranian relationship with Sudan, which is minor, has been present since 1989. But, so what? Iran of late is opening up to everyone. They've reconciled with Saudi Arabia, Morocco and even the Europeans. Since we are a professed Islamic state, what is so surprising about Sudan's relationship with Iran?

Moreover, Sudan has been shunned by some in the West, so it has turned East. Not only to Iran, but to Malaysia, Indonesia, Pakistan and China.

True, the visit of Rafsanjani did evoke massive, popular displays of support. But these were the reminiscences of the Iranian revolution coming back. Anyway, the program of cooperation between the two countries is not all that significant. It just provides for trade. Sudan will export meat, oil seed and cereal to Iran and will buy manufactured goods and petroleum products—hardly a revolutionary alliance.

Iran has absolutely no military presence in Sudan, despite rumors from neighboring countries about the presence of thousands of Iranian Revolutionary Guards.

Sudan itself cannot export revolution. No doubt, because of the

African and Arab aspect of Sudan as well as our well-articulated programs and theories, the Sudanese example does radiate. But we have no money to finance revolution abroad or spread it by military conquest. The Sudan is not engaged in subverting other nations.

As for harboring terrorists, let me say this: We have no interest in terrorism. The Koran is very explicit against individual acts of terrorism. It says that the Islamic cause must build patiently, even in the face of persecution, until acquiring statehood. Then the Islamic state is entitled to defend itself.

Most of the terrorist movements in the Middle East were far closer to European leftism and nationalism than to the tradition of Islam. They were inspired by groups in France, Germany and Ireland. As far as I am concerned, Islam can have nothing to do with terrorism.

The Islamic awakening has reached a new stage. It is no longer interested in confronting the West, in fighting with the West. The West is not our preoccupation. We are concerned with the constructive regeneration of our societies by mobilizing our souls and our minds, not fighting "Great Satans." Except when a policy is directed against Islam, the West is not the enemy for us.

---

*"The [military] regime is systematically dismantling the modern state of Sudan and creating a new, Islamic model."*

---

# Political Islam Is a Dictatorship in Sudan

Julie Flint

In June 1989, Sudan's first-ever democratically elected government was ousted by a military coup d'etat. The military government that now rules Sudan is heavily influenced by the National Islamic Front (NIF), an Islamic party led by Hassan al-Turabi that seeks to restructure Sudan according to Islamic law (*sharia*). In the following viewpoint, Julie Flint argues that the military government and the NIF are imposing an Islamic dictatorship on Sudan through repression and terror. This dictatorial style of government, according to Flint, is isolating Sudan from the world community, blocking economic development, and prolonging a civil war with non-Muslim forces. Flint is a freelance journalist covering the Middle East.

As you read, consider the following questions:

1. Why is the process of participatory democracy a "phony process," according to the author and the Western diplomat she quotes?
2. Why did the military government crack down on mosques, according to Flint?

Julie Flint, "Under Islamic Siege," *Africa Report*, September/October 1993. Reprinted with permission.

It was an act of enormous courage.

As we left Juba prison, where dozens of officers disappeared in the terror that followed an abortive rebel attempt to capture the city in 1992, a young private seemed to nudge against me. I looked at him, and looked quickly away again. He was staring straight ahead, his lips barely moving, and whispering: "I am afraid to talk. We have suffered very much. It is not over."

I have often wondered whether the dozens of minders and hangers-on accompanying our three-person delegation spotted him and, if so, what became of him. Later that day, in Juba's regional assembly, a young man slipped me a letter without breaking his stride or turning his head. It was nothing particularly sensitive—a plan for more humanitarian aid for the 250,000 people in the besieged city—but it did not go unnoticed.

"Who was that man?" deputy governor Angelo Beda asked many hours later. What man? "The one who gave you a letter in the assembly. . . . You see how it is: We are open and frank with you, but there is a fifth column among us."

## A State of Siege

Everyone in Sudan, it seems, feels under siege—the government that sees international disapproval crippling its attempt to liberalize the economy and so perhaps save its increasingly unpopular neck; the 3 million people in southern Sudan displaced by a ten-year-old civil war in which civilians are the deliberate targets of all parties; the factions of the Sudan People's Liberation Army (SPLA) [the rebel army of non-Muslims from southern Sudan] who are under fire for their own human rights abuses; the Nuba people [an ethnic group in northern Sudan] subjected to what [the human rights group] Amnesty International has called a campaign of ethnic cleansing; and ordinary Sudanese suffering under the heavy hand of Hassan Turabi's National Islamic Front (NIF)—the power behind the throne of a military government that everyone, everywhere tells you is profoundly un-Sudanese.

"We have never known a situation like this in our history," says a prominent opposition figure. "Today you are frightened to ask your brother if he is in the NIF." And then: "Please feel free to use my name. It is the least we can do today." The friend who arranged the meeting later sounded a note of caution: "Don't name him, please. He will be arrested."

The government of Sudan has stifled all opposition in the four years since Gen. Omar Hassan al-Bashir overthrew the democratically elected but deeply flawed government of Sadiq al-Mahdi [in 1989]. Political parties have been banned, political opponents silenced by death, torture, and imprisonment, and a process of "participatory democracy" set in motion "to give power back to the people"—a phony process that will ensure the NIF a stranglehold on a National Assembly that is expected to be operative by 1995.

"This whole system is a means of controlling the people—not of the people participating in the government," says a senior Western diplomat in Khartoum. "Even excluding all the coercion, there are so many appointees at the different levels that by the time it comes to the National Assembly, the majority will at some time have been voted for by an appointee."

University lecturers have either been dismissed or given a choice of collaboration, resistance, submission, or exile in what Africa Watch [a human rights group] has called a "ferocious" onslaught on higher education. Student and trade unions have been replaced with sham unions answerable to the NIF. (Leaders of the powerful railways syndicate were detained until "voting" was over.)

"Seventy percent of the workers were dismissed before the elections," says a former union leader jailed in or confined to Khartoum for most of the 1990s. "But even the remaining 30 percent were not given the freedom to vote: The candidates' list was prepared by the NIF." Many lawyers only learned of the so-called elections when they were already over. "The only lawyers who have seen the rules of the new Lawyers' Association are NIF members," says one of the old school. "The others were taken by surprise and appealed. But they were told this is not in the rules. We are witnessing an Orwellian transformation of society."

### Creating an Islamic State

Under cover of its rubber-stamp parliament, the Transitional National Assembly, the regime is systematically dismantling the modern state of Sudan and creating a new, Islamic model. Islamic banking systems have been introduced and Islamic law enforced. Although the regime has said *shari'a* will not be applied in the predominantly Christian south if peace is agreed with the divided SPLA, southerners are concerned that this promise is not yet guaranteed by law.

Old democratic institutions have new Islamic rivals. At least two security services directly responsible to the NIF have joined the traditional Sudan Security, creating what a former minister calls "a dictatorship without a dictator, a hydra with many heads." The paramilitary popular defense forces have been empowered and expanded, with a period of compulsory conscription for all students and government employees—including ministers. The newer popular police forces, described by the government as a kind of neighborhood watch, are viewed by foreign diplomats as a rival to the regular police and by ordinary citizens as a specifically Islamic police.

Underpinning these changes is a reign of terror unprecedented in Sudan. No one is not threatened by it. "What has happened in Sudan is horrible," says a former minister who was tortured intermittently for nine months, locked in a room the size of a cupboard with his hands tied to the wall so that only one foot could reach the ground. "It has nothing to do with the Sudanese tradition."

---

### Sudan Under the Islamists

Five years after the 1989 revolution in Sudan the Islamists have brought about almost the exact opposite of what, to judge from their prior writings, they intended. The civil war rages, the secret police operate without restriction, the press is censored, the military reigns, and political opponents of the Islamists and the military languish in ghost houses when they are not simply killed. It is true that life has never been easy in Sudan, and it would have been unrealistic to have expected any ideology to save the Sudanese from themselves. But by most measures—and especially by the measure of political oppression—Sudan is worse off as an Islamic state than it was before.

William Langewiesche, *The Atlantic Monthly*, August 1994.

---

Illustrating this, a father tells how security officials came to his home at 8:30 am to ask for his son. They said it was nothing serious; there had been some trouble at the boy's school and they needed to ask a few questions. It wouldn't take long. Ten hours later, three men emerged from the office where the father had been waiting all day and tossed an inert form he did not at first recognize into the back of a pick-up truck.

"You can take him home now," they said.

When he could talk, the boy said he had been taken into a room where eleven other youths were already lined up against the wall. The three men had come into the room and gone down the line hitting every boy in the stomach. Then they stripped the boys and lashed them with split bamboo canes before turning them out into the yard to stand staring into the sun for five hours. They were beaten if they closed their eyes and refused food and water.

Their "crime" had been to decide against enrolling in the Youth of the Nation, a paramilitary Islamic group.

On hearing this, the father returned to the security office in fury. "I have never wanted to believe these stories," he told the man who took his son away. "But now I do. I will kill you if my son is permanently injured. The only thing you have achieved by this is alienating twelve northern Muslim families."

In defense of the regime, a Western diplomat argues that it has a genuine concern for the poor—although patently not for the southern poor trucked out to fly-blown refugee camps in the desert outside Khartoum—and sees itself as a frontier state forging a new, Islamic model in Africa. "I do believe they think they are building a better society," he says. "But if they have to kill everyone to do it, they will."

## Cracking Down on Political Groups

Deafened by a chorus of international protest that has made desperately needed development aid conditional on human rights, the government changed its tactics. The norm now is not imprisonment and torture, but day-long detention that continues for weeks and months. A trade unionist who suffered this routine for seven straight months reported to security at 6 am every day and left at 5 pm. He is now confined to Khartoum, far from his home town and unable to work. "I have sold everything I have to sell," he says despairingly. "I can no longer afford to put my sons in school. Let all trade union organizations know these new trade unions are based on intimidation. The world should not recognize them."

In 1993, the government extended its crackdown on political organizations to religious groups as well, moving against the three main bases of traditional Sunni Islam—the Ansar, Khatmiya, and Ansar Sunna sects whose importance has increased as the noose has tightened around political groups.

The first step in this squeeze came early in 1993 with the effective takeover of the new Khatmiya headquarters in Khartoum North—a mosque whose opening had been postponed while the order's leader, Mohamed Osman Mirghani, then recently released from jail, rested outside the country. In Mirghani's absence, the governor of Khartoum ordered the mosque opened immediately under an imam of his choice, a NIF stalwart. Then it was the turn of the Ansar, whose headquarters in Omdurman, Khartoum's twin city, was raided on the eve of the Muslim holiday marking the end of the annual pilgrimage to Mecca. The contents of the site—the Khalifa mosque and the tomb of the Mahdi, the 19th century leader who led a nationalist revolt against the British—were looted and trucked away. Finally, the regime arrested the leader of the Saudi-backed Ansar Sunna, Sheikh Mohamed al-Haddiya, an outspoken septuagenarian orator, who had earlier been prevented from travelling to Saudi Arabia for the hajj.

Opposition sources, and some foreign diplomats, interpret the crackdown as a sign of panic, acknowledgment by the regime of its failure to create a popular base. But it was also, in the regime's terms, a necessary move to combat a new threat. The importance of the mosque, one of the few remaining channels of protest, could not have been highlighted more dramatically than it was in March 1993 when the Ansar issued a Ramadan call to the army to return to barracks and permit democracy or face a campaign of civil struggle.

## Sudan's Government Under Attack

Isolated in the Arab world, under increasing criticism in the international community, and burdened with an economy bled dry by the war in the south, even the government admits that Sudan is in poor shape. Economists lament the fact that export earnings no longer cover even oil imports. Foreign Minister Hussein abu Saleh complains publicly that the government is "besieged" and grumbles privately that Sudan's support of Iraq in the Gulf War was misjudged. Justice Minister Abdul-Azis Shiddu acknowledges that "there is no smoke without fire." Even Turabi admits that "things are not going very well."

But there appears to be little chance of change for the foreseeable future. "Turabi is a man with no limits," says one of the silenced majority. "He is the man who is willing to go to the last meter and even beyond it. As far as political power is concerned, he is as hard as steel."

With the army estimated to have been purged of 4,000 officers, 500 NCOs, and 11,000 rank and file, it is hard to see any immediate threat from the military despite growing popular discontent. (Inflation of roughly 20 percent a month has reduced the annual salary of a doctor to $400.) The first signs of public protest have been ruthlessly suppressed: Army troops shot dead ten people, including five children, in the town of Gedaref in January 1993 after spontaneous bread riots, and the government may have broken up a coup plot after the Ansar's Ramadan appeal to the army.

"People are against this regime, but haven't yet decided what the alternative is," says a veteran politician who is watched around the clock. "They know this government has guns and is prepared to use them. There is always the vague hope that a good officer will come up. But this officer is not there now. And if he is, he's in the street—not in the ranks."

# Periodical Bibliography

The following articles have been selected to supplement the diverse views presented in this chapter.

Frank C. Baldwin — "A Nation's Holy War," *The Christian Century*, July 13–20, 1994.

Massimo Dini — "The Growing Influence of 'God's Fanatics,'" *World Press Review*, March 1992.

John P. Entelis and Lisa J. Arone — "Algeria in Turmoil: Islam, Democracy, and the State," *Middle East Policy*, vol. 1, no. 2, Spring 1992. Available from 1730 M St. NW, Suite 512, Washington, DC 20036.

Abbas Hamdani — "Islamic Fundamentalism," *Mediterranean Quarterly*, Fall 1993. Available from Duke University Press, Box 90660, Durham, NC 27708.

Alfred Hermida — "The State and Islam," *Africa Report*, September/October 1994.

William Langewiesche — "Turabi's Law," *The Atlantic Monthly*, August 1994.

Ron Marchese — "Understanding the Arab World: Confusion and Misconception," *USA Today*, November 1992.

Bradford R. McGuinn — "Why the Fundamentalists Are Winning," *The New York Times*, March 22, 1993.

Judith Miller — "A Muslim Cleric Hones the Fusing of Religion and Politics," *The New York Times*, May 17, 1992.

Taslima Nasrin — "Sentenced to Death," *The New York Times*, November 30, 1993.

James North — "Fundamental Flaws," *In These Times*, May 17, 1993.

Jonathan Randal — "An Islamic Insurgency Reemerges," *The Washington Post National Weekly Edition*, June 13–19, 1994. Available from 1150 15th St. NW, Washington, DC 20071.

Abdul Aziz Said — "Islamic Fundamentalism and the West," *Mediterranean Quarterly*, Fall 1992.

Hasan Turabi, summarized by Louis J. Cantori and Arthur Lowrie — "Islam, Democracy, the State, and the West," *Middle East Policy*, vol. 1, no. 3, Summer 1992.

CHAPTER

2

# What Is the Status of Women Under Islam?

# Chapter Preface

In a story in the *New York Times Magazine*, Iranian-American writer Tara Bahrampour relates an account of her return to Iran, her first visit since the Islamic revolution of 1979. Her story provides an illustration of the paradox that exists for women living in the Islamic Republic of Iran.

Bahrampour recounts the prior warnings she received from other Western women who had traveled to the Islamic Republic: "No makeup, no perfume, no nail polish." Yet she finds her relatives in Iran, who are part of the middle class and not involved in the Islamic movement, are quite relaxed about wearing makeup, just as they were before the Islamic revolution. At a relative's wedding she attends, men and women wearing Western-style fashions dance to pop music, despite the laws prohibiting it. The wedding is suddenly disrupted by the *komitehs*, the paramilitary squads who act as "morals police," and a wave of panic grips Bahrampour and the other women. But once the *komitehs* leave, the music and dancing resume and the momentary panic is quickly forgotten.

Bahrampour also relates a persistent rumor told among the Iranian women of a young woman shot by the *komitehs* for refusing to properly veil herself in public. And yet, the young women with whom the author spends time casually allow their scarves to slip to their shoulders when no one is watching. "Don't worry, the women assure me, life here is not so frightening," she writes.

Bahrampour's story relates how her preconceptions about women in Iranian society were changed by her experiences. The viewpoints in the following chapter debate not only whether women are or will be repressed by religious laws in Islamic societies, but whether those societies should be judged according to Western values.

*"By continuing to work, walk on the streets, and choose their own style of dress, today many Algerian women continue to do 'daily battle.'"*

# Islamic Fundamentalism Represses Women

Karima Bennoune

Following riots in Algeria in October 1988, the Islamic Salvation Front (FIS), a political party that advocated an Islamic republic, quickly became one of the most powerful organizations in the country. In the following viewpoint, Karima Bennoune argues that the systematic attacks on women and women's rights carried out by Islamic fundamentalists in Algeria are a good predictor of what will happen if fundamentalists come to power. These attacks and the fundamentalists' interpretations of Islamic law that spurred them are political in nature, according to Bennoune; they are not a part of the "culture" of the Islamic world as some in the West believe. Bennoune is a lawyer and Arab-American activist who has worked for Palestinian rights.

As you read, consider the following questions:

1. What activities does Bennoune say are defined as "unclean" by fundamentalists?
2. What did the FIS say was the reason for Algeria's socioeconomic "predicament," according to the author? What was their solution?
3. According to Bennoune, is the conflict in Algeria between religious and secular forces? Explain.

From Karima Bennoune, "Algerian Women Confront Fundamentalism," *Monthly Review*, September 1994. Copyright ©1994 by Monthly Review Inc. Reprinted by permission of Monthly Review Foundation.

Algeria's current crisis has found its way to the front pages of many U.S. and European newspapers and magazines. Not surprisingly, the situation of Algerian women within that crisis and the assault on their rights by Algerian Muslim fundamentalists do not figure as central issues in the media portrayal of this moment in Algerian history. Press reports and those of major human rights organizations have shared this gynopia, and this particular aspect of their blindness has drastically altered the vision of Algeria offered for Western consumption, obscuring the nature of Algerian fundamentalism and the possible reasons for indigenous opposition to it.

While I was in Algiers, Algeria, in February 1994, the prominent leader of a women's group in Algeria, who herself has been placed on fundamentalist death lists and has had to leave her home for safety reasons, expressed to me her outrage at the recent reports of Middle East Watch for failing to address women's concerns. This is not a new phenomenon. When I first met her in 1992 she had stressed to me that when women activists had been protesting in the streets against the 1984 Family Code [which legalized polygamy, allowing men to marry up to four wives], they had been alone with the police and that no government and no international human rights organization had done or said anything to support them. In this viewpoint, I argue that situating the fundamentalist assault on women's rights at the center of an analysis of Algeria's current crisis is key to understanding it, and is a necessary component of any "human rights" critique.

## Women Targeted by the Fundamentalists

In fact, at least forty-eight Algerian women have been deliberately targeted and assassinated, principally by the two main armed fundamentalist groups, the Mouvement Islamique Armé (MIA) and the Groupe Islamique Armé (GIA). The women have primarily been shot or burned to death, while methods of decapitation and throat-slitting have been reserved for the male victims of the fundamentalist armed groups, including doctors, journalists, and professors. . . .

Women have been further pressured to cease performing certain activities seen as "unclean" by fundamentalists, such as teaching boys in school, owning or frequenting the hairdressers, or even going to the *hammam* or Turkish bath, which has been a part of many Algerian women's lives since at least the middle ages. In February and March 1994, the GIA also began a campaign of abducting and raping young girls and women. This has particularly occurred in Ain Defla and in Bouera, where even the wife of a non-fundamentalist imam was raped by members of an armed group.

Fundamentalist violence against women in Algeria is not a

new phenomenon. Its contemporary beginnings are to be found in the late 1970s, when Muslim fundamentalists began intimidating female university students on campuses throughout Algeria, including sometimes throwing acid on women students who refused to veil. The phenomenon has increased with a vengeance from that time to this. Initially, it was not taken seriously by the international human rights community or by the Algerian authorities. As emphasized by Khalida Messaoudi (a prominent woman activist and president of the Independent Association for the Triumph of Women's Rights), women were the first to be targeted by fundamentalist terrorists. Then later, beginning in 1992, mainly male journalists and intellectuals were targeted. Had the violence against women been taken seriously at the time, Messaoudi suggests, the nature of the fundamentalist agenda could have been clearly understood and perhaps the later bloodshed could have been averted. Instead, the "political" nature of this violence against women was deliberately obscured.

## The Emergence of Political Islam in Algeria

The Islamic Salvation Front (FIS) emerged as the major national opposition group in the late 1980s when political parties were legalized in the wake of the October 1988 repression [when hundreds were killed and many arrested as the Algerian military and police suppressed riots]. For the FIS, the political system which would save Algeria was to be found in what Andre Gunder Frank described as "a regress to an often largely mythical golden age–like seventh century Islam." The growth of fundamentalism into a powerful force coincided with the terrible socioeconomic crisis of the 1980s, induced by clumsy privatizations, the dismantling of the national economy, and widespread corruption in Algeria's new right-wing government. But the FIS actually had two contradictory bases. While religious fundamentalism seemed to many young people to offer an alternative non-Western vision of the good society, critiquing both social injustice and cultural Westernization, the middle class and merchant base of the FIS was dedicated to protecting property rights in the name of Islam and allowing Western multinational investment in Algeria. In fact, the first contemporary fundamentalist grouping in Algeria coalesced in opposition to President Houari Boumedienne's land reform plan in the 1970s.

The FIS's analysis of the Algerian predicament was that the reasons for the crisis were not socioeconomic but were to be found in the cultural and religious failings of the society. An exemplary slogan was: "Our crisis is a crisis of faith and morals." As the economic situation worsened, this "cultural" explanation turned the fundamentalist focus to women. The FIS was obsessed with women's behavior, such as working, housekeeping, childrearing, etc., and used so-called failings of women in these contexts as explanations for various social evils. This analysis suited the designs of the regime in power also because it diverted attention away from the socioeconomic crisis for which it was so obviously responsible.

Reprinted by permission of the *New Internationalist*.

Hence, the government of Chadli Benjedid (1979–1992) colluded with the FIS to keep any progressive/left forces in check. In fact, members of the right wing of the FLN (the ruling party from independence in 1962 to 1992 and the only legal party until 1989) began to express views similar to those of the fundamentalists, using and contributing to the political climate shaped by the FIS. For example, in December 1989, a pro-fundamentalist FLN deputy in the National Assembly proposed to solve the problem of unemployment by sending women back to the kitchen. In addition to its offensiveness, the proposal was absurd given that there were only approximately 365,000 working women in Algeria and well over 1.5 million members of the work force were unemployed.

In Algeria's first multiparty elections of June 1990 the FIS won control of the majority of Algerian municipalities due to popular frustration and the lack of any relevant alternative. This stunned the country and had a devastating impact on the lives of many women. One of the top leaders of the FIS, Abassi Medani (who is now serving a seventeen-year jail sentence for sedition), said, when asked about Algeria's constitutional provisions calling for equal rights between the sexes, that all law contrary to the *Sharia* [Islamic law] is unacceptable. Thus, in direct conflict with Algerian constitutional and statutory law, the FIS program was one of sexual apartheid which to varying degrees was implemented in the municipalities the party controlled.

FIS members and leaders were obsessed with what they called *mixité*, the mixing of the sexes outside of the family. Typical were the following comments published in the FIS newspaper: "Despite the disastrous consequences of this frightening epidemic [mixing of the sexes] in public that we see around the world, people do not wish to draw the appropriate conclusions and instead try to defend this cancer." In this context, the specter of women seducing married men and causing divorces was regularly raised.

To cure this social "malady," the FIS program included a proposal to stop "mixing" in the schools: separating boys and girls, excluding women from certain programs in higher education, and cutting back on women teachers being allowed to teach young men and thereby "poison" their minds. Meanwhile, fundamentalist teachers (of whom there were many) preached to children in classrooms that both of their parents would go to hell if their mothers did not veil or went swimming at the beach in a bathing suit.

Gender segregation was to extend to other public facilities. In hospitals the FIS hoped to have women doctors treat only women patients. They planned to have segregated buses for men and women, which would have greatly compounded the transportation crisis. Women were driven out of public facilities taken over by the FIS at the municipal level, like recreation and cultural centers. In their zeal to create a single sex public life, FIS-run city councils banned New Year celebrations, public dancing, mixed marriage ceremonies in hotels, the selling of alcohol, and the presence of women on beaches, as well as numerous concerts and plays.

### Systematic Harassment of Women by the FIS

The official program was coupled with the systematic harassment of women in neighborhoods where the FIS was powerful, especially women students, women going out to work, and women who refused to veil. A similar account of harassment was given to me by women of all socioeconomic backgrounds in Algiers and Constantine in May and June 1992. . . .

Khalida Messaoudi stressed to me that fundamentalist violence against women is part of political repression, rather than cultural repression which can be explained inherently by "Islam" itself. This distinction between "cultural" and "political" rights and rights violations is interesting. While it has been disputed by some, I think it illustrates several key points: (1) Feminist activists must often struggle to get the issues around which they work taken seriously at the international level, as such issues are sometimes dismissed as "cultural," meaning inherent, static or, at worst, unchangeable; (2) Muslim fundamentalism in the Algerian context is understood by its Algerian critics (including its feminist critics) to be a political rather than a religious issue. Thus the conflict is not between "the religious" and "the secular," but is rather a political struggle among Muslims over the political uses and interpretations of their religion, and over power. . . .

Algerian women have not been passive victims of these attacks and agendas. As during the nationalist struggle against France, when women played key roles, displaying their bravery and ingenuity, many Algerian women today have organized to confront the attacks on their rights, and used strategies of daily resistance to combat the fundamentalist platform. They have formed over thirty women's organizations, and played an active role in a panoply of non-governmental organizations around issues such as torture that multiplied in the wake of the October 1988 repression. Women intellectuals continue to research and publish on the status of women, a project which is becoming more dangerous.

Furthermore, women have been very active in the popular movement against fundamentalist violence, taking part in large numbers in the many demonstrations across the country. The largest of these public protests occurred on March 22, 1993, when hundreds of thousands marched in the streets in horror at the fundamentalist murders of a doctor and a former minister of education, and again one year later on March 22, 1994, when a huge number of Algerians protested the ongoing violence which has now claimed between 3,000 and 7,000 lives in just three years. During the 1994 demonstration, I was struck by the image of an unveiled woman carrying a sign which simply said, "We will not yield." There have also always been large numbers of women in the funeral processions for slain intellectuals, a particular target of the armed groups.

### Wearing Blue Jeans in Defiance

Algerian women have also contributed to the struggle against fundamentalism and repression by continuing to be productive members of society, despite the obstacles they face. Most young women do not veil, which one notices while driving through the streets, and many who once wore the *hijab* [veil] at the zenith of legal FIS power in the early 1990s have stopped doing so. Wearing blue jeans has become an act of defiance, as has wearing one's hair short or remaining single. Simply going to work has become a life-threatening activity for many women. A young researcher who works for the Center for the Study of Professional Formation and lives in a *quartier populaire*, or working-class area, told me of how she has to be careful when leaving her home to go to work. She must often take a taxi, which she can barely afford, to avoid waiting at the bus stop, and she can no longer leave early for fear of being alone on the street at the wrong time. Of course, the wrong time can come at any time, as it did for two little girls in her neighborhood who were run over and killed by the getaway car of fundamentalists leaving the scene of a shooting in February 1994. By continuing to work, walk on the streets, and choose their own style of dress, today many Algerian women continue to do "daily battle.". . .

## Violence Against Women Presages Future Violence

In closing, I urge all observers of the Algerian crisis to look at the experiences of women when attempting to understand what is happening in Algeria today and in determining just what is at stake in the struggle against armed fundamentalism. As an Algerian sociologist suggested, if Algerian fundamentalists have carried out this level of violence against women while struggling for power, one can but imagine the possible level of brutality to be enacted if these forces were to come to power. This is the reality which is, in part, obscured by omitting the deep-rooted anti-women agenda of the fundamentalist groups in Algeria from any examination of the current "Algerian drama." As a young Algerian woman researcher stressed to me when I visited her in February 1994, "Americans must learn about what is happening here before they judge if the rights of the fundamentalists are the ones really being violated. They must learn what the fundamentalists have done, the level of their propaganda against women—even in mosques."

The struggle against fundamentalism and fundamentalist violence in Algeria is deserving of, and in need of, support and international solidarity. The odd cultural relativism with which some leftists and some feminists in the West have decided that by questioning and opposing fundamentalism, Algerian women lose their "indigenous" status or become "Westernized" and thus not "authentic" is deeply disturbing and is a new type of racism. Such analysis also displays a remarkable lack of understanding of the situation as well as a lack of principle. As the CIA trained many of the killers in the fundamentalist armed groups, the attacks on Algerian women and others should be of particularly urgent concern to the U.S. left.

Based on my discussions with a wide range of women during my visits to Algeria in 1992, 1993, and February 1994, I have observed that many Algerian women believe in the key significance of their own situation. They see it as crucial to determining the outcome of the current crisis, understanding that, in the words of the Algerian writer Aicha Lemsine, "women are now the stake and symbol for the future course of Algeria. Changes in their status will signal the direction for Algeria's future: Islamic state or modern society."

---

*"Grasping the moment, women have forged a vocal voice, a visible (if veiled) presence, and a viable women's movement."*

---

# Islamic Government Need Not Repress Women

Nesta Ramazani

In 1979, Iran became the first Islamic republic when a revolution led by the Ayatollah Ruhollah Khomeini overthrew Shah Mohammad Reza Pahlavi. In the following viewpoint, Nesta Ramazani describes the development of women's rights in Iran in the aftermath of the revolution. According to Ramazani, despite some repression of women by Islamic extremists, a moderate pragmatist faction led by President Hashemi Rafsanjani found it necessary to increase political participation by women in order to promote economic and political development. Because of their participation in the revolution, argues Ramazani, women have been able to gain more rights under the Islamic government than they had under the secular government of the shah. Ramazani is a freelance writer who specializes in women of the Middle East.

As you read, consider the following questions:

1. According to Ramazani, what was the paradoxical relationship between the leaders of the Iranian revolution and women?
2. What has enabled women to turn the tables on "those who use religion to oppress them," according to the author?
3. What are the three considerations that call for optimism, according to the author?

From Nesta Ramazani, "Women in Iran: The Revolutionary Ebb and Flow," *The Middle East Journal*, vol. 47, no. 3 (Summer 1993), ©1993 by Middle East Institute. Reprinted with permission.

In discussions of the status of women in Muslim societies, it has long been axiomatic that secularism is the principal prerequisite for progressive reform in women's social, economic, and political lives. In light of the empirical evidence emerging from Iran, however, it might be prudent to reexamine that assumption. Paradoxically, and contrary to all expectations, this essentially theocratic state has been quietly introducing progressive reforms affecting women, even in areas of law pertaining to marriage, divorce, and child custody—the areas traditionally most resistant to change. Although secular purists, viewing the reformist measures through the perspective of feminism or Western liberal democracy, might consider the measures taken as inadequate, they nevertheless cannot deny that reforms have been effected.

### Extremists vs. Pragmatists

The clerical elite in Iran—both hard-line and pragmatist—have targeted women as an important social force. The hard-line clergy have advocated essentially repressive measures in the name of Islamic purity, while the more pragmatic clergy have supported moderately reformist laws, programs, and new institutions. The overall ascendancy of radical forces during the early phases of the 1979 revolution had a particularly deleterious impact on the lives of women. The pragmatic tendencies first identified in 1985, however, have grown considerably since the death of Ayatollah Ruhollah Khomeini in 1989, creating a climate more receptive to reform on issues affecting women. Many extremist policies of earlier years have been overturned, while others coexist with more moderate ones, fueling contradictions in word and deed in the Islamic republic. For example, women serve in the armed forces, but are restricted in what they may study in school; women have been elected in unprecedented numbers to the Majlis [Consultative Assembly], yet are cloaked in *chador*s; and women have won the right to claim "wages in cash" from husbands who file for divorce, but they still ride in the back of buses, segregated from men.

The reformist approach of the pragmatists, meanwhile, has had the unanticipated consequence of increasing the demands for change. As Eliz Sanasarian observes, every time the male elite compared Muslim women to Western women and argued that "women have been oppressed in the West but not in Islam, they raised awareness. Every time they reasserted female equality and praised women's abilities, they raised expectations. Every time they admitted that oppression of women is ongoing in Iranian society, they raised demands. . . . The state officials unwittingly entangled themselves in gender discourse."

The outcome of this dialectical relationship between the pragmatic political elite and women in Iran is potentially promising, as the attempts to coopt women, and the initiatives women are taking in response, are gaining momentum. That is not to say, however, that the pragmatists or women have clear sailing ahead. Quite the contrary, they are both under intense pressure from the conservatives, who still wield considerable power as allies of the influential *bazaaris* [commercial class] and as a strong force in the Majlis.

### Early Excesses and the Reformist Government

In the early years of the revolution, Iran's clerical leaders rescinded the shah's Family Protection Law, which included modest restrictions on polygyny. The clerics also reduced the marriageable age for girls, closed day-care centers and family planning clinics, banned abortions and birth control devices, and required *hejab* (modest dress) in public for all women. *Mut'a* (temporary marriage) was encouraged and all obstacles to polygyny removed. De facto segregation was instated at the universities, and women were barred from some fields of study. The clerics prohibited women from being judges, dismissing those already practicing that profession.

In rewriting the constitution, the revolutionary leaders encouraged motherhood and domesticity, stressing in the preamble the importance of the family as "the fundamental unit of society" and emphasizing a woman's "important duty" as "mother." Moreover, although Article 20 provides "equal protection of the law" for men and women, it states that "all human, political, economic, social and cultural rights will be based upon Islamic precepts," thus placing women in an unequal position with regard to polygyny, divorce, and child custody.

Paradoxically, at the same time that the revolutionary leaders were trying to domesticate women, they were also mobilizing them on a massive scale for political and military participation. Whereas in 1964 Ayatollah Khomeini had declared it "un-Islamic" for women to vote, in 1979 he urged them to vote in the first postrevolution parliamentary elections, declaring the vote a "religious, Islamic and divine duty." In 1984, at Khomeini's behest, the *basij* (paramilitary forces) started recruiting women. As the war with Iraq continued, Khomeini urged women to volunteer for military training in order to "double the strength of the men" already fighting. Four thousand females trained for information-gathering tasks and security missions as part of the *pasdaran's* volunteer mobilization force. Burdened by the war, the government started to replace male laborers with females; the number of women government employees actually increased. As a result of their involvement in these activities, women became a major political force whose support was useful to the revolutionary

regime. Even the hard-line elements of the leadership felt compelled, in their search for female support, to champion some new
rights for women.

Well before his accession to the presidency in 1989, Ali Akbar
Hashemi Rafsanjani was promoting reform measures to improve
the status of women. All of these reforms were rationalized
largely in terms of Islamic norms. In urging women to participate
in the economic development of Iran, for example, Rafsanjani,
while Majlis speaker, admonished them to do so "without the corruption" of Western societies; in encouraging women to join the
ranks of the military, he called on them to retain their "Islamic
morality"; and, in promoting greater female activity in the social
arena, he lauded the "progressive" Islamic code of ethics that
sanctions the full social participation of women. Rafsanjani believed that economic and political exigencies required a reorder-
ing of social relations between men and women. . . .

### Woman Power

Iranian women are gaining some forms of political power. In
the second round of Majlis elections in June 1992, nine of the
two hundred sixty-eight deputies elected were women. Of
these, two have degrees in philosophy and Islamic law, one in
Islamic culture, one in philosophy, one in midwifery, one in
French language and literature. One is a surgeon, another an
obstetrician. Not one is a secular feminist bent on overthrowing
the Islamic regime; all are ardent supporters of the propagation
of Islamic norms in their society. At the same time, however,
they are vocal supporters of rights for women. Deputy Nafiseh
Qiazbakhsh spoke of the "dangerous war" being conducted
against Islamic culture, while advocating better teacher training
and remedial education. Deputy Maryam Behruzi, while attacking the "cultural debauchery" being promoted through books
and films, declared that the "true status" of Islamic women
must be "worked on." Deputy Qodsiyeh Seyyed Alavi, while
calling on women to fight against "Western decadent culture,"
spoke of the scientific growth and development of women in the
medical field, in which women comprise 52 percent of all specialists in women's surgery. She called for expansion of educational opportunities for women.

The Islamic tenor of calls to improve the status of Iranian
women are not isolated incidents, nor are they the empty rhetoric
of a handful of women in high positions. Rather, they must be
seen in their social and historical context as part of a widespread
and unprecedented participation of women in Iranian society.
Paradoxically, under clerical rule women seem to have a greater
sense of participation than they had under the [Shah Reza] Pahlavi
dynasty, when all the models for appearance and behavior were

Western and irrelevant to native norms.

The clerical regime, like the Pahlavi regime, has engaged in both the coercion and the cooptation of women. Its attempts to cloak women in an Islamic identity distinct from the "tarnished" Western one promoted by the Pahlavis, however, has initiated a lively public debate on Islam and women's issues. The same leaders who have promoted women's hejab have encouraged women in education, work, and other social participation. Paradoxically, hejab has become the means to social activism. By wearing the badge of purity, women can move about freely. By wearing the badge of modesty, they may fight for women's rights. By wearing the badge of moral rectitude, women compel the state to back up its claims to the equality of men and women within Islam.

## Women's Social and Religious Organizations

By learning about Islam, women have been able to turn the tables on those who use religion to oppress them. Women's interest in informing themselves about Islam and its teachings is without precedent. Having expanded their spheres of activity through militant revolt and military participation, women have gone on to find other avenues in which to expand the parameters of their social participation. Some have joined women's organizations concerned with women's social and cultural affairs, such as the Association of Muslim Women, founded in 1989 by Zahra Mostafavi to fight for women's greater access to higher education. Others have joined Zeynab, a women's organization, which, among other activities, held an international meeting of Islamic scholars—all women—in Tehran in February 1992. The announced purpose of the meeting, reflecting that of the organization, was to "help bring about a profound educational change" in Iranian society and to study the application of Quranic teachings to the lives of women. Other women have been going to *jalaseh*s, religious gatherings given over to serious discussions and interpretations of the Quran and Islamic law, in which women are able not only to participate, but sometimes to play leadership roles.

In the past, female *mujtahid*s (religious scholars) and *qari*s (reciters of the Quran) were often daughters of clerics, tutored at home by their fathers. Learned in Islamic law, they enjoyed much prestige. Now, the establishment of a *hozeh-ye Islami*, a higher theological school, to train women in theology and jurisprudence has created new opportunities for women from many backgrounds to study the Quran and Islamic law. Others are studying Islamic law at universities. Such formal training lends new authority and weight to their interpretations of Islamic law, giving them ammunition to wage battles on matters of vital concern to women.

Many women have taken up the pen to explore the "true" standing of women in Islam. Among them Zahra Rahnavard and Tahereh Saffarzadeh stand out. Reexamining Islam, they claim that many extant Islamic practices derive from patriarchal interpretations of the Quran in male-dominated societies where the prevailing norms influenced men's largely biased interpretations of the holy book. They call for a reinterpretation of many current practices that are labeled "Islamic."

## Women Activists in the Islamic Republic of Iran

In the first phase of [the Iranian] revolution, women's status appeared to deteriorate due to the reversal of earlier reforms. Pressure from Islamist women activists and the demands of development have encouraged the government to revise some of its views and adopt a more compromising attitude on gender issues. Both the Islamic Republic and women Islamists have demonstrated considerable creativity in their attempts to modernize their Islamic doctrine. The regime's pragmatic approach, particularly since 1989, has repeatedly linked women's education with the creation of an Islamic society in which discrimination against women should not exist. Ayatollah Ruhollah Khomeini's daughter, who was known to have a very close relationship with her father, has a doctoral degree and is cited as living proof that the supreme leader of the revolution was a strong advocate of female education.

Homa Hoodfar, *Middle East Report*, September/October 1994.

Far from silencing women's voices, the revolution has resulted in a proliferation of books by and about women and an outpouring of "women's literature" without precedent in Iran's history. This cultural life has allowed women to write and publish in unparalleled numbers and to explore new themes, ideas, and modes of expression. Women have been scrutinizing the most intimate and personal matters as well as the broadest questions of life and culture. New publications have appeared, such as *Gahnameh-ye adabi va honari-ye khaharan* (*The Sisters' Literary and Artistic Proclamation*), that provide women a forum for their poetry, essays, and short stories. For the first time, women have begun writing autobiographies. The public reads their works avidly.

The government does not, however, tolerate all points of view, nor does the populace. The Ministry of Guidance has denounced some women writers, particularly those taking a Western-style feminist stance. It censored two works by Shahrnoosh Parsipour, author of *Women without Men*, labeling the author a "complex-ridden spinster." Recently an angry group of veiled women besieged the offices of *Gardoun*, a popular literary magazine, protesting the representation on its cover of a woman in a chador lying lifeless on the ground, appearing to symbolize the fall of Islamic values. . . .

## The Advancement of Women in the Theocratic State

The high visibility and compulsory nature of Islamic hejab in Iran has obscured the cautious reforms that the clerical leaders have been making gradually in the interests of the survival of their rule and revolution. Contrary to conventional wisdom, this essentially theocratic state has found the advancement of women compatible with its interests. The empirical evidence in support of this proposition in the case of Iran calls for an important reassessment of the correlation between secularism and reformism. The former may not be the prerequisite of the latter, if, indeed, religious reinterpretation can lead to adaptations to the realities of modern life.

The women of Iran, in turn, newly awakened to fresh possibilities, have taken up the gauntlet and, using the leadership's own rhetoric and logic, have held the government's feet to the fire in regard to implementing the "equality of men and women in Islam." They have seized the initiative to demand changes in education, in family laws, and in the workplace. Paradoxically, the very hejab imposed by the leaders has become a means to combat marginalization and increase female involvement in the social, political, and cultural life of the nation. Out of the ashes of the revolution may rise a new female identity, one whose cultural and ideological authenticity give it the legitimacy to question and contest many of the traditionally oppressive institutions supposedly sanctified by Islam—whether polygyny, divorce, or seclusion. Grasping the moment, women have forged a vocal voice, a visible (if veiled) presence, and a viable women's movement through which to realize their aspirations.

Iran's women now see themselves in a leadership position in the Muslim world. They sponsor conferences on Islam, discuss the real meaning of passages from the Quran, head cultural exchanges, and even criticize other Muslim countries for not living up to Islamic precepts—for instance, when they criticized Kuwait for not allowing women to vote. While Egyptian women, once at the forefront of the Middle Eastern women's movement. now find themselves suffering setbacks or treading water, Iran's women proudly point to the progress of women in their country as an example of the gains that women can make under Islamic leadership.

This does not mean that women are resting on their laurels. Much remains to be done. Attitudes toward women change only slowly and the battle is an uphill one. Islamic reforms have been marked by controversy, contradiction and strife. Further decline in economic conditions could affect women adversely, reducing educational opportunities and government support of programs. Even worse, an alliance between the radical and conservative forces may threaten the moderate clerics' hold on power and jeopardize the reformist approach to the status of women.

Yet, three basic considerations call for cautious optimism. First, conservative forces, if in power, cannot escape any better than the pragmatists from the pressures of economic realities if they wish to survive politically. Second, they cannot challenge the legitimacy of the interpretation of Islamic law by the pragmatic leaders. For the first time in Iran's modern history, clerics, as political leaders, have been reinterpreting Islamic law in light of modern life realities—a task that no secular leader could dare attempt. Third, and finally, the consciousness of large numbers of women has been raised irreversibly to the necessity of improving their status in Iranian society. The genie is out of the bottle, and is not likely to be forced back inside.

*"Women's liberation means the liberation from class oppression and patriarchal oppression."*

# Women Should Reject Islamic Gender Roles

Nawal el-Saadawi, interviewed by George Lerner

Under the influence of Islamic groups, the government of Egypt in 1985 passed Personal Status Laws that outlined gender roles and divorce laws reflecting conservative interpretations of *sharia*, or Islamic law. In the following viewpoint, Nawal el-Saadawi argues that these laws are based on patriarchalism, not on *sharia*. For women to be liberated, she believes, women must learn that the Islamic religion does not oppress them; it is the patriarchal structure of society perpetuated by the Islamic fundamentalist groups that oppresses them. This patriarchalism must be changed through reinterpretation of the religion, in her view. El-Saadawi is an Egyptian author and physician, and is the founder of the Arab Women's Solidarity Association. George Lerner is a freelance writer.

As you read, consider the following questions:

1. How does the author define "unveiling the mind?"
2. According to el-Saadawi, what is patriarchy based on?
3. What is the relationship between the family code of Egypt and the *sharia*, according to el-Saadawi?

Nawal el-Saadawi, interviewed by George Lerner in *The Progressive*, April 1992. Reprinted with permission.

*Nawal el-Saadawi, the author of more than two dozen books, is a champion of the women's liberation movement in Egypt. A physician by training, el-Saadawi, sixty, has used her experiences treating women of all social classes as a field study of Egyptian women.*

*In many novels and in such path-breaking nonfiction works as* Women and Sex *and* The Hidden Face of Eve, *el-Saadawi has decried the male domination of society and the practice of female circumcision, which persists to this day. Having written extensively of the pain and fear accompanying her own circumcision at the age of six, she has tried to educate and organize groups against the practice.*

*El-Saadawi challenges the righteousness of Islamic fundamentalists and the domination of political power by the Sadat and Mubarak governments of Egypt. Her progressive positions on women's roles have also alienated some on the Left. Resistance to her views after the 1972 publication of* Women and Sex *forced her from her position as director-general of Egypt's Ministry of Health. Several months before his assassination in October 1981, Anwar Sadat imprisoned el-Saadawi, along with a thousand other activists, in an attempt to suppress all opposition. Following her release by President Hosni Mubarak, she founded the Arab Women's Solidarity Association (AWSA) with the aim of attaining political power for women.*

*We spoke in her Cairo home shortly after the Egyptian Ministry of Social Affairs closed the AWSA office, citing the organization's failure to comply with administrative requirements.*

## The Arab Women's Solidarity Association

*George Lerner: What were some of your ideas in founding the AWSA?*

Nawal el-Saadawi: Half of our society is women. They should start to speak for themselves, to write for themselves, to think for themselves, and to correct the laws that oppress them. We need advancement of women; we need women to participate in changing the society, to fight against class oppression and patriarchal oppression. We also need to create union among women, to create political power. We have two slogans: Unveiling of the Mind, creating awareness among women, and Union and Solidarity to bring political power for women.

We founded the Association in 1982, but the Minister of Social Affairs, who is a woman, refused to register it until 1985. On June 15, 1991, the Vice President issued a decree to close the AWSA in Egypt. We are now taking the government to court because this is against the law. The government closed the Egyptian association, but it cannot close the International Arab Women's Solidarity Association, which has status with the United Nations and a board from many Arab nations.

*In your writing, you link political power to the domestic role of women within a patriarchal system. How do you propose changing*

81

*women's roles in Egypt?*

By changing their image. If a woman thinks she was created by God to stay at home and serve her husband, then she can never do anything. We are trying to change this image, to unveil her mind, to tell her, "No, you are not here to be just a wife and a mother, to cook and clean, to be a servant in the house. You are here as a human being to participate politically in the government of your country, to speak up and to write and to challenge." Women are changing their roles, and are now starting to understand that their roles in life are not limited to the home.

*When you wrote* The Hidden Face of Eve *in 1980, women made up 9 per cent of the Egyptian work force. Do women have more access now to job opportunities and education?*

I come from a village where all my aunts and my grandmothers worked in the fields and received no wages. Housewives work very hard, but receive no wages. What happened when women went out to work under the class-patriarchal system? The women's work outside the house became an extension of their duties inside the house. They brought the money back to their husbands and the husbands oppressed them. We have to change this. Women should work outside the house and be paid. This work should help them to have a new awareness and new economic and political power.

*Was this new awareness behind the founding of the AWSA?*

They closed the association because it was the only feminist group in Egypt and in the Arab world. We had seminars on topics ranging from the Gulf war to women killing their husbands, to sex, to politics, to economics, and more. We discussed everything in a scientific and free way, bringing together the Right and Left, the governmental and nongovernmental. Everyone was talking about our seminars. The government didn't like that.

*How successful have you been in appealing to women across social classes?*

We brought in women from the upper classes who were very much against the marriage law and against oppression within marriage. Still, they were the privileged class. Peasant women, poor women came to us because they were oppressed economically by class, because they were oppressed by their husbands and by their fathers.

## Feminism and Islam in Egypt

*How would you define feminism in Egypt?*

Feminism to us is a very English word. We call it women's liberation because we don't have feminism in Arabic. Women's liberation means the liberation from class oppression and patriarchal oppression. We were attacked by different groups. The Right said we were Marxists, the dogmatic Left said we were

Westernized, and the fundamentalists thought we were atheists.

*You describe early Islam as having been a force of liberation for women. In the West, some people conceive of Islam as being oppressive towards women, as represented by the veil.*

Many people in the West think Arab women are oppressed because of Islam. This is not true. When I compared the Koran to the Christian Bible, to the Old Testament, or to the Hindu Bhagavad Gita, and when I examined the relationships of these religions to women, I discovered that Islam is less oppressive to women than Christianity or Judaism. The concept of virginity, of oppression, and of the superiority of men is imbedded in Judaism and Christianity. These themes are also in Islam, but much less so. Mohammed was very progressive. He spoke very highly of women; he loved women. Sexual relations are very flexible in Islam.

*What changed in Islam after Mohammed's death regarding the status of women?*

Religions usually start progressive. They start as revolutions against poverty and against oppression, but after they become established they become oppressive. Mohammed was a poor man who fought for the oppressed groups; for slaves and for women. In his later life, and after his death, Islam began invading countries to kill people and to get them inside Islam. Then the oppression started.

*Are there any people or institutions that interpret Islam in a progressive way, a way liberating towards women?*

Many people are doing that; Fatima Mernissi in Morocco, Rifat Hassan in Pakistan, and many other women writers. Sheikh al-Ghazalli in Egypt is quite progressive, relative to the other Sheikhs. They are not purely religious men or women. They may be sociologists who are studying religion. Religion is a social phenomenon; why should it be restricted only to the so-called theologists? Man created God; God did not create man. Sociologists, writers, and other thinkers should reinterpret Islam.

*So the liberation of women involves the reinterpretation of religion?*

Exactly. We are always linking religion to politics to sex. We are talking about the three taboos: religion, sex, and politics. This to us is feminism or women's liberation, the unveiling of the mind.

## The Veil and the Patriarchal Society

*How do you see the origin of the veil? Why did patriarchal society develop the veil?*

Veiling occurred in history before Islam, before Christianity, and before Judaism. It came with the evolution of slave society and with patriarchy: monogamy for women and polygamy for men.

Patriarchy is based on monogamy for women. If a woman

83

were to marry two husbands, the whole patriarchal structure would collapse, because fatherhood would never be known. So the husband is very sensitive about his wife; she is his private property. He must cover her so that no other man will see or touch her. He wants to give his inheritance to his children, so he must be sure that nobody has touched his wife, that those children are his children, and that he is the father. That is the basis of patriarchy.

Rachid Kaci, *Caricatures Arabes*, 1988, by permission of l'Institut du monde arabe.

*So women become a kind of private property, a kind of capital?*
Exactly. She becomes an instrument to bear children, to work in the house. When she is divorced, the man takes the children

and gives his name to them. Her name is lost in history.

*At the same time, you've described the role of men as a legalized sexual licentiousness.*

If a man has sexual relations with four wives or ten wives, this will never threaten patriarchy because fatherhood still will be known. But if his wife has sexual relations with another man, then fatherhood comes under doubt.

*Couldn't a conservative Islamic theologian justify patriarchy by pointing out that Mohammed had twelve wives?*

Mohammed married many women because in his time men married many women. He tried to restrict the number. Like female and male circumcision, polygamy started in the slave systems. In Islam, Mohammed tried to diminish female circumcision. He said, "Do not cut the whole clitoris, cut just a piece."

He was trying to diminish the number of wives, to diminish polygamy, and to diminish slavery. We have to judge Mohammed in the context of history, not by our criteria. In the Arabian desert where men were really corrupt, he was one of the most honorable men.

*Why do you think there is a difference between the practice of male and female circumcision? While young girls are circumcised in secret, boys are circumcised amidst celebrations.*

In some societies, women are circumcised with celebration. But generally the rite is secret because it is offensive and painful. Inside themselves, people think it's wrong. I saw a woman crying when she allowed her daughter to be circumcised. She couldn't help it. She said, "That is what God said." But God has nothing to do with it.

## Writing About Women's Issues

*You gained much renown after the publication of* Women and Sex.

It was the first book in Arabic to speak about clitoridectomy and virginity in a scientific way. And they banned it. They allow pornography, but they don't allow scientific books on sex. That is the paradox of patriarchy and class.

*Wasn't* Women and Sex *banned for some time?*

All my books were banned for eleven years under Anwar Sadat. I had to publish in Lebanon. I call the eleven years of Sadat [1970–1981] the dark years, which ended with his putting me in jail. First, I was dismissed as the director-general of the Ministry of Health in 1972.

*After the publication of* Women and Sex?

And also the publication of the magazine *Health*. I was editor of *Health* and founded the Health Association. I lost my job, lost my magazine, my writings were censored, and then it ended with my landing in jail. I was never given a platform, never allowed to speak on television or radio. . . .

*In the novel* Woman at Point Zero, *the prostitute Firdaus is sentenced to death for killing a pimp. What impact did this woman, whom you actually met in prison, have on the women's liberation movement?*

Firdaus is a martyr, a model of fighting to the last moment. She challenged the government, the president, the whole system, and paid with her life. Death makes her much more alive than if she had stayed. If Firdaus had signed the petition [for presidential clemency] and survived, if she had said pardon me, nobody would write about her. I admire her because few people are ready to face death for a principle.

## Women as Slaves

*Firdaus said only the prostitute is free, because she controls her own money and life. Do you agree?*

Firdaus did not say that. She said a free prostitute is free, but there are also slaves among prostitutes. I think the prostitute is a slave, sometimes more of a slave than the wife. Firdaus said I want to be a free prostitute, not a slave. That's why, when the pimp tried to control her, she killed him. All her life she sought freedom, independence, dignity, and love, and always men interfered: her father, her husband, and then the pimp. She found that she had to be either an oppressed wife or an oppressed prostitute, no alternative.

*Then where can women find independence, freedom, dignity, and love? Considering Firdaus's example, do you see any hope for a different future?*

In her case, the way was blocked because she was poor, because she was a prostitute. You cannot transcend your life, you cannot get away from your material limitations.

Hope comes from the power of people who die and do not bend their heads. She could have lived if she had signed the petition, but she said no. She gives hope to women and to men that there are people who can say no and pay with their lives.

I just finished a novel, *The Innocence of the Devil*. It will be published in Beirut [Lebanon] because nobody here wanted to publish it. In it, the Devil says no to God and pays all his life without having the chance to defend himself. Why should people pay by being imprisoned? Sheriff [el-Saadawi's husband] spent thirteen years in prison. Why should he have to pay that price? It's like killing him.

At the end of my novel *Two Women in One*, the heroine is put in jail. Everyone asks me where the hope is in that. The hope is that people are ready to go to jail for what they believe in. Firdaus was ready to die for what she believed in. . . .

*Was it your experience in prison under Sadat that inspired you to found the AWSA?*

I never joined a party or group in my life. I was a writer, an independent. But when I was in jail, I started to think that we cannot liberate women as individuals and writers. We must have collective political work; we must have political power. So I came out of jail and started the AWSA. The jailing opened my eyes to the power of collective work.

## Combating the Government and the Fundamentalists

*How much success have you had in combating the government and conservative religious forces on legal grounds?*

We, the AWSA, fought to totally change the family code. We lost because the government was not with us. Before 1985, we had a relatively better family code [laws concerning marriage, divorce, and child custody]—still oppressive, but better. In 1985, the law changed for the worse, because of the pressure of the Islamic groups on the government. We made a big row but we failed. The police and government threatened us.

*Did it become easier for a man to get a divorce?*

It became easier for a man to marry more than one wife and more difficult for the first wife to divorce. According to the previous law, if my husband marries another wife, I can automatically get a divorce. According to the existing law, I must go to court and prove that this second wife causes me harm. Most of the judges look at the material harm, not the psychological harm. If I say that I hate his second wife, the judge will tell me that my husband is still spending money on me, that I am living in the same apartment, that nothing happened to me. They don't respect the emotions of women.

The family code of Egypt is one of the most backward in the Arab world. It has nothing to do with Islamic law; Islamic Sharia is much more progressive than Egyptian law. It is related to slavery or the Pharaonic period.

*What about the fundamentalist groups?*

It is also related to the effect of fundamentalist groups and the dominant role of Saudi Arabia and the Americanization of Egypt. This is the paradox. America, through Saudi Arabia, has encouraged the most fanatic right-wing fundamentalist Islamic groups against the socialist groups, the communist groups, and the Nasserist [secular nationalist] groups.

This result of American and Saudi Arabian efforts is to oppress women, even though America speaks about democracy and human rights.

*Is there any international body that can unite women—perhaps the United Nations?*

I don't think so. I don't believe in the U.N. I wrote a letter to [former U.N. Secretary-General Javier] Perez de Cuellar asking him to resign after the Gulf war. Now we hear that he is connected to the 1991–1992 Bank of Credit and Commerce International (BCCI) scandal.

All my life savings were in that bank, the BCCI in London. I became penniless in a minute. Now I read how this bank was used by governments, by presidents, by the Central Intelligence Agency, and by Arab millionaires to kill people in Afghanistan, in Iran, in the Gulf, and in Nicaragua. How these people used my money, the royalties from my books! For thirty years I sweated to write books, and this bank used all that money on those corrupt people.

I have two crises: the closure of the Association and the loss of my life savings. Yet I feel that I am winning because this exposes the corruption of the whole international system. So I am a victim not only of the Egyptian government, but also of the whole international corruption of this system.

*Has this corruption become clear since 1991 in particular?*

The Gulf war exposed everyone. Also, the collapse of the Soviet Union exposed the gigantic corrupt power of the United States. We are now seeing the ugliness of the sole remaining superpower—how criminal and corrupt it is. BCCI is linked to the corruption in the United States and in Britain and in Afghanistan and in the Third World. My money was there, an innocent novelist putting her money in this corrupt bank. This is a story. . . .

*In 1980, you wrote of the Iranian revolution as an anticolonial, positive force of change. Would you see it in the same way now?*

It was aborted. The colonial powers played a role to shift it from a political and economic revolution to a religious revolution. The capitalist ruling powers are much happier with a religious, fanatic revolution than a socialist revolution.

The Iranian revolution was a mixture of the Left and the enlightened mullahs. They were fed up with the Shah and American domination. Millions of Iranians went out into the streets for bread and money and for equal justice, not for veiling their women. This revolution failed totally. I don't think any fundamentalist, fanatic, religious state will survive, because it's against nature, against the mind. Khomeini was terrible. He was against thinking, against humanity.

*How much progress has the women's liberation movement made?*

It's a gradual process. Revolution does not come in one or two nights.

The coming generation has a future much better than ours. I chose a difficult way in life and paid a high price. When I was writing I was digging into rock, trying to push my way. My generation made a path through the rock as writers and novelists. My daughter's generation has a path to follow. Of course it's rough, but they have a way, at least. In my case, there was no way.

*"Islamist women have decided to be more modest. They not only adopt a specific clothing style, but also speak of their inner modesty."*

# Women Can Embrace Islamic Gender Roles

Sherifa Zuhur

An Islamic movement in Egypt that includes women has been growing since the early 1980s. In the following viewpoint, Sherifa Zuhur describes the attitudes and beliefs of young Egyptian women, some of whom belong to the Islamic movement. Many young women, she argues, reject both the passive role of women that Westerners associate with Islam and the Westernized view of "liberated" women that previous generations of activists espoused. Islamic "feminists," according to Zuhur, differ from the previous generation of feminists in their view of the role the state can or has played, their stronger rejection of the West, and their diversity. Zuhur teaches history at Indiana State University and is the author of *Revealing Reveiling: Islamist Gender Ideology in Contemporary Egypt.*

As you read, consider the following questions:

1. What aspects of Islamic separation of the sexes most alarm Western women, according to Zuhur?
2. According to the author, what is the contradiction of Western feminism?
3. What two features of Islamic feminism must be noted in a serious study, according to Zuhur?

Excerpted from Sherifa Zuhur, "The 'Woman Question' Revised in Egypt," in *Proceedings of the Twenty-First Annual Conference of the Association of Muslim Social Scientists*, edited by Mona M. Abul-Fadl, published by the International Institute of Islamic Thought, Herndon, VA, 1993. Reprinted with Permission.

Women's self-identification is a crucial part of the Islamist equation. Do they see themselves as members of a coherent ummah [community of Muslims] or as individuals competing with each other for the relatively scarce pool of public goods (or status, or wealth)? Though they do not generally believe they are extensions of their men, as the West would have us believe, they believe in placing community values and spirit before their own aspirations. Whether they actually enact these values is another matter.

Most women do not perceive themselves as passive members of society, though many wish they were heard more clearly by the powers that be. Some younger women [in Egypt] I studied, unveiled and veiled, felt that they alone, as individuals, could never question their society's customs, although they recognized the ways in which certain practices limit female behavior. The new ideal that Islamist women hold of themselves is not identical. Most share concerns with virtue, morality, nurturing of others, and some believe in activist reform.

## Historical Context

Islamists have espoused a particular ideology of social and familial relations. Although their idealization of gender has been accused of ahistoricity, their followers are women in a particular historical moment who have molded the movement, in some respects, to their own lifestyles. The gender dimension is not neatly divided from other Islamist goals, but is part of a revitalizing process seeking to invigorate the ummah's conscience. Many see it as merely a reassertion of patriarchy. Others have looked at subsets of women too narrowly, choosing their focus from decade-old profiles of the movement and looking only at women's economy and family profile rather than their conception of their faith, its centrality to their lives, and to expression of gender identity.

What have we learned about the configuration of gender, identity, and Islamism from them and those who have observed them? And, what have Islamist women learned about those who criticize them? We have learned that gender issues are considered core values to the society and therefore to its identity. The Middle Eastern state, in general, sought to expand sex-role definitions, primarily, in the interest of production and, secondarily, in the interest of controlling religious elites, and only thirdly for the cause of "human development." Islamists and many ordinary citizens saw that certain groups of women benefited more from these policies than others, but also saw that the West and international agencies had defined a particular agenda for women that coincided with increased immigration, more nuclear family arrangements, increasing social divisions, and inflation.

Islamist women, whether activist or not, relate a theory of gender and family relations with political overtones. They are aware that the ideal Muslim woman—the sort of woman they aim to be—is not like that image the state projected to them in their childhood, through school, and over the airwaves. They say that they will no longer emulate the western women's career-motivated path. Neither do they believe in the integrity of the active elite Egyptian women, who have shaped another popular image of what powerful women can be and how they should appear. Although they are accused of "going back to the dark ages," these women's interest in piety, social worth, and their education prevent them from merely picking up a lifestyle from the medieval period or from their urban lower-class sister, the *bint al balad*.

## *Hijab* and Women's Rights

Islamist women have decided to be more modest. They not only adopt a specific clothing style, but also speak of their inner modesty. Many promote more active means of separating the sexes, such as separate facilities, seating, classes, or services for women. These two aspects of separation—one concealing the body, the other establishing spatial boundaries between unrelated women and men—are the aspects of gender and Islamism that most alarm western women and some non-Islamist Arab women. I have elsewhere written a great deal about the symbolic power of the *hijab* [veiling]. While I have tried to explain women's sense that veiling and segregation demonstrate a commitment to a society organized around virtue, I have worried, along with non-Islamist women, that these symbols represent a contraction of sex-roles that will limit many women unnecessarily. Most western writers see a direct connection between the reimposition of veiling or the introduction of the *hijab* (as in Iran, Afghanistan, and as proposed by the Islamic Salvation Front (FIS) in Algeria) with the sternest aspects of the Shari'ah [Islamic law] and the real abuse of women, including Pakistani political rapes. They cannot understand how their representations of the new Islam and women affect Muslim readers, who point out that the progressive and beneficial aspects of Muslim gender ideology are never the focus of attention.

In the small study I completed, I found ample evidence that the conception of sex-roles on the part of young Islamist women has indeed contracted, to the point that many fields (i.e., engineering, certain medical specialties, and the sciences) are again considered unwomanly. Many women hoped to marry instead of working in their discipline. Women were not keen on breaking new barriers and downplayed their own achievements. Only a small number of women countered this trend, indicating their interest in actively pursuing their careers instead of marriage, hoping to travel, study foreign languages, and perhaps modify other Islamist views of gender. (Incidentally, most of the women of the latter group were daughters of working women.) I wondered if the anticareer aspect of Islamist gender ideology was really so beneficial to a movement that will require every ready hand and talent if it is not to be subverted by material interests, as have so many other groups of young and idealistic believers.

## Islamic Feminism?

Islamists have expressed an ideology of gender that is not free from contradictions. However, the gender ideology promoted by many western feminists is also contradictory in some ways, dependent as it is on the formal transformation of existing institutions, reliance on male backup and acquiescence within the home, and bringing two strands of feminism into focus. The two philosophical strands are supported by those who believe that women are merely socialized into gender roles and must break with domestic tradition and those who believe that women's nature really must emerge whether through motherhood, a better and more gentle style of interaction, or compensatory practices. In my opinion, the contradictions are quite overwhelming, yet western feminism is convinced that it is a universal principle.

Women of color within the West and women of the Third World have broken away from mainstream feminism, attacking it in several ways over the last twenty-five years or so. "International feminism," composed of its problematic western definitions, perpetuates racism and class divisions to some degree. Even western women of color have problematic definitions of the societal features oppressing Third World women, since they believe that certain practices infringe on women's human rights and that these beliefs are, in turn, conditioned by their conceptions of sexual identity and a broad range of role options for women.

Others within the field of Middle Eastern women's studies fight over who may study women in the Middle East, over the set features of "patriarchy," and how inevitably it affects women's range of actions. Islamist women have not participated in many of these debates. How can they then be said to comprise a new Islamic feminism?

While many Islamist women would not describe themselves as being "feminist" and do not care for the term, many are certainly what African and other Third World women are calling "womanist." Womanism here represents an acceptance of the complementary relationship of the sexes as well as the maternal nature and strengths and weaknesses of typical (but not all) women. If that sounds like a basis for conservative Islam or for the views of, for example, Ayatollah Khomeini on women that begin this way, one may be missing the second part of the formula. "Womanists" believe that women should be supported by society, protected against abuse, and enabled to fulfill their potential to the benefit of their families, peers, co-workers and society at large. Many hold that interpretations of Islam and even legal applications were somewhat corrupted by abuses of power and other regional legal and ideological systems. Some suggest reconsidering the hadith and rejecting all sources but the Qur'an, or concentrating on the Qur'an and the Sunnah. Others promote a more thorough revision of traditional legal restrictions of women, saying that this would comply with the spirit of the early Islamic era, but they do not believe Islam, with its many protective amendments of pre-Islamic women's status, is inherently antiwoman.

## Women and the State

So far, I might be describing many Egyptian non-Islamist (but Muslim) female activists as easily as the ordinary Islamist woman. Where they first diverge is in their assessment of how well the secular state has introduced and enacted "womanish" policies and how divisive socially these policies have been. Islamist women are not wrong if they see that the primary beneficiaries of these policies have been elite women and that their entry into a politically and economically active social life has deeply troubled many conservative (though not necessarily Islamist) men. Furthermore, the state's policies in this regard were never enacted in consultation with its people, were incompletely realized, and were initiated mainly with economic rather than human goals in mind.

When I conducted interviews with young Islamist women [in Egypt], many were dubious about state-led reforms. Although most felt women should be protected by law with regard to equal pay and hiring procedures, some young women felt that many women abused their maternity privileges by leaving work for too long, sometimes returning and then deciding to have another child. (Incidentally no older women in my survey agreed with them.) They also were dubious about the impact of the Personal Status Laws and the subsequent amendments of 1985 [defining women's rights in marriage and divorce]. Some felt that more equitable divorce procedures for women were called for because men had historically abused their privileges. Others felt that the rule regarding the right to retain the family home was more fair to women but could only create heightened conflict due to the housing shortage. Some believed that the reforms were categorically illegitimate, since the state had stepped into the province of the ulema—they felt that only an "Islamic" state had the right to sweep away years of Shari'ah tradition. Many did not know that some Islamist women fought along with non-

Islamist women to save various features of the reforms.

Of these varying viewpoints, only some can be categorized correctly as Islamic feminist. Those who propose a wholesale return to the home and the maternal role bring up other problematic issues. This emphasis of the reproductive rather than the productive role of women is loudly heard throughout the Muslim world, not only in Egypt. Islamists and conservatives fault many working women for a) neglecting their families, b) behaving immodestly, whether through display (*tabarruj*) or interaction with male colleagues, c) behaving in the moody or temperamental fashion that proves women's susceptibility to stress combined with the hormonal effects of their reproductive cycle, d) becoming infertile, less fertile, or less inclined to have children, e) being self-centered, f) being ever-more materialistic, and g) taking on male characteristics, such as being more assertive, aggressive, or ambitious. Women are also accused of being unpatriotic and antinationalist in supporting a western mode of female behavior. While some Islamists feel that a lot of the above is nonsense and that women can work so long as they fulfill their family duties, they appear to be the "liberals" or "moderates" in this regard. Others argue that women simply must go home. . . .

## Islamist Women and Western Commodities

One dimension of Islamic feminism shared by many women who have adopted the veil is a reaction to the commodification, in the economic and cultural senses, of women. Here, some western feminists recognize views similar to theirs. Beauty myths and ideals are not created in the best interest of women, for they idealize the unattainable and the unnatural (at least for many women). In the West, they market the perfect young female body, separating it from its intellectual, emotional, or spiritual functions. Women are then taught that they are incomplete and ugly if they cannot replicate that physicality. Young veiled women said that they had decided to remove themselves from the game of appearances seduction and the implications of wealth and status that dress implies by following God's rules of covering, which honor their minds and souls. After all, men could pay more attention to what they had to say without the distraction of tight or revealing clothing.

Some women argued that the commodification process goes deeper—that women need to do without products made in the West, fast-frozen food as well as cosmetics—moving to an economic plane. By returning to their homes instead of working full-time, women could do without labor-saving products and could perform their own household duties instead of paying for maids and/or child care. Of course some women follow the argument only as far as it affects their appearance and would not think of changing their other consumption patterns. Both levels can be seen as a sort of feminism if it can concentrate, as one respondent put it, "on what is inside a woman's head instead of what is on top of it."

---

## The "Hijab" Offers Women Dignity

Throughout the Arab Middle East, young women are donning black cloaks that render their bodies formless and the "hijab," a scarf that hides the hair, ears and forehead. In many cases, they are the granddaughters of women who threw off the veil in the 1920s and 30s as a rejection not only of Western colonial rule, but also of male domination.

What accounts for such a reversal—a reversal at very least in the tactics of political and personal liberation, and perhaps in the very definition of both? The answers reveal much about what Islamic fundamentalism offers the modern Middle Eastern society and psyche, male as well as female.

First, the many (and often competing) strands of politically militant Islam offer women a form of dignity and protection, although that seems a paradox to Westerners who think of dignity as a synonym for equality. Modern Middle Eastern cities are crowded, uncomfortable places with far too little housing and services that are hopelessly overwhelmed. . . .

Wearing the hijab lets women move about the city unmolested and unharassed by the young men and teen-age boys who have poured into the capital from the countryside in search of work. It sends an unmistakable signal to every male: This is a devout woman. Leave her alone. It permits women to ride public buses jammed, sardine-like, with passengers, without being gawked at, poked or fondled. It is, in this sense, a pragmatic response to the disadvantages of modernity.

Judith Miller, *The New York Times*, December 27, 1992.

---

If one were to seriously consider Islamic feminism or womanism as contained in Islamist *women's* philosophies in Egypt, two features must be noted. First of all, women diverge from the opinions cited by notable Islamist writers and leaders in some cases. If they do not diverge in theory, they do in practice. Women recognize the economic necessity for increased income, delayed marriage, and the benefits of education with regard to discipline and broadening of the mind, even in "male" fields. Therefore women work, although they criticize working women, and utilize child care, although they note its shortcomings as well.

Secondly, women don't always agree with each other, though

one may have that impression at first. In fact, we would have to talk about a liberal Islamist feminism, a moderate Islamist womanism, and a conservative Islamist position on gender. This range could be expected in a society like Egypt, whose early feminist movement was linked to nationalist activity and has spanned decades of debate.

## The Human Rights Dimension

The gender aspect of human rights is said to be universal, but it has been dominated by western discourse. Nonetheless, Islamist women who believe in Islam's benefits for women cannot go without recognizing the abuses of the system. Polygamy may be better than divorce, as it requires a man to provide financially for his "old" wife, but it has shaken and emotionally depleted many women. Although the Qur'an limits polygamy in the eyes of some, men who can afford it and who claim the ability to "deal equally" with their women can indulge in it so long as it is legal. Is this part of the justice Islamists seek? Some liberal Islamist feminists think not.

Female circumcision is another practice that continues in Egypt today, despite laws against it. The Prophet acknowledged but did not approve of the custom; nevertheless, people incorrectly refer to it as an Islamic protection of virtue, even calling one method *shar'i* circumcision. Ignoring the issue, labeling it a western concern, or railing at Egyptian writers who brought it out in the open does nothing to alleviate the health and well-being of the women affected. Many Islamist women will not discuss the matter.

Other issues are up for debate. In most cases, the arguments for social leveling and equal applications of *'adalah* [social justice] apply to men and men, not men vs. women. Many Islamists say that justice is for all, but that men and women cannot interpret or experience that justice identically, since the sex roles accepted by society have shaped their responsibilities and respective needs.

## Modernity

Far from a retreat to the archaic past, Islamists utilize modern language, referents, and methodology. Women, when commenting on gender, more often discuss western disorders than medieval models. Many are, after all, graduates of institutes that revere technology. And if not, they are affected by a society shaken by it. Crime, communal strife, drugs, and moral decay are all features that have particular effects on the gender balance. Women note the western cities in which single women (and single men) inhabit single apartments, shop alone, and find loneliness only alleviated by the drone of their television sets.

Many have lived or traveled extensively in the West and discuss the problems of abortion, infertility, young women's bulemia and anorexia (brought on by the sick beauty image) in detail, and more convincingly than their own media sources. Others bring up that modern problem—democracy—noting that the West criticizes their society for its weak attempts. Yet it is the West that continues to profit from the balance of trade and holds stability to be far more valuable than a democratization that might empower the Islamists instead of the "allies."

## The Future

Where are these women going, they and their comrades? Certain issues are potentially explosive or divisive. Others are not, for the range of women who identify with Islamist ideology is so broad. Western women and non-Islamist Egyptian women fear the spread of the *hijab* more than the antiproductive features of Islamist ideology. Perhaps it is the latter that should command more attention. Both are complex matters that involve a social tolerance of dissent that is, of course, related to the degrees of suppression or openness available to political life. Would non-Islamist women fear the Islamists less if they did not worry that their code of modesty would be extended to all women?

A great deal hinges on the mutual perceptions of Islamists and the West. Must they only see each other as a challenge or a threat? Can Islamists see more than Crusader or paternalism impulses? Can the West identify what it really sees instead of what it would like the world to look like? Can women recognize that difference is not made of false consciousness but of diverse consciousness?

# Periodical Bibliography

The following articles have been selected to supplement the diverse views presented in this chapter.

Fatima B. — "Wearing the Veil, Under Penalty of Death," *Los Angeles Times*, April 1, 1994. Available from Times Mirror Square, Los Angeles, CA 90053.

Tara Bahrampour — "Hers: Under Wraps," *The New York Times Magazine*, July 10, 1994.

Ann Louise Bardach — "Tearing Off the Veil," *Vanity Fair*, August 1993.

Ethan Bronner — "Unveiled," *The New Republic*, June 8, 1992.

John F. Burns — "A Writer Hides. Her Country Winces," *The New York Times*, July 31, 1994.

Kim Edwards — "The Body as Evil," *Utne Reader*, May/June 1992.

Ellen Gruenbaum — "The Islamist State and Sudanese Women," *Middle East Report*, November/December 1992.

Sondra Hale — "The Rise of Islam and Women of the National Islamic Front in Sudan," *Review of African Political Economy*, July 1992.

Mahin Hassibi — "Sexual Apartheid in Iran," *On the Issues*, Fall 1994.

Homa Hoodfar — "Devices and Desires: Population Policy and Gender Roles in the Islamic Republic," *Middle East Report*, September/October 1994.

Jules Inda — "Behind the Veil Debate," *Utne Reader*, March/April 1992.

Suad Joseph — "Gender and Civil Society," *Middle East Report*, July/August 1993.

Louise Lief — "An Old Oasis of Tolerance Runs Dry," *U.S. News & World Report*, August 29–September 5, 1994.

Sarah Miles — "Breaking Points," *New Internationalist*, January 1992.

Judith Miller — "Women Regain a Kind of Security in Islam's Embrace," *The New York Times*, December 27, 1992.

Hisham Sharabi — "Modernity and Islamic Revival: The Critical Task of Arab Intellectuals," *Contention*, Fall 1992. Available from Indiana University Press, 601 N. Morton St., Bloomington, IN 47404.

# Can Democracy Coexist with Islam?

**Islam**

# Chapter Preface

"Can fundamentalism and democracy co-exist?" is the subtitle of a May 1992 article by *Washington Post* reporter Caryle Murphy. The question is a timely one for countries of the Middle East that have witnessed in the 1990s both growing demands for democratic reforms and the growing popularity of Islamic movements espousing conservative (fundamentalist) religious and political agendas.

Observing the two concurrent trends, *New York Times* writer Judith Miller contends that democratic elections in the Middle East are likely to bring to power "militant Islamic regimes that are, in fact, inherently anti-democratic." Islamic movements are antidemocratic, in Miller's opinion, because they deny the civil rights of ethnic and religious minority groups—an "essential component of liberal democracy," in Miller's words. Further, according to Miller, the Islamic movements repudiate the United Nations Universal Declaration of Human Rights—the international standard of civil, social, and political liberty—as contradictory to *sharia*, Islamic law.

Others do not believe that Islamic movements are inherently antidemocratic. Emad Eldin Shahin, an expert on contemporary Islamic movements, sees "common grounds between Islam and democracy." Democratic governments, in Shahin's view, can differ in orientation, structure, and practice, and need not follow the Western model of liberal, secular democracy. Islamic movements accept the democratic concepts of political pluralism—the existence of a variety of political parties, including secular ones—and the transfer of power from one party to the next, according to Shahin, as long as these concepts do not undermine Islamic values. Therefore, Shahin concludes, "Islamic principles could give rise to a representative, pluralistic, and just political system in which the government is accountable to the people and the individual's fundamental rights are respected."

The viewpoints in the following chapter explore whether Islam, given its historical traditions and its goals, is compatible with democracy.

> "Liberal democracy, however far it may have
> traveled, however much it may have been
> transformed, is in its origins a product of
> the West."

# Islam Has Weak Democratic Traditions

Bernard Lewis

Islamic countries have long histories of authoritarian rule. In the following viewpoint, Bernard Lewis argues that liberal democracy—as defined in an American sense with an emphasis on property and human rights—is a product of Western culture and history. It would be difficult for Islamic countries that do not share this history and culture to develop Western-style liberal democratic institutions, according to Lewis. However, Lewis believes that worldwide trends toward democracy and modernization make democratic development in the Islamic world possible though not inevitable. Lewis is professor emeritus of Near Eastern studies at Princeton University and author of *Islam and the West*.

As you read, consider the following questions:

1. How does Lewis define *jihad*? Why do fundamentalists promote *jihad*, in his opinion?
2. How does Lewis define the "legal person"? Does Islam recognize a legal person, in Lewis's view?
3. According to Lewis, how do Islamic law and Islamic history differ on recognizing private property?

Excerpted from Bernard Lewis, "Islam and Liberal Democracy," *The Atlantic Monthly*, February 1993. Reprinted by permission of the author.

There has been much discussion of late, both inside and outside the Islamic world, about those elements in the Islamic past and those factors in the Muslim present that are favorable and unfavorable to the development of liberal democracy. From a historical perspective it would seem that of all the non-Western civilizations in the world, Islam offers the best prospects for Western-style democracy. Historically, culturally, religiously, it is the closest to the West, sharing much—though by no means all—of the Judeo-Christian and Greco-Roman heritage that helped to form our modern civilization. From a political perspective, however, Islam seems to offer the worst prospects for liberal democracy. Of the forty-six sovereign states that make up the international Islamic Conference, only one, the Turkish Republic, can be described as a democracy in Western terms, and even there the path to freedom has been beset by obstacles. Of the remainder, some have never tried democracy; others have tried it and failed; a few, more recently, have experimented with the idea of sharing, though not of relinquishing, power.

Can liberal democracy work in a society inspired by Islamic beliefs and principles and shaped by Islamic experience and tradition? It is of course for Muslims, primarily and perhaps exclusively, to interpret and reinterpret the pristine original message of their faith, and to decide how much to retain, and in what form, of the rich accumulated heritage of fourteen centuries of Islamic history and culture. Not all Muslims give the same answers to the question posed above, but much will depend on the answer that prevails. . . .

## Are Liberal Democracy and Islam Compatible?

There is an agonizing question at the heart of the present debate about democracy in the Islamic world: Is liberal democracy basically compatible with Islam, or is some measure of respect for law, some tolerance of criticism, the most that can be expected from autocratic governments? The democratic world contains many different forms of government—republics and monarchies, presidential and parliamentary regimes, secular states and established churches, and a wide range of electoral systems—but all of them share certain basic assumptions and practices that mark the distinction between democratic and undemocratic governments. Is it possible for the Islamic peoples to evolve a form of government that will be compatible with their own historical, cultural, and religious traditions and yet will bring individual freedom and human rights to the governed as these terms are understood in the free societies of the West?

No one, least of all the Islamic fundamentalists themselves, will dispute that their creed and political program are not compatible with liberal democracy. But Islamic fundamentalism is

102

just one stream among many. In the fourteen centuries that have passed since the mission of the Prophet, there have been several such movements—fanatical, intolerant, aggressive, and violent. Led by charismatic religious figures from outside the establishment, they have usually begun by denouncing the perversion of the faith and the corruption of society by the false and evil Muslim rulers and leaders of their time. Sometimes these movements have been halted and suppressed by the ruling establishment. At other times they have gained power and used it to wage holy war, first at home, against those whom they saw as backsliders and apostates, and then abroad against the other enemies of the true faith. In time these regimes have been either ousted or, if they have survived, transformed—usually in a fairly short period—into something not noticeably better, and in some ways rather worse, than the old establishments that they had overthrown. Something of this kind is already visibly happening in the Islamic Republic of Iran.

The question, therefore, is not whether liberal democracy is compatible with Islamic fundamentalism—clearly it is not—but whether it is compatible with Islam itself. Liberal democracy, however far it may have traveled, however much it may have been transformed, is in its origins a product of the West—shaped by a thousand years of European history, and beyond that by Europe's double heritage: Judeo-Christian religion and ethics; Greco-Roman statecraft and law. No such system has originated in any other cultural tradition; it remains to be seen whether such a system, transplanted and adapted in another culture, can long survive.

Leaving aside the polemical and apologetic arguments—that Islam, not Western liberalism, is the true democracy, or that Western liberalism itself derives from Islamic roots—the debate about Islam and liberal democracy has focused on a few major points.

## The "Legal Person"

Every civilization formulates its own idea of good government, and creates institutions through which it endeavors to put that idea into effect. Since classical antiquity these institutions in the West have usually included some form of council or assembly, through which qualified members of the polity participate in the formation, conduct, and, on occasion, replacement of the government. The polity may be variously defined; so, too, may be the qualifications that entitle a member of the polity to participate in its governance. Sometimes, as in the ancient Greek city, the participation of citizens may be direct. More often qualified participants will, by some agreed-upon and recurring procedure, choose some from among their own numbers to represent them. These assemblies are of many different kinds, with differently defined electorates and functions, often with some role in the making of decisions, the enactment of laws, and the levying of taxes.

The effective functioning of such bodies was made possible by the principle embodied in Roman law, and in systems derived from it, of the legal person—that is to say, a corporate entity that for legal purposes is treated as an individual, able to own, buy, or sell property, enter into contracts and obligations, and appear as either plaintiff or defendant in both civil and criminal proceedings. There are signs that such bodies existed in pre-Islamic Arabia. They disappeared with the advent of Islam, and from the time of the Prophet until the first introduction of Western institutions in the Islamic world there was no equivalent among the Muslim peoples of the Athenian boule, the Roman Senate, or the Jewish Sanhedrin, of the Icelandic Althing or the Anglo-Saxon witenagemot, or of any of the innumerable parliaments, councils, synods, diets, chambers, and assemblies of every kind that flourished all over Christendom.

---

### Islamic Movements and Liberal Democracy

Although they are quick to take advantage of expanded rights, such as greater press freedoms and opportunities to contest elections, the Islamists are not well disposed to liberal democracy, either by ideological inclination or social base.

Indeed, many of these movements look very much like the governments they oppose. They obtain significant resources from patrons abroad with which they construct and sustain their domestic clienteles. In rejecting the prevailing system, they aspire to an alternative no more "liberal" or "democratic" than the regimes that spawned them.

In their debates about political and moral authority, neither the existing regimes nor their opponents speak of establishing institutions by which government might be held accountable.

Lisa Anderson, *Dissent*, Fall 1994.

---

One obstacle to the emergence of such bodies was the absence of any legal recognition of corporate persons. There were some limited moves in the direction of recognition. Islamic commercial law recognizes various forms of partnership for limited business purposes. A *waqf*, a pious foundation, once settled is independent of its settlor, and can in theory continue indefinitely, with the right to own, acquire, and alienate property. But these never developed beyond their original purposes, and at no point reached anything resembling the governmental, ecclesiastical, and private corporate entities of the West.

Thus almost all aspects of Muslim government have an intensely personal character. In principle, at least, there is no state, but only a ruler; no court, but only a judge. There is not even a *city* with defined powers, limits, and functions, but only an assemblage of neighborhoods, mostly defined by family, tribal, ethnic, or religious criteria, and governed by officials, usually military, appointed by the sovereign. Even the famous Ottoman imperial divan—the *divan-i humayun*—described by many Western visitors as a council, could more accurately be described as a meeting, on fixed days during the week, of high political, administrative, judicial, financial, and military officers, presided over in earlier times by the Sultan, in later times by the Grand Vizier. Matters brought before the meeting were referred to the relevant member of the divan, who might make a recommendation. The final responsibility and decision lay with the Sultan or the Grand Vizier.

## God's Polity

One of the major functions of such bodies in the West, increasingly through the centuries, was legislation. According to Muslim doctrine, there was no legislative function in the Islamic state, and therefore no need for legislative institutions. The Islamic state was in principle a theocracy—not in the Western sense of a state ruled by the Church and the clergy, since neither existed in the Islamic world, but in the more literal sense of a polity ruled by God. For believing Muslims, legitimate authority comes from God alone, and the ruler derives his power not from the people, nor yet from his ancestors, but from God and the holy law. In practice, and in defiance of these beliefs, dynastic succession became the norm, but it was never given the sanction of the holy law. Rulers made rules, but these were considered, theoretically, as elaborations or interpretations of the only valid law—that of God, promulgated by revelation. In principle the state was God's state, ruling over God's people; the law was God's law; the army was God's army; and the enemy, of course, was God's enemy.

Without legislative or any other kind of corporate bodies, there was no need for any principle of representation or any procedure for choosing representatives. There was no occasion for collective decision, and no need therefore for any procedure for achieving and expressing it, other than consensus. Such central issues of Western political development as the conduct of elections and the definition and extension of the franchise therefore had no place in Islamic political evolution.

Not surprisingly, in view of these differences, the history of the Islamic states is one of almost unrelieved autocracy. The

105

Muslim subject owed obedience to a legitimate Muslim ruler as a religious duty. That is to say, disobedience was a sin as well as a crime.

Modernization in the nineteenth century, and still more in the twentieth, far from reducing this autocracy, substantially increased it. On the one hand, modern technology, communications, and weaponry greatly reinforced the rulers' powers of surveillance, indoctrination, and repression. On the other hand, social and economic modernization enfeebled or abrogated the religious constraints and intermediate powers that had in various ways limited earlier autocracies. No Arab Caliph or Turkish Sultan of the past could ever have achieved the arbitrary and pervasive power wielded by even the pettiest of present-day dictators.

## Private Property and Rights

The impediments to the development of liberal institutions were not merely political. The small-scale autocracy of the home, especially the upper-class home, founded on polygamy, concubinage, and slavery, was preparation for an adult life of domination and acquiescence, and a barrier to the entry of liberal ideas. Women—particularly the mothers, sisters, wives, and daughters of rulers—have played a much more important role in Muslim history than is usually conceded by historians. But they were until very recently precluded from contributing to the development of their society in the way that a succession of remarkable women have contributed to the flowering of the West.

The economic basis of Western-style liberal democracy was early recognized in the West. British, American, and French democrats alike insisted on the right to property as one of the basic human rights that safeguard and are safeguarded by free institutions. It also forms an essential component of civil society as conceived by European thinkers. For some time the rise of socialist ideas, parties, and governments weakened the belief in private property as a liberal value. Recent events have done much to restore that belief.

Islamic law unequivocally recognizes the sanctity of private property, but Islamic history reveals a somewhat different picture, in which even a rich man's enjoyment of his property has never been safe from seizure or sequestration by the state. This chronic insecurity is symbolized in the architecture of the traditional Muslim city, in which neighborhoods, and even the houses of the wealthy, are turned inward, surrounded by high blank walls. Marx and Engels themselves recognized that their canonical sequence of ruling classes defined by production relationships might not apply to non-Western societies. They sketched the theory of what they called "the Asiatic mode of production," in which there was no effective private ownership of land, and

106

consequently no class war—just a simple opposition between the terrorized mass of the population and the all-encompassing state power, bureaucratic and military.

Like many of their other insights, this is a caricature, not a portrait, but also like their other insights, it is not without some basis in reality. Comparing the relationship between property and power in the modern American and classical Middle Eastern systems, one might put the difference this way: in America one uses money to buy power, while in the Middle East one uses power to acquire money. That is obviously an oversimplification, and there are significant exceptions on both sides. The misuse of public office for financial gain is not unknown in the United States; the use of money to buy into the political process is not unfamiliar in the traditional Middle East. But these are marginal, in the main small-scale, departures from the norm. In the vast American political and economic system the money made through the actual exercise of power is relatively unimportant—no more than small-time peculation. In the Middle East money can buy only the power of intrigue, not of command.

Perhaps the most striking manifestation of this difference between the two systems is in the merchant class, and its place in the society and polity. Muslim societies, both medieval and early modern, often included a rich and varied industrial and commercial life, and evolved a wealthy and cultivated merchant class. But with brief and insignificant exceptions—as, for example, in a disputed borderland between rival states, or in an interregnum between the collapse of one regime and the consolidation of another—they were never able to match the achievement of the rising European bourgeoisie in the creation of the modern West. One reason is that a large proportion of them were non-Muslims, principally Christians and Jews, and therefore precluded from any decisive role in the political process. But far more important was the chronic, permanent insecurity, the sequence of upheavals and invasions, the ever-present threat of expropriation or destruction.

## Modernization and Other Democratic Trends

These traditional obstacles to democracy have in many ways been reinforced by the processes of modernization, and by recent developments in the region. As already observed, the power of the state to dominate and terrorize the people has been vastly increased by modern methods. The philosophy of authoritarian rule has been sharpened and strengthened by imported totalitarian ideologies, which have served a double purpose—to sanctify rulers and leaders and to fanaticize their subjects and followers. The so-called Islamic fundamentalists are no exception in this respect.

107

Self-criticism in the West—a procedure until recently rarely practiced and little understood in the Middle East—provided useful ammunition. This use of the West against itself is particularly striking among the fundamentalists. Western democracy for them is part of the hated West, and that hatred is central to the ideas by which they define themselves, as in the past the free world defined itself first against Nazism and then against communism.

The changes wrought by modernization are by no means entirely negative. Some, indeed, are extremely positive. One such improvement is the emancipation of women. Though this still has a long way to go before it reaches Western levels, irreversible changes have already taken place. These changes are indispensable: a society can hardly aspire realistically to create and operate free institutions as long as it keeps half its members in a state of permanent subordination and the other half see themselves as domestic autocrats. Economic and social development has also brought new economic and social elements of profound importance—a literate middle class, commercial, managerial, and professional, that is very different from the military, bureaucratic, and religious elites that between them dominated the old order. These new groups are creating their own associations and organizations, and modifying the law to accommodate them. They are an indispensable component of civil society—previously lacking, yet essential to any kind of democratic polity.

## The Ruler's Contract

There are also older elements in the Islamic tradition, older factors in Middle Eastern history, that are not hostile to democracy and that, in favorable circumstances, could even help in its development. Of special importance among these is the classical Islamic concept of supreme sovereignty—elective, contractual, in a sense even consensual and revocable. The Islamic caliphate, as prescribed and regulated by the holy law, may be an autocracy; it is in no sense a despotism. According to Sunni doctrine, the Caliph was to be elected by those qualified to make a choice. The electorate was never defined, nor was any procedure of election ever devised or operated, but the elective principle remains central to Sunni religious jurisprudence, and that is not unimportant.

Again according to Sunni doctrine, the relationship between the Caliph and his subjects is contractual. The word *bay'a*, denoting the ceremony at the inauguration of a new Caliph, is sometimes translated as "homage" or "allegiance." Such translations, though no doubt reflecting the facts, do not accurately represent the principle. The word comes from an Arabic root meaning "to barter," hence "to buy and to sell," and originally referring to the clasping or slapping of hands with which in ancient Arabia a deal was normally concluded. The *bay'a* was thus conceived as a contract by which the subjects undertook to obey and the Caliph in return undertook to perform certain duties specified by the jurists. If a Caliph failed in those duties—and Islamic history shows that this was by no means a purely theoretical point—he could, subject to certain conditions, be removed from office.

This doctrine marks one of the essential differences between Islamic and other autocracies. An Islamic ruler is not above the law. He is subject to it, no less than the humblest of his servants. If he commands something that is contrary to the law, the duty of obedience lapses, and is replaced not by the right but by the duty of disobedience.

Muslim spokesmen, particularly those who sought to find Islamic roots for Western practices, made much of the Islamic principle of consultation, according to which a ruler should not make arbitrary decisions by himself but should act only after consulting with suitably qualified advisers. This principle rests on two somewhat enigmatic passages in the Koran and on a number of treatises, mainly by ulama [religious scholars] and statesmen, urging consultation with ulama or with statesmen. This principle has never been institutionalized, nor even formulated in the treatises of the holy law, though naturally rulers have from time to time consulted with their senior officials, more particularly in Ottoman times.

### Pluralism in Islamic Law

Of far greater importance was the acceptance of pluralism in Islamic law and practice. Almost from the beginning the Islamic world has shown an astonishing diversity. Extending over three continents, it embraced a wide variety of races, creeds, and cultures, which lived side by side in reasonable if intermittent harmony. Sectarian strife and religious persecution are not unknown in Islamic history, but they are rare and atypical, and never reached the level of intensity of the great religious wars and persecutions in Christendom.

Traditional Islam has no doctrine of human rights, the very notion of which might seem an impiety. Only God has rights—human beings have duties. But in practice the duty owed by one human being to another—more specifically, by a ruler to his subjects—may amount to what Westerners would call a right, particularly when the discharge of this duty is a requirement of holy law.

It may be—and has been—argued that these legal and religious principles have scant effect. The doctrine of elective and contractual sovereignty has been tacitly ignored since the days of the early caliphate. The supremacy of the law has been flouted.

Tolerance of pluralism and diversity has dwindled or disappeared in an age of heightened religious, ethnic, and social tensions. Consultation, as far as it ever existed, is restricted to the ruler and his inner circle, while personal dignity has been degraded by tyrants who feel that they must torture and humiliate, not just kill, their opponents.

And yet, despite all these difficulties and obstacles, the democratic ideal is steadily gaining force in the region, and increasing numbers of Arabs have come to the conclusion that it is the best, perhaps the only, hope for the solution of their economic, social, and political problems. . . .

All in all, considering the difficulties that Middle Eastern countries have inherited and the problems that they confront, the prospects for Middle Eastern democracy are not good. But they are better than they have ever been before. Most of these countries face grave economic problems. If they fail to cope with these problems, then the existing regimes, both dictatorial and authoritarian, are likely to be overthrown and replaced, probably by one variety or another of Islamic fundamentalists. It has been remarked in more than one country that the fundamentalists are popular because they are out of power and cannot be held responsible for the present troubles. If they acquired power, and with it responsibility, they would soon lose that popularity. But this would not matter to them, since once in power they would not need popularity to stay there, and would continue to govern—some with and some without oil revenues to mitigate the economic consequences of their methods. In time even the fundamentalist regimes, despite their ruthless hold on power, would be either transformed or overthrown, but by then they would have done immense, perhaps irreversible, damage to the cause of freedom.

But their victory is by no means inevitable. There is always the possibility that democrats may form governments, or governments learn democracy. The increasing desire for freedom, and the better understanding of what it means, are hopeful signs. Now that the Cold War has ended and the Middle East is no longer a battlefield for rival power blocs, the peoples of the Middle East will have the chance—if they can take it—to make their own decisions and find their own solutions. No one else will have the ability or even the desire to do it for them. Today—for the first time in centuries—the choice is their own.

*"The Islamic heritage, in fact, contains concepts that provide a foundation for contemporary Muslims to develop authentically Islamic programs of democracy."*

# Islam Has Strong Democratic Traditions

John O. Voll and John L. Esposito

In the following viewpoint, John O. Voll and John L. Esposito argue that Islam and Islamic culture contain many democratic concepts, even if these concepts do not conform to the Western model of democracy. According to Voll and Esposito, the emergence of Western democracy resulted from a complex process involving the redefinition and recombination of democratic, nondemocratic, and antidemocratic traditions. They argue that a similar process is occurring in the Islamic world, as Muslim thinkers reinterpret Islamic history and traditions in an effort to develop an authentically Islamic form of democracy. Voll is a professor of history at the University of New Hampshire and author of *Islam: Continuity and Change in the Modern World*. Esposito is a professor of religion and international affairs at Georgetown University and author of *The Islamic Threat: Myth or Reality?*

As you read, consider the following questions:

1. According to Voll and Esposito, was Christianity compatible with democracy in the West? Explain.
2. How do Voll and Esposito define *shura*, *ijma'*, and *ijtihad*?
3. On what grounds does Muhammad Iqbal, quoted by Voll and Esposito, denounce Western democracy?

From "Islam's Democratic Essence" by John O. Voll and John L. Esposito, originally published in the *Middle East Quarterly*, September 1994. Reprinted with permission.

Is democracy incompatible with Islamic revivalism? Many in the West think so, arguing as Gilles Kepel does that "the rejection of even a chimerical notion of democracy is actually inherent in Islamic religious doctrine." Others like Samuel P. Huntington hold that "deeply ingrained Islamic" cultural traditions are a "negative condition" that "may prevent democratic development." These pessimistic views make two faulty assumptions, however: that democracy is possible only in one form, and that Islam can be expressed in only one way.

The Islamic heritage, in fact, contains concepts that provide a foundation for contemporary Muslims to develop authentically Islamic programs of democracy. This broader understanding of democracy has important implications for U.S. policy toward the Muslim world. American support for democracy in the Muslim world must recognize the possibility of many different formats for popular political participation. Washington need not back specific movements but it should support the possibility of their participation in emerging democratic political systems.

## The Roots of Democracy

Widespread acceptance of democracy as a legitimate basis for political order is a phenomenon of the modern era. It tends to be forgotten that as late as the end of the eighteenth century, most Western political thinking was based on principles other than democracy. Paul E. Corcoran writes that

> From the perspective of twenty-five hundred years of Western political thinking, almost no one, until very recently, thought democracy to be a very good way of structuring political life . . . the great preponderance of political thinkers for two-and-a-half millennia have insisted upon the perversity of democratic constitutions, the disorderliness of democratic politics and the moral depravity of the democratic character.

"Divine right" of monarchs remained an issue in European politics until just two centuries ago. Even in the United States, the Founders had at best ambiguous views about democracy. Michael Levin observes that while "the absence of entrenched aristocratic and ecclesiastical power gave the United States a propitious basis from which to move towards modern democracy," this "was certainly not a path the founders intended to explore."

The emergence and acceptance of democratic theories, institutions, and practices in the West involved, as it does today, a complex process of redefining and combining nondemocratic, even anti-democratic, traditions with existing democratic customs, often of a consensual nature. In the early modern and modern eras, this heritage was reformulated in light of new perceptions about social, religious, and political needs and rights. For example, the "idea of popular sovereignty was simply incompatible with the theocentric concept of princely power and the increasingly rigid imperial structure of the Roman Church," according to Corcoran, but this did not prevent people who still believed themselves to be Christian from creating democratic systems in Western Europe and North America.

Most societies have indigenous traditions that incorporate decision making by consultation and some popular participation. In Western Europe, the reconceptualization of premodern traditions played an important role in the development of modern democratic institutions. Hugh Chisholm, a prominent scholar of English history, wrote in the classical eleventh edition of the *Encyclopaedia Britannica* that "we find in the Anglo-Saxon polity, as developed during their rule in England, all the constituent parts of parliament." The assemblies of yeoman peasants like the *things* of Scandinavia were reenvisioned as precursors of modern parliaments, as reflected in the very names of the parliaments in Norway (*Storting*) and Iceland (*Althing*). The modern democratization processes even involve reconceptualizing what may have been anti-democratic themes, combining these with the protodemocratic and democratic elements in every tradition. The Magna Carta, now seen as a major document in the history of Western democracy, was a royal promise of privilege made to a group of nobles.

Thus, indigenous concepts and institutions can interact with the experiences and structures of the modern era, creating the potential for democratization in contemporary societies. This background has positive implications for understanding the process of democratization throughout the world and its implementation today. Although the ruling elites in most major societies had significant reservations about democracy, according to Steven Muhlberger and Phil Paine, "most people in the world can call on some local tradition on which to build a modern democracy. . . . The evidence is clear that both the idea and the practice of democracy are foreign to no part of the world."

## Islamic Heritage

What elements in the Islamic tradition have Muslim thinkers redefined and reconceptualized in the service of democracy? Despite the great dynamism and diversity in contemporary Muslim political thought, certain concepts are central to the political positions of virtually all Muslims. According to Abul Ala Maududi (1903–1979), a major Sunni thinker of India, then Pakistan, who established the leading South Asian Islamic revivalist organization, the Jamaat-i Islami, the "political system of Islam has been based in three principles . . . *Tawheed* [*tawhid*] (Unity of God), *Risalat* (Prophethood) and *Khilafat* (Caliphate). It is difficult to appreciate different aspects of the Islamic polity without fully understanding these three principles."

*Unity of God.* Muslims unanimously agree on the unity of God as the central concept of Islamic faith, tradition, and practice. Ismail Raji al Faruqi, a Sunni Islamic scholar and activist, writes that at "the core of the Islamic religious experience . . . stands God Who is unique and Whose will is the imperative and guide for all men's lives." Similarly, the modernist Sunni intellectual Fazlur Rahman holds that this doctrine "is central to the Qur'an— without which, indeed, Islam is unthinkable." Ayatollah Khomeini, a Shi'i theologian, addressed Muslims as "followers of the school of *tauhid* [*tawhid*]."

---

## Religion and the "Voice of the People"

In the mid-nineteenth century Pope Pius IX was still denouncing the democratic revolutions of 1848 and dismissing liberal democracy as an "error". Only in the late nineteenth century did the notion of Christian democracy fully take hold in parts of Catholic Europe. In Britain in the seventeenth century and in France in the eighteenth, the notion of representative government was still doing battle with the Divine Right of Kings. But an idea triumphed which was rooted, ultimately, in Athens or the Roman Republic (albeit these states had plenty of noncitizens and slaves), namely the concept of *vox populi, vox dei,* "the voice of the people is the voice of God." No monarch or elite speaks for God, but rather the people themselves.

This idea is not, as some Westerners seem to imagine, alien to Islam. Some Islamic liberal modernizers have sought to identify the Muslim concept of *shura,* or consultation, with the basic idea of democracy. Others have pointed to the tradition of the Prophet Muhammad that "my people will never agree in an error." By extension, what the people agree on, must not be an error.

Michael Collins Dunn, *Middle East Policy,* vol. 1, no. 2, Spring 1992.

---

Building on the base of the imperative will of God for all aspects of human life, in political philosophy this imperative means that there can be only one sovereign, and that is God. Some non-Muslim analysts, as well as old-fashioned conservative Muslims and extremist fundamentalists, argue that *tawhid* makes "Islamic democracy" a self-contradiction: the sovereignty of God contradicts the sovereignty of the people. Thus, Maududi maintains that the profound tie between God and political legitimacy means that

> Islam, speaking from the view-point of political philosophy, is the very antithesis of secular Western democracy. . . . [Islam]

altogether repudiates the philosophy of popular sovereignty and rears its polity on the foundations of the sovereignty of God and the vicegerency (*Khilafah*) of man.

However, contemporary Muslims like Maududi do not reject democracy; they do insist that it be framed within *tawhid*.

A more apt name for the Islamic polity would be the "kingdom of God" which is described in English as a "theocracy." But Islamic theocracy is something altogether different from the theocracy of which Europe has had bitter experience. . . . The theocracy built up by Islam is not ruled by any particular religious class but by the whole community of Muslims including the rank and file. The entire Muslim population runs the state in accordance with the Book of God and the practice of His Prophet. If I were permitted to coin a new term, I would describe this system of government as a "theo-democracy," that is to say a divine democratic government, because under it the Muslims have been given a limited popular sovereignty under the suzerainty of God. The executive under this system of government is constituted by the general will of the Muslims who have also the right to depose it.

In this system, "every Muslim who is capable and qualified to give a sound opinion on matters of Islamic law, is entitled to interpret that law of God when such interpretation becomes necessary. In this sense the Islamic polity is a democracy. . . ."

### Risalat and Khilafat

*Human agency.* Prophethood and Caliph are the concepts of the human agents involved in implementing the Islamic message. Prophethood refers to the belief that God reveals His will to humans through specific individuals recognized as prophets. Muslims believe that God's comprehensive revelation was made through Muhammad and recorded in the Qur'an. This provides the primary foundation for all Islamic institutions.

Caliph, the second major concept defining activities of humans, has two important meanings and usages. The first, most common meaning is the title "successor" to the Prophet Muhammad as the leader of the Islamic community. Thus, the political system of the early Islamic state was the caliphate. The Ottoman sultan was the last Muslim ruler widely to be recognized with the title of caliph; the office and title were subsequently abolished with the establishment of the Turkish Republic in 1924.

The second meaning relates to the Qur'anic usage of the term caliph, dating from before the death of Muhammad and the establishment of the political caliphate. In the Qur'an, caliph refers to all humans, identifying them as the deputies or agents of God on earth. During the second half of the twentieth century, this Qur'anic meaning has received increased emphasis by Muslim revivalist thinkers. They are moving away from the caliphate as a ruling system toward a vision of the role of all humans in politics. As such, it provides a possible foundation for an Islamic democratic perspective. Maududi utilized this concept of caliphate as a basis for finding democracy in Islam:

> The real position and place of man, according to Islam, is that of the representative of God on this earth, His vicegerent [caliph]; that is to say . . . he is required to exercise Divine authority in this world within the limits prescribed by God.

This interpretation has specific implications for the political system in that

> The authority of the caliphate is bestowed on the entire group of people, the community as a whole, which is ready to fulfill the conditions of representation after subscribing to the principles of *Tawheed*. . . . Such a society carries the responsibility of the caliphate as a whole and each one of its individual [*sic*] shares the Divine Caliphate. This is the point where democracy begins in Islam. Every person in an Islamic society enjoys the rights and powers of the caliphate of God and in this respect all individuals are equal. . . .

### Operational Concepts for Islamic Democracy

Several Islamic concepts have a key role in the development of Islamic democracy: consultation (*shura*), consensus (*ijma'*), and independent interpretive judgment (*ijtihad*). These terms have not always been identified with democratic institutions, and even today have a variety of usages. Nonetheless, like reinterpreted concepts such as citizen and parliament in the Western tradition, they have become crucial concepts for the articulation of Islamic democracy.

*Consultation.* Advocates of Islamic democracy have sought to broaden the traditional understanding of consultation, understood to be by the ruler with his populace. Fazlur Rahman argues that the classical doctrine of consultation was in error because it presented consultation as the process of one person, the ruler, asking subordinates for advice; in fact, the Qur'an calls for "*mutual advice* through mutual discussions on an equal footing." He goes so far as to state that those who deny the Muslim community its democratic voice "are willingly or unwittingly guilty of rendering Islam null and void."

The importance of consultation as a part of Islamic systems of rule is widely recognized. Muhammad Hamidullah places consultation in a generally accepted framework:

> The importance and utility of consultation cannot be too greatly emphasized. The Quran commands the Muslims again and again to take their decisions after consultation, whether in a public matter or a private one . . . the Quran does not prescribe hard and fast methods. The number, the form of election, the duration of representation, etc., are left to the discre-

116

tion of the leaders of every age and every country. What is important is that one should be surrounded by representative personalities, enjoying the confidence of those whom they represent and possessing integrity of character.

Baqir as-Sadr, a political theorist executed by the Iraqi government in 1980, relates consultation to the rights of the people: "The people, being the vicegerents of Allah, have a general right to dispose of their affairs on the basis of the principle of consultation," and this should involve "the formation of an assembly whose members are the real representatives of the people."

---

## Democracy and Islam

There is no inherent incompatibility between democracy and Islam. Like all scripture, the Quran can be interpreted to support many different types of political behavior and systems of government. It contains no direct support for democracy, the closest statement being an indication that "what is with God is better and more lasting for those . . . who [conduct] their affairs by mutual consultation [*shura*]." As would be expected, its emphasis lies much more on the pious qualities expected of a ruler than on the way in which rulers should be chosen. . . .

The conflict arises when the particular form of political Islam precludes the procedural essence of democracy, the repeated provision of debate and choice between a free range of options. When political Islam, in the name of cleaning out the stables of corruption and alienation, promises to install a system where only those who subscribe to the true path are allowed into the contest for power, then the incompatibility arises. When parties led by devoted leaders inspired by religious beliefs vie among others for a role in government, there is no incompatibility.

I. William Zartman, *The Annals of the Academy of Political and Social Science*, September 1992.

---

The popular caliphate in an Islamic state is reflected especially in the doctrine of mutual consultation (*shura*). All Muslims as vicegerents (agents of God) delegate their authority to the ruler and it is their opinion that must also be sought in the conduct of state.

*Consensus.* The Prophet Muhammad is believed to have said, "My Community will not agree upon an error." Accordingly, consensus has for centuries provided the ultimate validation of decisions in Islam, especially among Sunni Muslims. "Sunni Islam came to place final religious authority for interpreting Islam in the consensus (*ijma'*) or collective judgment of the community." Subsequently, "consensus played a pivotal role in the development of Islamic law and contributed significantly to the corpus of law or legal interpretation," according to John L. Esposito. However, only learned scholars (the *ulama*) had a role in reaching consensus; the general public had little significance. When the scholars reached consensus on a subject, it usually ended the debate.

In modern times, Muslim thinkers have imbued the concept of consensus with new possibilities. It need not be static; Hamidullah sees consensus as offering "great possibilities of developing the Islamic law and adapting it to changing circumstances." Further, consensus can provide an effective basis for accepting majority rule. As Louay M. Safi notes, the "legitimacy of the state . . . depends upon the extent to which state organization and power reflect the will of the ummah [the Muslim community], for as classical jurists have insisted, the legitimacy of state institutions is not derived from textual sources but is based primarily on the principle of *ijma'*." Thus, consensus offers both legitimation of Islamic democracy and a procedure to carry it out.

### Individual Interpretation

*Independent judgment.* Many Muslim thinkers believe the exercise of informed, independent judgment to be the key to implementing God's will. Virtually all Muslim reformers of the twentieth century show enthusiasm for the concept of independent judgment. Muhammad Iqbal (1875–1938), one of the major figures in modern and modernist Islam, in the 1930s called for "the transfer of the power of Ijtihad from individual representatives of schools to a Muslim legislative assembly." According to Khurshid Ahmad, vice-president of the Jamaat-i Islami, "God has revealed only broad principles and has endowed man with the freedom to apply them in every age in the way suited to the spirit and conditions of that age. It is through the *Ijtihad* that people of every age try to implement and apply divine guidance to the problems of their times." Advocacy of independent judgment can be a call for radical reform, as it is for Altaf Gauhar:

> In Islam power flows out of the framework of the Qur'an and from no other source. It is for Muslim scholars to initiate universal *Ijtihad* at all levels. The faith is fresh, it is the Muslim mind which is befogged. The principles of Islam are dynamic, it is our approach which has become static. Let there be fundamental rethinking to open avenues of exploration, innovation and creativity.

Consultation, consensus, and independent judgment provide the basic concepts for understanding the relationship between Islam and democracy in the contemporary world, and an effective foundation to build an Islamic basis for democracy. . . .

Islamist movements have taken the lead in combining Western

experiences and concepts with an affirmation of key concepts arising out of the fundamental sources of Islamic faith and experience. Movements like an-Nahda in Tunisia, the Muslim Brethren of Jordan and Egypt, and the Jamaat-i Islami in Pakistan affirm that democratization consists of more than simply importing a set model from the West. Not anti-modern or anti-Western, they are postmodern in their view that emerging global human order transcends the era of Western domination.

The global dynamics of democratization reflect the dramatic changes of the present. Throughout the world—including the Western democracies—the effort to create more effective democratic structures continues apace. (In the United States, we witness everything from "reinventing government" to term limits.) These efforts attest to the fact that there is no universally accepted or clearly defined model of democracy, even of Western democracy, that can simply be adopted by people engaging in democratization. The difficulties of the new democratic regimes in Eastern Europe as well as the Muslim world reflect the problems and complexities of the global experiences of democratization.

Many Muslims are actively engaged in defining Islamic democracy. They believe religious resurgence and democratization are complementary; they are contradictory only if democracy is defined according to specific Western standards.

Muslims need to develop Islamic programs of democracy, for this allows them to escape simply borrowing Western-based definitions of democracy. Doing so shifts the debate from the legitimacy of importing foreign political institutions to the best way of increasing popular participation.

From a global perspective, the efforts of Muslims to develop authentic and viable forms of Islamic democracy have great significance. Their utilization of traditions of consultation and consensus reflect concerns that are prominent in Western efforts to create more effective forms of participatory democracy. The increasing density of intercommunication and networks of relationships among democratic, democratizing, and nondemocratic societies around the globe makes efforts anywhere important for actions and developments everywhere. Muslims have important contributions to make in the process of reconceptualizing democracy, especially in the area of consensual participation and nonadversarial democratic structures.

*"Islamists are now trying to reconcile moral and religious tenets with modern life, political competition and free markets."*

# Islam Is Evolving Toward Democracy

Robin Wright

In January 1992, a military coup in Algeria prevented the completion of democratic elections that would have brought the Islamic Salvation Front (FIS) to power. In the following viewpoint, Robin Wright argues that the Algerian election was a good test case for the compatibility of political Islamic parties and democracy. Islamic political parties, wrongly perceived by the West as inherently extremist and antidemocratic, recognize that extremism in the 1980s was too politically costly, she argues, and they are now seeking to work within the democratic system. The West ought to have more strongly opposed the coup and upheld the elections, she believes. Wright is a reporter for the *Los Angeles Times* and author of *Flashpoints: Promise and Peril in a New World*.

As you read, consider the following questions:

1. According to Wright, what does religion provide to societies struggling toward democracy?
2. What does Wright say the FIS offered in the 1991 election that the ruling party could not? What did the FIS not offer?
3. According to the author, what are the West's two alternatives for responding to growing Islamist sentiment?

From "Islam, Democracy, and the West" by Robin Wright. Reprinted by permission of *Foreign Affairs*, Summer 1992. Copyright ©1992 by the Council on Foreign Relations, Inc.

More than fifteen years after the Iranian Revolution wrought the world's first modern theocracy, Islam is once again emerging as a powerful political idiom. Not only in the Middle East, but from north and west Africa to the former Asian republics of the Soviet Union, from India to western China, Islam is increasingly a defining force in evolving political agendas. The new burst of activism has reached such proportions that, with the demise of communism, Islam is increasingly—and erroneously—being perceived as one of the future ideological rivals to the West.

The latest phase began in the late 1980s. It varies distinctly from the Islamic experience in Iran [led by Ayatollah Khomeini] in 1979, in Lebanon [led by Hezbollah] after 1982 and among a host of smaller cells in Egypt, Saudi Arabia, Kuwait, Syria and elsewhere during the late 1970s and early 1980s. The two most conspicuous differences are the constituency and tactics of the new Islamists.

## The Second Resurgence of Islam

The first phase was more often associated with Shiite Muslims, Islam's so-called second sect. Besides the Iranian Revolution, groups such as Lebanon's Hezbollah and Iraq's Dawa, which also operated on the Shiite-populated eastern shores of the Arabian peninsula, accounted for the most visible and enduring activism. The recent resurgence of Islam, however, is more prevalent among the mainstream Sunni, who account for at least 85 percent of the world's one billion Muslims. The Sunni are also spread more widely through the seventy-five nations that constitute *Dar al Islam*, or House of Islam. With the exceptions of Lebanon, Iraq, Iran and Yemen, the Sunni dominate countries stretching from Africa to the Levant, the Arabian peninsula, across the southern tier of the new Commonwealth of Independent States, into western China, south Asia and as far east as Indonesia, the most populous Muslim state.

Unlike the extremism that typified the first resurgence—in political upheavals as well as suicide bombings, hijackings and hostage seizures—the new Islamic activism is now characterized by attempts to work within the system rather than outside it. Since 1989, for example, Islamists from diverse groups have run for parliament in Jordan and Algeria. Indonesia's largest Muslim movement, which has support from up to forty million people, held peaceful rallies in 1992 to urge democratic reforms in the authoritarian state. Since the dismemberment of the Soviet Union in 1991, Islamists in the former Central Asian republics have petitioned for legal recognition, to end years as underground movements, so they can run for public office.

Reasons for the new preference for ballots over bullets vary within each country and movement, but they generally reflect an acknowledgement that the costs of extremism in the 1980s proved too high. Iran's isolation, for example, forced it backward economically, not forward. Also the demise of communism starkly illustrated the joint dangers of totalitarian rule and confrontation with the West. Islamists have not failed to recognize that pluralism and interdependence are the catchwords of the 1990s.

## The Maghreb (Northern Africa)

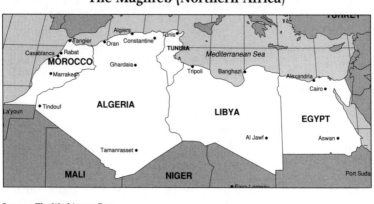

Source: *The Washington Post.*

Cooperation has by no means fully replaced confrontation. But in key regions Islamists are no longer simply striking out angrily at what they do not like. After centuries marked mainly by dormancy, colonialism and failed experiments with Western ideologies, many Islamists feel they have a mandate to create constructive alternatives. Further pressed by the same factors that have led to political and economic transformations globally, a growing number of Islamists are now trying to reconcile moral and religious tenets with modern life, political competition and free markets. Few Islamists, as yet, have suitable or complete answers. The common campaign slogan, "Islam is the solution," remains simplistically inadequate.

### Religion and Societal Change

Politicized Islam is not alone. At the end of the twentieth century, religion has become an energetic and dynamic force for change worldwide. Among the struggling societies attempting both to rid themselves of bankrupt or inefficient systems and to find viable alternatives, religion provides ideals, identity, legitimacy and an infrastructure during the search. In varying degrees, Buddhists in east Asia, Catholics in eastern Europe, Latin America and the Philippines, Sikhs and Hindus in India and even Jews in Israel have turned to their faith to define their goals and to mobilize.

The various attempts within Islam, however, also reflect a deeper quest—one that could make the Islamists' impact broader or more lasting, because Islam is the only major monotheistic religion that offers not only a set of spiritual beliefs but a set of rules by which to govern society. Besides the challenge of finding a place in the new global order, Islam is now at a pivotal and profound moment of evolution, a juncture increasingly equated with the Protestant Reformation. The traditional role of the faith, its leadership, organization, priorities and interpretation, are also under scrutiny.

The changing focus is reflected even in the names. The first phase of the Islamic resurgence was often symbolized by a host of groups in Lebanon, Egypt, and Israel's occupied territories named Islamic Jihad, or Holy War, while the latest activism is most noted for groups—from Tunisia to Tajikistan—called the Islamic Renaissance Party. The challenge is as much within Islam as in the countries and systems in which Muslims live. In many ways Islamic societies now find themselves in the opening rounds of what the West went through in the sixteenth and seventeenth centuries in redefining both the relationship between God and man and between man and man.

The challenge for Islamists is all the greater because the political climate—at home and in the international arena—is hardly conducive to reforms or experimentation, much less full expression. The specter of Iran's revolutionary excesses and Lebanon's terrorist zealotry continues to color local and Western attitudes toward Islam. Despite the growing body of evidence to the contrary, Islam is still widely—and again wrongly—perceived as inherently extremist. Despite the many shades and shapes of Islamic activism, it is also still wrongly treated as a single or monolithic force. . . .

## The Case of Algeria

Algeria has become the primary test case for the compatibility of Islam and democracy. Islamic activism emerged in Algeria when President Chandli Bendjedid ended socialist one-party rule after growing public discontent was capped in 1988 by riots in which at least 400 people were killed. In the first phase of a three-part transition the Islamic Salvation Front (FIS) won a stunning upset in the 1990 local elections, capturing more than 60 percent of regional assemblies and 55 percent of municipal councils. The National Liberation Front (FLN), which had ruled since leading Algeria's eight-year war against French colonialism [1954–62], came in an embarrassingly poor second.

The election, the first free multiparty poll since independence in 1962, was as much a rejection of the FLN as a vote of support for the Islamists. Almost three decades of inefficient and increasingly corrupt rule had finally caught up with the FLN. By 1992 at least 14 million of Algeria's 25 million population were estimated to live below the poverty line. With a $25 billion foreign debt that consumed almost 70 percent of its oil revenues, the government had little left to address mass grievances over chronic housing shortages, unemployment, substandard education and social services and limited development. And with 65 percent of the population under the age of thirty, the majority had no memory of, much less nostalgia for, the Algerian revolution.

In contrast the energetic Islamists offered a legitimate and familiar alternative, if not a very detailed program. Their appeal was also reflected in their response to a strike called during the election by gas stations, newspapers and even trash collectors. After mounds of garbage accumulated on the streets of the Mediterranean capital, Islamists mobilized supporters to clean up the refuse with their hands. The Islamists' commitment was in stark contrast to the malaise within the FLN.

Because of the large rejectionist vote in local elections, the second phase of the transition, elections for parliament, was expected to be a more accurate reading of the public's political will. In the first round in December 1991, which fielded more than fifty parties, FIS captured 188 of the 231 seats decided, only 28 short of a majority. This time the FLN came in third, with only 15 seats, trailing after the Berber-dominated party, the Socialist Forces Front, which won 25. Hamas, another Islamic party, came in fourth. Although the FIS total was a million less than during the local elections, it appeared set to win a decisive parliamentary majority in the second round for 199 undecided seats scheduled for January 16, 1992.

## Algerian Elections Suspended

The two elections represented a political milestone. No Islamic party since the Iranian Revolution had won such an overwhelming victory, and no Islamic party had ever definitively defeated a long-dominant power through democratic means.

But the world's first Islamic democracy never had a chance to prove itself. Five days before the second round of elections, a "white coup" led by Defense Minister Khaled Nezzar forced Bendjedid to resign. He was replaced with a five-man High State Council, and elections were then suspended. Over the following weeks, the FIS leadership was detained and the party banned. At least 8,800 sympathizers or supporters of both FIS and Hamas—some claimed the figure was as high as 30,000—

were also rounded up by late March 1992 and dispatched to detention camps in the southern Sahara desert. In an attempt to revoke the results of the 1990 local elections, dozens of mayors and many regional assembly leaders who had won power on the FIS ticket were also arrested; the assemblies were dissolved.

Islamists were the target, but democracy was the ultimate victim. The Algerian junta has hinted that it might follow through with the final phase of the transition, presidential elections; but FIS is unlikely to be included. Indeed the new government's strategy is to use the interim—with the help of foreign aid and loans and by selling off oil and gas rights—to address the grievances that led the electorate to vote for FIS. The council also reportedly favors rewriting the constitution to prevent future attempts by Islamists to enter politics. On April 29, 1992, Algeria's Supreme Court ordered the FIS dissolved.

## Pluralism and Suppression in Algeria

The junta, however, is unlikely to survive. The Algerian coup was in many ways like the abortive Moscow putsch [that attempted to overthrow Mikhail Gorbachev] in 1991; although the process may take longer, it will fail for similar reasons. Bendjedid's phased transition to pluralism produced more than just multiple parties. From a handful of newspapers under state control, Algeria's press soared to dozens of diverse and increasingly outspoken publications. Once-cloistered debate moved into open forums, while public interest groups, including a human rights movement, began to flourish. Most of all, Algerians, particularly the disaffected, tasted empowerment and liked it; its indefinite suppression will eventually produce a backlash.

The junta's tactics have also been crass. To lead the new ruling council, the military brought back Mohammed Boudiaf, an aging revolutionary hero who fell out with his cohorts in 1963 and has lived in exile ever since. The detentions were ruthless. When security forces were unable to find a wanted Islamist, they merely picked up another family member. Many detainees have undergone summary trials and have been sentenced to two to twenty years in prison. The government also banned all public gatherings around mosques and even moved to replace 40 percent of the leaders of Algeria's 9,000 mosques; scores of *imams* (Islamic religious leaders) were among those detained. Algerians have not experienced such repression since the war for independence.

But the junta is most likely to fail because it has given new legitimacy to the very force it sought to suppress—Islam. After the coup, the FLN fragmented into factions for and against the putsch, while opposition parties were unable to mobilize effectively against the junta. In the disarray, FIS was left as the force

125

pushing hardest for democracy.

The movement's remarkable discipline after the coup helped. Despite the riot police and army cordons around key mosques, FIS leaders repeatedly urged restraint. "The army has a scenario for us, but it is a role we will not play. We will not respond to provocation," acting FIS leader Abdelkader Hachani told thousands of the faithful at Friday prayers [at the Bab el-Qoed mosque during the week of the coup]. Although FIS is a multi-faceted movement with factions that favor different levels of activism, as well as differing versions of Islamic democracy, it was visibly united in trying to prevent bloodshed.

---

### Democratic Islamic Politicians

A fundamentally important question is whether experiments in democratization, as are now under way in Jordan, Yemen, Kuwait and Lebanon, will domesticate the populist Islamist movements which often comprise the most significant challenger for popular legitimacy, while simultaneously serving as an important motivation for government action. Put another way, does the political process instill pragmatism and a political logic of give-and-take that will slake all but the most ardent activist? The evidence is mixed, but promising. In each of the four countries mentioned, recent elections have brought Islamists into the political process, and in each of these cases Islamist politicians have proved willing to play by the rules.

Augustus Richard Norton, *New Perspectives Quarterly*, Summer 1993.

---

Even after the mass arrests, FIS demands two months after the coup were limited to release of political detainees, an end to persecution of Islamists, a dialogue with all political parties and resumption of elections. Notably it did not call for jihad. Most of the sporadic hit-and-run attacks, particularly against Algerian security forces, were linked to a host of small and loosely organized Islamic extremist cells not under FIS control. Among them were Hijra wa Takfir, or Sin and Atonement, and the Afghans, so-named for their participation in the Afghan war against Soviet occupation in the 1980s; many were reportedly trained by the CIA in Pakistan. Despite the temptation, FIS did not abandon democracy to achieve its goals.

### The Lack of a Western Response

For the Arab and Muslim worlds, Algeria is not simply a test case of the affinity of Islam and democracy. It is also a test of whether the West can reconcile with Islam. On that count the

West's record is only marginally better than the junta's.

After the Algerian coup, Western reaction was notable largely for its passivity. The U.S. State Department officially "regretted" the suspension of the democratic process in Algeria and then fell silent. Several Western governments allowed the junta's representatives to pay official visits to explain their plans and goals. Some even considered aid. A consortium of European and American banks provided $1.45 billion to help Algeria spread out the servicing of its debt.

Before the U.N. General Assembly in fall 1991, President George Bush said: "People everywhere seek government of and by the people. And they want to enjoy their inalienable rights to freedom and property and person." The United States, he added, supported those rights globally. If Algeria is any example, however, there is an implicit exception: any country where Islam is the winner of a democratic election.

The lack of U.S. response, at a time when the Bush administration was active and outspoken in advocating political pluralism, makes it appear that the White House preferred a police state to an Islamic democracy. Indeed the absence of an international outcry or Western condemnation—as there was, for example, after Peru's president Alberto Fujimora suspended the constitution and dissolved parliament in April 1992—has encouraged the junta to pursue its course, a fact FIS has publicly noted. The FIS platform remains uncomfortably vague. Its achievements in Algeria's municipalities during eighteen months in power were mixed, in no small part because of disputes with FLN governors over budget allocations and priorities. Despite FIS reassurances, other Algerian parties feared the Islamists would eventually ban them and declare a theocracy, as happened in Iran. . . .

## The Clash of Islam and the West

The West and Islam have reached a crossroad in their relationship. The clash since 1979—epitomized by the antagonism between the United States and Iran—need no longer serve as the paradigm. Unfortunately, despite the strong evidence of Islam's political appeal and its future potential, the United States and its Western allies still have no more tangible strategy to contend with Islam than they did after Ayatollah Ruhollah Khomeini forced the shah of Iran from the Peacock throne in 1979.

As Islamist sentiment grows, the West has two stark alternatives: one is to use this important juncture—when both democracy and Islam are growing—to press Muslim-dominated countries toward political pluralism and then to accept the results of free and fair democratic elections. By having sided with democracy from an early stage, the West will then be in a stronger position to hold new Islamic governments accountable if they abuse or abandon democratic principles—without being seen as anti-Islamic.

The incentive is to ease tensions between Western and Eastern cultures and countries. The next few years will be as important for democracy's evolution as for Islam's. For two millennia democracy has taken root only in Western cultures. One of the next major global challenges will be determining whether democracy is adaptable to Eastern countries, including Islamic and Confucian societies, and vice versa. This is a moment to encourage, rather than obstruct, Islam's expression in pluralist forms.

The second alternative is to try to counter or contain Islamist movements by backing or aiding governments that repress them. Such a policy could become as costly and prolonged as fighting communism, and potentially more difficult. Challenging an ideology that is supported by a failed economic system is one thing; demonizing a centuries-old faith and culture is another. Moreover, as in the Cold War, the United States would have to cultivate some unsavory allies along the way. Many of the regimes most committed to blocking Islamist movements—ranging from Syria's Hafez al-Assad to Libya's Muammar al-Qaddafi—are also opposed to democracy.

This alternative—an implicit or declared policy of stopping Islamist movements before they rise to power—could also realize the West's greatest fears: unity of the diverse and disparate Islamist groups into an anti-Western force and the use of extremist and terrorist tactics. Finally, the broader danger is that trying to obstruct Islamists will, in turn, lead to a new East-West divide with far deeper passions—and a bloody history—behind it.

The Islamic resurgence clearly presents a challenge to the West. But it also provides enormous opportunity.

*"Fundamentalists insist they have not demanded free elections in order to promote democracy or the individual freedoms that underpin it, but to promote Islam."*

# Islam Is Not Evolving Toward Democracy

Martin Kramer

In December 1991, in the first democratic parliamentary elections ever held in Algeria, an Islamic political party won a landslide victory. Some Western experts argued that the election was a hopeful sign for democracy in Islamic countries. In the following viewpoint, Martin Kramer argues that the belief among Western scholars that Islamic fundamentalist movements represent the emergence of "Islamic democracy" is refuted by the pronouncements of the fundamentalists themselves. Though Islamic political parties are competing in elections, he argues, they have not abandoned their goal of establishing Islamic regimes that will be fundamentally hostile to the West. Kramer is a professor in the school of government at Georgetown University in Washington, D.C.

As you read, consider the following questions:

1. According to the author, how did extremist groups transform themselves into populist movements?
2. What gives the fundamentalists their electoral advantage, in Kramer's analysis?
3. According to Hassan al-Turabi, quoted by Kramer, is a multiparty system consistent with Islamic beliefs?

From Martin Kramer, "Islam vs. Democracy." Reprinted from *Commentary*, January 1993, by permission; all rights reserved.

For most of the 1980s, those who saw Islamic fundamentalism for what it is saw groups as violent and dogmatic as any in the world. These were people who mixed nostalgia with grievance to produce a millenarian vision of an Islamic state—a vision so powerful that its pursuit justified any means. Angry believers invoked this Islam when they executed enemies of the revolution in Iran, assassinated a president in Egypt, and detonated themselves or abducted others in Lebanon. Their furious words complemented their deeds. They marched to chants of "Death to America" and intimidated all opponents with charges of espionage and treason. They did not expect to be understood, but they did want to be feared, and feared they were, by Muslims and non-Muslims alike.

Yet their violence failed to overturn the region. While fundamentalists did seize the state in Iran, in most Arab countries they lurked about the edges of politics. They were often dangerous, and always fascinating, but they posed no mortal threat to the established order.

## Fundamentalism in the 1980s

By the decade's end, however, many of these same groups had managed to transform themselves into populist movements, and even win mass followings. They did so by riding a huge tide of discontent, fed by exploding populations, falling oil prices, and economic mismanagement by the state. While regimes fumbled for solutions, the fundamentalists persuaded the growing numbers of the poor, the young, and the credulous that if they only returned to belief and implemented God's law, the fog of misery surrounding them would lift.

Islam is the solution, ran the fundamentalist slogan. What that meant, no one would say. . . .

A great deal of solid scholarship on these movements appeared during the 1980s, making it difficult to view them benignly. Their theories of *jihad* and conspiracy, embedded in wordy tracts, received critical scrutiny. True, Edward Said, Columbia University's part-time professor from Palestine, presented a contrary view in *Covering Islam*, a book which bemoaned the Western media's treatment of Islam. The book was much admired by the Islamic Jihad in Beirut, prolific deconstructionists (of U.S. embassies) who circulated it among Western hostages for their edification. But the violence of the fundamentalists made them a difficult sell, and when in 1989 they filled the streets to demand the death of the novelist Salman Rushdie, they bit the hands even of those few Western intellectuals who had tried to feed them. As the decade closed, Islamic fundamentalism could count on few foreign friends.

Meanwhile, even as Islam's fundamentalists were demanding

the death of Rushdie, a longing for democracy (and capitalism) swept across Latin America, Eastern Europe, and the Soviet Union. Throughout the Middle East and North Africa, rulers took fright at the scenes of revolution from Romania and East Germany, and proceeded to initiate tightly controlled experiments in political pluralism. At the time, the architects of these experiments had no sense of the fundamentalists' appeal; they thought that the openings would work to the benefit of parties advocating liberal reform.

## Democratic Sentiments?

In a 1989 interview quoted by John Esposito and James Piscatori [in the *Middle East Journal*, (Summer 1991), Tunisia's Rached] Ghannouchi said that "the state is not something from God but from the people," a perfectly democratic sentiment. But in a speech to his followers distributed in Paris in March 1991, Ghannouchi said, "We must call into question the credibility of Western democracy. For my part I have serious doubts, just as I doubt all the ideas imported from the West concerning public liberties, the rights of man, international law. . . . They are nothing but myths and nonsense destined to put us to sleep." Did Ghannouchi's attitude towards democracy change in two years' time, or does he say something different to sympathetic Western scholars than to his own followers?

Michael Collins Dunn, *Middle East Policy*, vol. 1, no. 2, 1992.

But it was the fundamentalists who led the dash through the newly opened door. The first of a succession of surprises occurred in Egypt's parliamentary elections in 1987, when a coalition dominated by the fundamentalist Muslim Brethren emerged as the biggest opposition party in a contest gerrymandered to assure victory for the ruling party. The fundamentalists also outdistanced all other opposition parties in the 1989 elections for Tunisia's parliament, although a winner-take-all system gave every seat to the ruling party. That same year, the fundamentalists nearly captured the lower house of Jordan's parliament, in that country's first general election since 1967. Then, in 1990, the fundamentalists swept the countrywide local elections in Algeria.

Given these successes, almost overnight fundamentalist movements became the most avid and insistent supporters of free elections—an unpatrolled route to the power that had hitherto eluded them. Liberal Arab intellectuals, who had lobbied for democratic reforms and human rights for much of the 1980s, now retreated in disarray, fearful that freer press and elections might play straight into the hands of fundamentalists.

For Western theorists of democracy, it was as if the Arabs had defied the laws of gravity. Few admitted the bind as frankly as Jeane Kirkpatrick, who said:

> The Arab world is the only part of the world where I've been shaken in my conviction that if you let the people decide, they will make fundamentally rational decisions.

Most theorists, however, refused to be shaken. In order to synchronize the Arab predicament with the march of democracy, they developed a convenient theory—the theory of initial advantage.

## The Theory of Initial Advantage

The fundamentalists, according to this theory, enjoyed an advantage in the first stages of democratization: they knew how to organize, to stir emotions, to get out the vote. But "as civil society is enlivened," announced one political scientist, "it is only natural that the influence of the Islamist groups will be challenged." Then their appeal would fade, once the people enjoyed a full range of options. In the privacy of the voting booth, the voters would become rational actors and elect liberals and technocrats who proposed serious answers to the crisis of Arab society.

Algeria's parliamentary election, first scheduled for June 1991 and then postponed until December, was to have proved the point. According to the theorists, Algeria had the best chance of giving birth to a liberal democracy. More than any other Arab country, Algeria enjoyed an intimate connection with Europe, and its elites were at home with the ways of the West. True, the new Algerian voter had already given one sweeping victory to the Islamic Salvation Front (known by its French acronym, FIS) in local elections. But expert opinion declared the FIS victory a "protest" against the corruption of the ruling party, not a vote for a stern regime of Islamic mores. Anyway, ran the argument, the FIS had lost its initial advantage, first by mismanaging the municipalities where it had assumed authority, and then by backing Saddam Hussein in his Kuwait blunder.

"Saddam's defeat has turned the Algerian political situation upside down," announced *L'Express*, "leaving the FIS in the worst position of all." It was safely predicted that Algerians would turn away from the sheiks in the upcoming parliamentary elections—a fair and free ballot, structured in technical consultation with the best Parisian authorities in the *sciences politiques*. "The FIS can now count on only a die-hard bloc of unemployed urban youths," opined an American political scientist in the *Journal of Democracy*, who found it "unlikely that the FIS will gain enough votes to dictate the makeup of the new government." Such confident assurances helped to anesthetize

Algeria's elite, who secretly worshiped foreign expertise and looked surreptitiously to the foreign press to explain their own predicament to them.

Thus, Paris and Algiers were both astonished when the FIS won a landslide victory in the first round of the parliamentary election, nearly burying Algeria's regime and its Westernized elite. The Sudan's Turabi was right for once when he claimed that any observer with insight should have been able to predict the outcome: "The Western media wished this not to be so, so they hid the facts from everyone, so the results came as a surprise." But the self-deception went beyond the media, to the battery of democracy doctors who had ministered to the ailing Algerian polity. Their theory of initial advantage proved to be an immense blind spot, large enough to conceal a near-revolution.

## The Fundamentalists' Electoral Advantage

Algeria confirmed something that has been demonstrated in study after study of fundamentalist movements: fundamentalism is no fad, but the preference of a generation. It will not stop on a dime—on the failure of Saddam's *jihad*, or the scandal surrounding Islamic banks in Egypt, or haphazard garbage collection in fundamentalist-run towns in Algeria. Nor do the fundamentalists now need a detailed plan to alleviate suffering, because they possess potent words, and those words vest suffering with meaning. In a Western polity, the Pied Pipers of the disaffected young could not hope to win power in a landslide vote. But the explosion of the young population in the Arab world has given this generation an immense electoral advantage. After Algeria's parliamentary election, the bleak reality could not be denied: free elections in the Middle East and North Africa were more likely to produce fundamentalist rule than not.

The failure to anticipate the FIS victory should have cut deeply into the credibility of Western democracy doctors, with their blithe promise that the fundamentalist appeal would fade in a truly free ballot. But they have rebounded with a new discovery. Fundamentalism, they now claim, is destined not to disappear but to triumph, because *it* is the yearning for democracy in Islamic camouflage.

Those who claim credit for this discovery muster three arguments in support of their contention that Islam has become the "Cause of Good," and that Islamic movements therefore deserve the sympathy the West has bestowed on democracy movements elsewhere. Paradoxically, each of these arguments has already been systematically refuted—by the fundamentalists themselves.

The first argument holds that Islamic fundamentalism, whatever its past, has entered upon an evolution, and has already started to reconcile Islam with democratic values. As one academic apologist claims:

> Many Islamic activists have "Islamized" parliamentary democracy, asserting an Islamic rationale for it, and appeal to democracy in their opposition to incumbent regimes.

The distortion here does not lie in the claim of compatibility between Islam and democracy. Although the dominant interpretation of Islam has historically sanctioned authoritarian rule, the reinterpretation of Islamic sources, done with enough imagination, could conceivably produce an opposing argument for Islamic democracy. Here and there, intrepid Muslims have searched the divine word of the Qur'an, the traditions of the Prophet, and the early history of Islam in order to establish the democratic essence of Islam, buried deep beneath the chronicles of despotism.

But these are not the Muslims leading the fundamentalist movements now bidding for power. Fundamentalists insist they have not demanded free elections in order to promote democracy or the individual freedoms that underpin it, but to promote Islam. Indeed, when leading fundamentalist thinkers do address the broader question of democracy, it is not to argue its compatibility with Islam but to demonstrate democracy's inferiority to Islamic government. Such a virtuous government, they affirm, can rest only on obedience to the divinely-given law of Islam, the *shari'a*.

A deception lurks in any description of the fundamentalists as being committed to the rule of law, for the *shari'a* is not legislated but revealed law; as such, in the eyes of the fundamentalists it has already achieved perfection, and while it is not above some reinterpretation, neither is it infinitely elastic. If anything, fundamentalist exegesis has rejected reformist attempts to stretch the law much beyond its letter and has even magnified the differences between Islamic and universal law.

## Islamic Principles of Inequality

At the heart of these differences reside Islamic law's principled affirmations of inequality, primarily between Muslims and non-Muslims, secondarily between men and women. This has made fundamentalists into the most unyielding critics of the Universal Declaration of Human Rights, which guarantees the freedom to choose one's religion and one's spouse. Both freedoms indisputably contradict Islamic law, which defines conversion out of Islam as a capital offense, and forbids marriage between a Muslim woman and a non-Muslim man. (In 1981, the leading fundamentalists met in Paris and put out an Islamic Universal Declaration of Human Rights, which omitted all freedoms that contradicted the *shari'a*.)

The *shari'a*, as a perfect law, cannot be abrogated or altered, and certainly not by the shifting moods of an electorate. Accordingly, every major fundamentalist thinker has repudiated popular sovereignty as a rebellion against God, the sole legislator. In the changed circumstances of the 1990s, some activists do allow that an election can serve a useful one-time purpose, as a collective referendum of allegiance to Islam, and as an act of submission to a regime of divine justice. But once such a regime gains power, its true measure is not how effectively it implements the will of the people but how efficiently it applies Islamic law.

The ideal of Islamic government most often evoked by the fundamentalists harks back to the notion of a just commander, ruling in consultation with experts in the law. There is a revulsion against the combat of parties and personalities in democratic politics, well expressed by the Sudan's Turabi, fundamentalism's best-known spokesman in the West. In a tract on the Islamic state, Turabi explains that such a state, once established, really has no need of party politics or political campaigns. While Islamic law does not expressly oppose a multiparty system,

> this is a form of factionalism that can be very oppressive of individual freedom and divisive of the community, and it is, therefore, antithetical to a Muslim's ultimate responsibility to God.

As for elections:

> In Islam, no one is entitled to conduct a campaign for themselves directly or indirectly in the manner of Western electoral campaigns. The presentation of candidates would be entrusted to a neutral institution that would explain to the people the options offered in policies and personalities.

Through this elaborate hedging, Turabi arrives at a tacit legitimation of one-party rule, which is the actual form of government he now justifies and supports in the Sudan.

Of the vast complex of democratic values and institutions offered by the West, the fundamentalists have thus seized upon only one, the free plebiscite, and even that is to be discarded after successful one-time use. They remain ambivalent, if not hostile, to party politics, and they spend much of their intellectual energy arguing that the reckless expansion of freedom can only harm the collective security of Islam. When asked which existing regime most closely approximates an ideal Islamic order, fundamentalists most often cite the governments of the Sudan or Iran—the first a military regime, the second a hierocracy ruled by an increasingly autocratic cleric, and both first-order violators of human rights.

## Uniformity vs. Diversity

The second argument holds that Islamic fundamentalism drives many movements and represents a wide spectrum of views, not all of them extreme. Because of its diversity, the past or present performance of fundamentalism in one setting says nothing about its future performance in another. And this diversity also rules out domino-like progress: the world does not face an Islamintern [comparable to the Soviet Comintern of the 1920s], but a variety of local movements.

The concept of a diverse fundamentalism has wound its way to Washington, where it achieved full flower in a June 1992 speech by Edward Djerejian, Assistant Secretary of State for Near Eastern and South Asian Affairs:

> In countries throughout the Middle East and North Africa, we thus see groups or movements seeking to reform their societies in keeping with Islamic ideals. There is considerable diversity in how these ideals are expressed. We detect no monolithic or coordinated international effort behind these movements. What we do see are believers living in different countries placing renewed emphasis on Islamic principles, and governments accommodating Islamist political activity to varying degrees and in different ways.

But this claim for the diversity of fundamentalist movements—again labeled expectantly as movements of reform—is most convincingly countered by the fundamentalists themselves, with their uncanny knack for refuting every Western argument made on their behalf. Turabi put it best, in an interview granted just after the FIS success in the first round of the Algerian parliamentary election. The awakening of Islam, he said, has produced a movement notable for its *uniformity*. If there appear to be differences, that is because "God in His wisdom is varying and distributing the phenomenon to let people know that it is coming everywhere at all times."

## The International Islamic Movement

The leading fundamentalists insist that their movement is pan-Islamic as a matter of principle. The borders that separate their countries, drawn up by European imperial fiat, do not bind them morally or limit them politically. And in practice, fundamentalist movements have an irresistible tendency to think and act across borders. Over the past decade, the international traffic among Islamic fundamentalists has grown intense. Fundamentalist leaders jet from conference to conference to open channels that will assure the rapid transmission of ideas and mutual aid. They learn from one another, imitate one another, and assist one another.

The greatest success of their joint efforts has been the aid they collectively mobilized for the Afghan *mujahideen* during the 1980s—aid that included money, materiel, and thousands of volunteers who fought in the Islamic *jihad* against the Soviet occupation. No less striking has been the success of the Islamic

Republic of Iran in implanting the indomitable Hezbollah, a fundamentalist movement faithful to Iran's revolution, on Lebanese soil, where it has waged a largely successful *jihad* against American, French, and Israeli forces.

Thanks to the jet, the cassette, and the fax, pan-Islam is no longer a bogey but a growing reality. Turabi, for example, categorizes Islamic fundamentalism as a "pan-national movement," and the Sudan's policy reflects it. The Sudan has run Algerian voting data through its computers for the FIS, it has provided diplomatic passports for foreign fundamentalists, and it has brought the foremost fundamentalists to Khartoum to create an Islamic Arab Popular Conference, of which Turabi is secretary. Iran is still more active, not only continuing to finance Hezbollah in Lebanon, but also including a line item in its budget for support of the Palestinian *intifada*—monies which have gone largely to fundamentalists who battle the peace process. Visitors to Khartoum and Teheran, and even to Amman, are astonished at the odd mix of foreign fundamentalists who can be spotted in hotel lobbies and government ministries.

There is, in short, much ado about something, part of which is visible aboveboard in publicized visits and conferences, part of which is arranged in the conspiratorial fashion mastered by the fundamentalists during their long years underground. And so the apologists, preoccupied with imaginary changes in the substance of the fundamentalist message, overlook perhaps the most important transformation of all: the emergence of a global village of Islamic fundamentalism.

## Fundamentalism vs. the West

According to the final argument, fundamentalism, whatever the dangers it might pose to freedoms or borders, still poses no real threat to Western interests or to the stability of a new world order. The fundamentalists' goals cannot be achieved in defiance of the West. States which have sold oil to the West will still sell it; states which have needed Western aid will still need it. Once in power, promises another Western apologist, fundamentalists will

> generally operate on the basis of national interests and demonstrate a flexibility that reflects acceptance of the realities of a globally interdependent world.

But where their apologists see an interdependent world, the fundamentalists themselves see a starkly divided world. During the Gulf crisis, they championed the view that any partnership between believers and nonbelievers constituted a violation of divine order. Therefore, while Saddam may have done wrong when he invaded Kuwait, King Fahd, who depended on "American 'Crusaders' to defend Saudi Arabia, most certainly sinned.

Ma'mun al-Hudaybi, official spokesman of the Egyptian Muslim Brotherhood, announced that "Islamic law does not permit any enlisting of assistance from polytheists [*mushrikun*]." According to Rashid al-Ghannushi, the exiled leader of the Tunisian fundamentalist movement, Saudi Arabia had committed a colossal crime. Of Saddam, no friend of Islam before the crisis, he said:

> We are not worshiping personalities, but anyone who confronts the enemies of Islam is my friend and anyone who puts himself in the service of the enemies of Islam is my enemy.

For fundamentalists, the identity of the enemy has remained constant since Islam first confronted unbelief. In *their* vision of interdependence, Islam will indeed sell its oil, provided that it is allowed to invest the proceeds in instruments of war which will enable Muslims to deter any form of Western intervention. This proliferation will eventually create a world order based not on American hegemony but on a restored balance of power—and terror. As Hezbollah's mentor, Fadlallah, says in a transparent reference to military might and the eventual acquisition of nuclear weapons:

> We may not have the actual power the U.S. has, but we had the power previously and we have now the foundations to develop that power in the future. . . .

## The Real Values of Fundamentalists

Democracy, diversity, accommodation—the fundamentalists have repudiated them all. In appealing to the masses who fill their mosques, they promise, instead, to institute a regime of Islamic law, make common cause with like-minded "brethren" everywhere, and struggle against the hegemony of the West and the existence of Israel. Fundamentalists have held to these principles through long periods of oppression, and will not abandon them now, at the moment of their greatest popular resonance.

These principles bear no resemblance to the ideals of Europe's democracy movements; if anything, they evoke more readily the atavism of Europe's burgeoning nationalist Right. The refusal to see Islamic fundamentalism in this context, or to take seriously the discourse of the Islamists, is evidence of the persistent power of the West to create a wholly imaginary Islam. In this instance, the myth of fundamentalism as a movement of democratic reform assures the West that no society on earth has the moral resources to challenge the supremacy of Western values: even Islam's fundamentalists, cursing the ways of foreigners, will end up embracing them. This is a reassuring gospel, but it necessarily ignores Islam as it is actually believed and practiced by the fundamentalists, and this denial has sowed the seeds of future disillusionment.

*"Islam has no specific and rigid opinion regarding the most desirable forms of government or on the question of separation of 'mosque' and state."*

# The Islamic World Needs Secularism

Asád AbuKhalil

Secular government—the separation of church and state—is a hallmark of Western liberal democracy. Some Western scholars believe there is no distinction between "mosque" and state under Islam and that Islam is therefore incompatible with democracy, according to Asád AbuKhalil. In the following viewpoint, AbuKhalil argues that only Islamic fundamentalists prescribe a religious state; most of the people of the Islamic Arab world are striving toward secular, Western-style democracy with elected representatives, accountability of the elected, and guarantees of human rights. AbuKhalil is an adjunct professor of Arab Politics at Georgetown University and a scholar-in-residence at the Middle East Institute in Washington, D.C.

As you read, consider the following questions:

1. According to AbuKhalil, what does the Quran deal with and how does it refer to politics?
2. What are the underlying causes behind the emergence of political Islam, according to AbuKhalil?
3. According to the author, how is democracy defined by today's Arab intellectuals?

Asád Abukhalil, "A Viable Partnership: Islam, Democracy, and the Arab World," *Harvard International Review*, vol. 15, no. 2 (Winter 1992/93). Reprinted with permission.

Westerners often maintain that the Arab world has not been affected by popular expressions for democratic change. The absence of democracy in the Arab world and the prevalence of oppressive regimes in the region has led people to attribute the political situation to religious and cultural factors. There are several noted Middle East experts in the US who insist that democracy does not exist in the Arab/Islamic context because Arab/Islamic civilization has been inclined toward authoritarian rule. These experts also argue that Islam and democracy are fundamentally incompatible. There are some who insist that the very nature of what they call "the Arab/Islamic" mind is not conducive to representative governments. This latter view, however, is too blatantly prejudicial to deserve a response.

Apologists for Arab regimes sometimes claim that this Arab government or that Arab government is indeed democratic. In reality, there is no Arab government today that can be said to be democratic. Absolutist rule seems to be prevalent in the Arab region, although there are some governments that are more absolutist and oppressive than others. The absence of democratic governments, however, should not be construed as a sign that the Arab people are themselves hostile to the concept of democracy.

## Aspiring to Democracy

Democracy, as an aspiration and not as a political actuality, is now sweeping the entire region. Since the early 1980s, Arab men and women have clearly voiced their deep desire for democratic changes in their respective countries. Developments dealing with democratic aspirations in the Arab world do not receive the wide sympathetic coverage that democratization movements in other parts of the world do. It is unlikely that the Western press will pay more attention to reform in the Arab world because democratization in that area will likely produce forces and movements that, for political and not religious or cultural reasons, express antipathy to the US and its interests. Unlike in East-Central Europe, democratization in the Arab world is not synonymous with pro-Americanism. The Arab people are generally very critical of US military and political involvement in the region, which they blame for the longevity of some of the most unpopular Arab regimes—such as the Persian Gulf regimes.

Over the past several years, political changes have taken place in several Arab countries that are now leading to democratization of one form or another. Democratization of the political system occurred in Jordan, Algeria (until the process was aborted by a military *coup d'etat* in January 1992), Yemen and Lebanon (despite the 1992 election irregularities and Syrian and Israeli heavy-handedness in that country). It should be emphasized

140

that these governments democratized their systems not for their love of democracy *per se* but rather as a direct result of democratic movements consisting of men and women who made their desire for fundamental political changes very clear. In both Algeria and Jordan, security services used deadly force against pro-democracy demonstrators, but the news was not widely publicized in the West because of a still pervasive lingering hostility to Muslims and Arabs. Moreover, it is often mistakenly assumed that Muslims only demonstrate to show opposition against the US and/or Israel.

It should be noted that Arab citizens have opposed their governments, even in Iraq, despite the ruthless oppressiveness of some Arab regimes. In February 1982, for example, the Syrian government crushed a popular rebellion in the city of Hamah, killing more than 15,000 people in the process. Similarly, the Iraqi government has killed many civilians in its ongoing campaign against dissent. It is rather bizarre that the Arab people and Islamic religion are still held responsible for the tyrannical governments under which they are forced to live.

## Islam and Democracy

Discussion of politics in the Arab context often focuses on the question of Islamic resistance to democracy. The characterization of Islam as "a way of life" has negatively influenced most Western analysis of Islam and politics. The idea that in Islam there is no separation between "church" and state leads people to assume that secularism is inapplicable in all regions where Muslims predominate. But any religion—more precisely, any of the three major monotheistic religions—if applied fully in the 20th century, is incompatible with democracy and secularism. Similarly, a religion is a way of life if one attempts to apply religious laws—and only religious laws—to all facets of social life. To be sure, Islam has been used by governments for centuries for political purposes, and it has consequently affected various aspects of Muslim life. But the questions of Islam and democracy as well as of Islam and secularism are often discussed in ways that imply a peculiar anti-democratic streak in Islam.

In reality, the teachings of the three major monotheistic religions would appear anachronistic if one attempted to live today only according to religious laws. Islam, contrary to claims made by its apologists and critics, has no opinion on the central questions of secularism and democracy. It is only the strict religious orthodoxy that has been trying to force upon believers the myth of "Islamic answers to all of today's problems." The Qur'an, which is the only book accepted by Muslims as the word of God, has very little to say about matters of government. Most of the Qur'anic verses—over two thirds according to one esti-

141

mate—deal with matters of ethics and spirituality, while later Qur'anic revelations deal with everyday life. The Qur'an lacks references to politics, with the exception of some very general and vague references to *shura* (consultation) and obedience to "those in charge." These references are hardly the Islamic recipe for a better government that Muslim fundamentalists claim they are. In other words, Islam has no specific and rigid opinion regarding the most desirable forms of government or on the question of separation of "mosque" (there was no religious hierarchy in early Islam) and state. It was post-Muhammad rulers and jurists who wished to re-interpret and in some cases mis-interpret Islamic texts for the purely political purpose of legitimizing governments-in-power. The marriage between the political elites and the clerical establishments in past and present day Arab politics explains the obscurantism and dogmatic adherence to a one-dimensional interpretation of Islamic sources.

## Political Islam

The rise of Islamic fundamentalism in the Arab and Muslim worlds should not be attributed to religious fervor. The underlying causes behind the emergence of "political Islam" are not theological or religious, but rather socioeconomic and political in nature. Many members of fundamentalist organizations were formerly members of leftist and sometimes atheist communist organizations. The demise of the leftist model worldwide and the resentment aimed against Arab governments left the Muslim and Arab masses with one, largely untried, practically novel model. The attractiveness of Islam rests on its ability to appeal with its language and simplicity to millions of people and on its effectiveness as a political vehicle of change. As such Islam ceases to be a body of theological teachings and becomes an ideology of provocation that is intended to embarrass and delegitimize dominant Arab governments.

Moreover, traditional Western hostility to Islam and the antipathy among most Arab people to the political, military and economic interests of the US makes the Islamic weapon all the more appealing. The fixation among Western governments with "an Islamic threat" and the negative reaction to the fall of the Shah of Iran intensified Muslim anger against what is perceived to be a Western stigmatization of everything Islamic. Furthermore, many Arabs and Muslims resent the staunch Western support for the government of Saudi Arabia and other Gulf states, as well as Western identification with Israel. The Arab Gulf regimes represent to many Arabs the monopolization of a nation's wealth by a small family elite, the ostentatious squandering of government funds and the hypocritical exploitation of Islamic slogans by corrupt elites who preach one thing and practice another.

The events in Algeria in 1992 are destined to increase the appeal of Muslim fundamentalists in the region. In Algeria, a Muslim movement won through what was considered a relatively fair and honest election process. The military establishment in Algeria chose to cancel the election results and launch a *coup d'etat* that imposed a crackdown against Muslim activists. There was widespread popular Arab criticism of Western indifference to the crackdown in Algeria. Arabs now believe that the US and other Western governments tolerate oppression and the abolishment of election results if the victims are Muslim fundamentalists. Many Arabs charge that the US is not consistent in its verbal—albeit timid—commitment to the spread of democratic ideals in the region. There is a popular perception in the Arab world today that the US only cares about human rights violations in countries that are not politically friendly with the US. Western toleration of the Algerian coup will only reinforce Muslim/Arab suspicions about fundamental Western hostility to Islamic governments. Fundamentalists are already using the Algerian example to demonstrate the limitations of "working within the system."

## Islam and Political Parties

A contradiction lies at the heart of the political ideology of all Islamist movements. They assert that there is only one source of law (the Quran), and that sovereignty belongs to God. But once in power, sovereignty has to be exercised, one way or another. From the moment that it constituted itself as a political party, the Islamist movement [in Algeria] put itself forward as a candidate for the exercise of sovereignty. By winning the legislative elections of December 26, 1991, the Islamic Salvation Front (FIS) put itself in the position where it had to form a government and rely on the apparatus of state to direct the country.

Lahouari Addi, *Middle East Report*, March/April 1992.

But a fundamentalist seizure of power in one or more Arab countries cannot be postponed indefinitely. Much of the popularity of Muslim fundamentalism stems from its anti-establishment position. Islamic fundamentalists will not be discredited until they seize power. Fundamentalist movements have been operating on the basis of catchy but hollow slogans. The slogan "Islam is the solution," which was basically the program of the fundamentalists in Algeria, will eventually lose its appeal when people begin looking for real solutions to their acute social and economic problems. The fundamentalists are mistakenly assuming that their Islamic character will shield them from criticism once they hold the reins of power. When this writer asked Sheikh Muhammad Husayn Fadlallah (the "spiritual guide" of the Party of God in Lebanon, better known by its Arabic name, Hizballah) about his program for the impoverished Shi'ites of South Lebanon, he answered, "We do not need programs. We have the Qur'an." While clerical leaders can afford to claim to rely solely on the Qur'an in their lives, poor peasants and workers can not use the Qur'an to pay their bills and feed the children. The crisis of legitimacy for the fundamentalists will be created by their attitude toward dissent, their dogmatic view of social and economic problems and by their exclusive composition that alienates many of the qualified (non-clerical) experts and technocrats.

## Arab Discourse on Democracy

The subject of democracy and openness has been the focus of Arab intellectual debates since before the demise of communist rule. The Gulf War and the weakness of the Arab regional system exposed the need for political reforms and regional integration. The opportunistic exploitation of Islam by Saddam Hussein and the Saudi royal family and the defeat of tyrannical regimes in Eastern Europe only increased the demands for democratization and regional integration. While some Western analysts still insist that Arab nationalism is dead, the popular Arab reaction to the Gulf War reflected a unified mass reaction among the Arab masses of the *Mashriiq* (the East) and the *Maghrib* (the North African region) which has been rare in contemporary Arab history. The failure of Saddam Hussein's brutal invasion of Kuwait (which was presented by Hussein as "unity" with Kuwait and a rectification of colonial territorial inventions) and the collapse of the Soviet Union made it clear that unity-through-coercion will not last. Most Arabs now understand that unity without democracy will be short-lived.

The ideological debate in the Arab world today, particularly in the scholarly writings published by the Center of Arab Unity Studies in Beirut and by publishers of Arabic materials in London, focuses on the way in which Islam, Arab nationalism and democracy can be linked together harmoniously. Strict Islamic fundamentalists refuse to recognize forces of national loyalty because they see in Islam the only acceptable bond of collective allegiance. Furthermore, some Islamic fundamentalists see in Arab nationalism a secular danger to their aim of imposing Islamic religious laws on all citizens. Even some secular Arab nationalists are now trying to appease the fundamentalists by resorting to Qur'anic language and by avoiding a confronta-

tion with the sectarian forces in the Arab world. Democratic en-
thusiasts have tried to reconcile Islam and democracy by simply
maintaining that democracy is consistent with Islam because
the Qur'an emphasizes the necessity of *shura* among Muslims.
And the fundamentalists themselves are recognizing—at least
verbally—the Arab population's thirst for democracy by pledg-
ing their commitment to the electoral process. Democracy is
now central as a theme in Arab novels, poetry, movies and
plays. The Iraqi press is now carrying articles about democracy,
not so much because the government is willing to democratize,
but because the regime is trying hard to win legitimacy. All
Arab governments are now making promises of democratization
an integral part of their political rhetoric.

Democracy in the Arab world is now understood by Arab intellectuals and people to mean real, effective institutions. No
longer will the Arabs be misled by rubber-stamp parliaments or
advisory councils such as the newly established one in Saudi
Arabia. Arabs are now insisting on institutional democracy. In
July 1991, a group of more than four hundred *Ulama* [religious
scholars], jurists and university professors emphasized to the
King of Saudi Arabia in a confidential memorandum that the
proposed advisory council (which the King had been promising
for several years) "should not be a mere rubber-stamp formality,
as is the case in some countries." Democracy in the past was
stigmatized in the minds of some Arabs due to their Western
colonial heritage. Arabs after World War II were too proud to accept being seen as imitators of Western models and institutions.
Arabs today are clearer and more specific about their political
expectations. In today's Arab writings on the subject, it is clear
that democratization means Western-style institutions, parliamentary representation, a one-person-one-vote electoral system,
freedom of expression for political organizations, accountability
of the elected, an independent judiciary and individual rights.
The hollow slogans of *shura* arrangements often used in Arab
Gulf regimes will not deceive or satisfy the Arab people.

## Freedom Through a Secular Legal Code

While there is evidence of the spread of ideas of democratization in the Arab world, there are still some strong forces at play
against the democratic trend. Not only are Arab governments
still violently resisting the relinquishment of power which they
had all attained illegally and/or violently, but there are various
groups and minorities still being oppressed in various parts of
the Arab world: women and homosexuals everywhere in the region; Kurds in Syria, Iraq and Lebanon; Blacks in Mauritania
and Sudan; Berbers in North Africa; Palestinians in the Gulf,
Lebanon, and in the Occupied Territories; Christians, particu-

145

larly Copts, in Egypt, and all Jews still living in Arab lands; and in general all the citizens of the oppressive Arab regimes. The Arab world will not be free merely with the elimination of the oppressive ruling governments. It will be free only when all Arab citizens, regardless of gender, religion, sexual orientation, racial background, ethnic affiliation, tribal lineage and political identification are equal before the law. This will not be achieved until the juridical hegemony of Muslim laws (*shari'ah*) is lifted and secular status laws are finally codified.

*"Secularism has yet to be accepted by most Muslims, while the Islamic revival has yet to live up to its heady promises."*

# The Islamic World Does Not Need Secularism

Greg Noakes

Many scholars argue that religion (and Islam in particular) impedes social and economic development. They advocate secular solutions for the problems faced by developing societies such as those in the Islamic world. In the following viewpoint, Greg Noakes argues that attempts to impose secularization to promote development in the Islamic world have failed to take root; yet Islamic revivalism has failed to outline a plan for dealing with practical matters. Contemporary Islamic thinkers, according to Noakes, have embraced the concept of *ijtihad* (individual intellectual effort) as a way of identifying Islamic, rather than secular, solutions to modern social, economic, and political problems. Noakes is the news editor of the *Washington Report on Middle East Affairs*, a nonpartisan monthly magazine.

As you read, consider the following questions:

1. What, according to Noakes, do secularists say is necessary for democratic development in the Islamic world?
2. According to Noakes, what are some of the arguments of Muslims concerning the compatibility of democracy and Islam?

Greg Noakes, "Secularism and the Islamist Challenge," *Washington Report on Middle East Affairs*, September/October 1993.

Throughout the 20th century, Muslim societies have been torn between the impulse of secularism and the attraction of Islamic renewal. Both systems are seen by their proponents as the key to solving the Muslim world's social, political and economic problems. Secularism has yet to be accepted by most Muslims, however, while the Islamic revival has yet to live up to its heady promises.

Contemporary Islamic thinkers have seized upon the concept of *ijtihad*, or individual intellectual effort, in order to reinterpret their religious and cultural traditions, meet the challenges of modern life with solutions that draw upon Islam for their source, and fulfill the aspirations of their coreligionists.

## Islam and Secularism

"Islamic secularism" is a concept which plays well both in university lecture halls and the give and take of a council of ministers charged with administering a modern nation. In such environments, many scholars and analysts see Islam as a brake on society, impeding the economic and social development of Muslim states.

In the West, the notion that religion should guide society was weakened during the Renaissance, dealt a crushing blow in the Age of Enlightenment and drew its last gasp as the French Revolution put a dramatic end to the "divine right of kings." The course of progress in Western historiography mirrors the story of secularization; man assumes his role as the measure of all things and religion becomes a matter of private devotion.

For a number of modern thinkers, both Muslim and non-Muslim, Islamic society, too, is badly in need of a reformation, or better yet a renaissance, to break religious shackles that keep the Muslim world backward and ignorant. If Muslims are to develop, the secularists argue, Islam must be relegated to the private sphere and rational humanism allowed to guide society.

So much for the lecture hall. In practice, secularization has yet to succeed to any significant degree in most of the Muslim world, though not for lack of effort. Non-Muslims attempted to impose secularism in the Soviet Union and Communist China as a policy directive of the highest order. China's Muslims remain oppressed, but the rapid resurgence of Islam as a faith, political platform, and source of sociocultural identity in Central Asia after seven decades of Marxist-Leninist rule indicates the failure of Communism to stamp out the "opiate of the people."

The 1950s and '60s were the heyday of modernization theory in the West, and particularly in the United States. Where Moscow and Beijing sought to tear Muslims from their faith, Washington expected they would wean themselves voluntarily from "reactionary" Islam.

In the post-World War II era, modernization theorists talked about the educational power of mass media, surveyed individual attitudes toward social change and "modernization" and generally attempted to remake the Muslim world in the West's image.

## Naive "Modernization"

Daniel Lerner, a leading architect of modernization theory, rather patronizingly wrote that the West would transform the Arab world through "a rationalist and positivist spirit against which Islam is absolutely defenseless." Some thirty five years later, modernization theory is a curious relic of a bygone age of naiveté, shattered by realities it had failed to take into account.

Some Muslim rulers adopted the secularist model as well, following either the authoritarian or liberal path to "modernity." Mustafa Kemal Ataturk's scorched-earth Westernization of Turkey in the 1920s is an example of the first approach. Turks were forced to use a European alphabet and wear European clothes, shrines and religious brotherhoods were closed and the number of mosques limited by government decree. Resistance to such enforced secularization was met with repression, and occasionally with death.

---

## Islam vs. Liberalism

The Islamic mainstream has come to accept crucial elements of political democracy: pluralism (within the framework of Islam), political participation, government accountability, the rule of law and the protection of human rights. But it has not adopted liberalism, if that includes religious indifference. Change is more noticeable in the domain of political organization than of social and religious values. Having said this, it cannot be emphasized strongly enough that what we are observing [in the Islamic movement] is thought in progress, responding to a considerable extent to societal conditions and government policies. It is to a large extent not abstract but political, even activist, mobilizing thought, shaped and influenced by a political environment that in virtually all cases is neither liberal nor genuinely pluralistic, let alone democratic.

Gudrun Krämer, *Middle East Report*, July/August 1993.

---

In Tunisia, Habib Bourguiba followed a kinder, gentler program. While Mustafa Kemal proclaimed Turkey a secular republic, Islam remained the state religion in Tunisia. Bourguiba built mosques rather than closed them. Yet he also dissolved the Zitouna University, a seat of Islamic learning since the Middle Ages; prohibited women from wearing the *hijab* ("veil"); and in

1961 called on Tunisians not to observe the Ramadan fast—one of the five pillars of Islam—in order to wage "the struggle against underdevelopment."

The policies of Ataturk and Bourguiba transformed their nations. Eventually, however, they also produced two of the more active and organized Islamist movements of the past twenty years. Again the seeds of secularism fell on barren ground.

## The Strength of Islam

The strength of attachment and depth of feeling that most Muslims associate with their faith dispelled the secularist dream, at least for the foreseeable future. The victory of the Islamic Salvation Front (FIS) in the first round of Algeria's aborted parliamentary elections [in December 1991] came as a surprise only to those observers whose social circles were limited to the garden of the Hotel Aurassi in Algiers. Talking to ordinary Algerians, one sensed strong support for the FIS, not because of specific policy proposals but "because we are Muslims and we must have Islam" to solve the country's problems.

Muslims are fond of saying that Islam is applicable in all places in all times. The problem is: Which Islam? Is it the anachronistic legalism of a scholarly tradition which declared the "door of individual interpretation" closed a millennium ago, the ethereal Islam of the mystics, or perhaps Islamic modernism, "fundamentalism," liberalism, conservatism or traditionalism?

Proclaiming, as many contemporary Islamist groups do, that "Islam is the solution!" is really no solution at all. Slogans don't repay foreign debts, build housing and infrastructure, feed the hungry, spark investment, regulate societies or solve foreign policy disputes. The problem of Muslim decline, seized upon by the secularists with such alacrity, is a real dilemma that must be addressed. The answers, unfortunately, are not ready-made.

How can Muslims, confronted by modern challenges yet clearly opposed to the secular solutions of the West, respond? The answer most contemporary Muslim thinkers propose is that of *ijtihad*, the "individual intellectual effort" opposed by conservative sheikhs for so long.

## *Ijtihad* as Islamic Democracy

*Ijtihad* comes from the same Arabic root as *jihad*, and both have the sense of "effort" or "struggle." *Ijtihad* is an intellectual struggle to use reason and knowledge to arrive at an appropriate solution to a given situation or question. Originally the term applied to Islamic law, but contemporary Islamists have extended it to all forms of religious discourse and thought: politics, economics, social affairs and, of course, law and theology.

*Ijtihad*, for these Islamists, is a method to preserve Islamic principles while still meeting contemporary challenges and adapting Islamic teachings to new situations. In some ways it is a purifying process of reducing Islam to its essence. Some features of modern Muslim society, whether local cultural practices or imported ideological models, can be rejected as un-Islamic. Other elements are value-neutral, and may be retained or rejected according to the needs and preferences of society. There are also elements of Muslim society that are judged to be inherent in an Islamic order, and must be maintained or revivified so that society fosters the expression of Islamic principles and practice.

Again, the theoretical construct works flawlessly in the faculty lounge or the pages of a manifesto. In practice, however, the process is a daunting one, and the advocates of *ijtihad* are divided over both ideological and utilitarian issues. There is heated debate about what yardsticks should be used to measure Islamic society, how much change can be accommodated, and the methodology through which that change can be implemented.

Even the choice of issues to be debated is open to discussion. Is architecture value-neutral, for instance? If not, what constitutes "Islamic architecture"?

Across the Middle East, men don long white *thobes* and women cover their hair as outward expressions of their commitment to Islam. Yet a leading North African Islamist proclaims that if the Prophet Muhammad were living today he would wear a wool business suit and fly the Concorde. So is traditional clothing, banned by Ataturk and prescribed by some Islamists, an essential element of Muslim society or is it a matter of no particular religious, political or social concern?

### Practical Concerns

The questions being debated among Islamists are as complicated as human society itself. Thinkers and scholars see their theories collapse in the face of complex social realities. An examination of five areas of practical concern for proponents of *ijtihad* also reveals some of the larger issues with which they are grappling.

One of the fiercest debates among Islamists concerns the compatibility of democracy and Islam. Some argue that democracy is unbelief and denies the sovereignty of God, while others say that the people should have a say in government through the Islamic concept of *shura*, or consultation, and develop models of how this *shura* should work and to whom it should apply.

Still other Islamists believe that Western democracy is perfectly compatible with an Islamic state, and in fact is an ideal form of government. The issue of democracy's acceptability, with or without modifications in form or terminology, raises a question about the integration of non-Islamic elements into an Islamic system. If democracy is acceptable or, according to some, essential to the maintenance of an Islamic order, what other theories and systems developed outside of the Islamic system should be adopted?

Attitudes toward women are another issue. Most Islamist thinkers argue that women must participate fully in society, whether in education, professional careers or political activity. The denial of a woman's rights as guaranteed by the Qur'an and the Prophet is unconscionable, and these rights must be reinstated before an Islamic society is realized.

Other thinkers and many rank-and-file Islamists, however, have adopted the attitude that a woman's place is in the home, that public life should be the preserve of men and that women should be subservient. Some base these views on interpretations of Islamic texts, but most refer to traditional sex roles and argue that they should be maintained to protect society.

---

## Democratization That Is Neither Western Nor Secular

The most significant debates taking place in the [Islamic Arab] region today are not about secularization versus promotion of Islamic forms of government. Rather, they are about the democratization of existing governments in a manner consistent with Islamic law, a process which, though informed by Western democratic experiences, is viewed as neither Western nor secular.

Azizah Y. al-Hibri, *Case Western Reserve Journal of International Law*, no. 1, 1992.

---

In matters of gender, there is a clear differentiation between the ideas and rhetoric of the intellectuals, which stress that women must play an active role in national life, and the restrictive attitudes of many ordinary Muslims. This dichotomy within the Islamist movement begs the question of whether the intellectual ideal can be implemented in the face of traditionalist values. *Ijtihad* is a tool of change, but there are clearly limits as to how much change is realistically possible.

Another issue which Islamists are tackling is the extent to which Islam is applicable in certain fields, and the possibility that certain spheres of activity may be beyond "Islamization." Science and technology are the best examples of this. Physics experiments produce the same results whether performed by a Muslim or a non-Muslim scientist. The process for operating a fax machine, an Abrams tank or a television set is the same in the Muslim world as anywhere else, and Islamists must decide whether an "Islamic science" really exists or is just a hollow vanity.

Discussion of economic matters has led Islamists to another dilemma. Islam forbids the payment or acceptance of usury, which most Islamic scholars agree applies to ordinary banking interest. Islamists, so far, have wrestled in vain with the place of an interest-free economic system within an increasingly interdependent global economy based on interest.

At this stage of economic development it is clearly impossible for the Muslim world to break away from the larger worldwide system, but how can the participation of Muslim states, institutions and individuals in that system be squared with Islamic economic principles? There are some external limits to the Islamist project that must be recognized and either acknowledged or overcome by Islamist intellectuals.

## Internal Constraints

Finally, there are internal constraints in Middle Eastern society that complicate the practical application of the Islamist agenda. The most obvious is the presence of non-Muslim minorities in many Muslim nations. Most Islamists agree that non-Muslims should not be subject to Islamic law, but are less clear about the relationship between a central Muslim administration and non-Muslim communities.

Some want to resurrect the *dhimmi* system, where non-Muslims were protected minorities subject to an additional tax but free of requirements like military service. Others see non-Muslims as full partners in an Islamic system where only areas like family life and social customs would be excluded from Islamic rules. There is at best an ambivalence about the issue, but it is a crucial concern in the application of any kind of Islamic system. How the issue is eventually resolved will have an important, probably decisive, influence on the relations between Islamic civilization and non-Muslim societies, virtually all of which have their own Muslim minorities.

The complicated issues of the admissibility of outside concepts, ideological cohesion, scope of activity, and external and internal constraints seem insurmountable to many observers. Islamists, though, argue that any social system or political ideology is subject to the same problems and that Islam is better equipped than most to meet these challenges. By using *ijtihad* to answer the twin questions of what is Islam and how should it be applied, Islamists believe that they can construct an Islamic system based on eternal principles yet fully capable of meeting the social, political, cultural, and economic needs of the contemporary Muslim world.

# Periodical Bibliography

The following articles have been selected to supplement the diverse views presented in this chapter.

Lisa Anderson — "Liberalism, Islam, and the Arab State," *Dissent*, Fall 1994.

Patrick Clawson — "Liberty's the Thing, Not Democracy," *Middle East Quarterly*, September 1994. Available from 1920 Chestnut St., Suite 600, Philadelphia, PA 19103.

Michael Collins Dunn — "Revivalist Islam and Democracy: Thinking About the Algerian Quandary," *Middle East Policy*, vol. 1, no. 2, 1992. Available from 1730 M St. NW, Suite 512, Washington, DC 20036.

John L. Esposito and James P. Piscatori — "Democratization and Islam," *Middle East Journal*, Summer 1991.

Alexander Flores — "Secularism, Integralism, and Political Islam," *Middle East Report*, July/August 1993.

Youssef M. Ibrahim — "An Islamic Fundamentalist Abroad Talks Freely of Limits on Freedom," *The New York Times*, January 9, 1994.

G.H. Jansen — "Islam and Democracy: Are They Compatible?" *Middle East International*, 29 May 1992. Available from 1700 17th St. NW, #306, Washington, DC 20009.

Gudrun Krämer — "Islamist Notions of Democracy," *Middle East Report*, July/August 1993.

Kishore Mahbubani — "The Dangers of Decadence: What the Rest Can Teach the West," *Foreign Affairs*, September/October 1993.

Judith Miller — "The Challenge of Radical Islam," *Foreign Affairs*, Spring 1993.

Caryle Murphy — "Islam's Uneasy Balance," *The Washington Post National Weekly Edition*, May 25–31, 1992. Available from 1150 15th St. NW, Washington, DC 20071.

Augustus Richard Norton — "Inclusion Can Deflate Islamic Populism," *New Perspectives Quarterly*, Summer 1993.

I. William Zartman — "Democracy and Islam: The Cultural Dialectic," *The Annals of the American Academy of Political and Social Science*, November 1992.

Sami Zubaida — "Islam, the State & Democracy: Contrasting Conceptions of Society in Egypt," *Middle East Report*, November/December 1992.

# Does Political Islam Promote Terrorism?

**Islam**

# Chapter Preface

On July 18, 1994, a car bomb demolished the Argentine-Israeli Mutual Association, a cultural exchange organization in Buenos Aires, killing nearly one hundred people. Weeks later, in August 1994, two car bombs exploded in London, one at the Israeli embassy and another at a Jewish charity shop. An Iranian expatriate by the name of Manoucher Motamer, seeking asylum in Venezuela, alleged that Iran was responsible for all three bombings.

"An accusing finger is pointing directly at Iran as having considerable responsibility for the . . . terrorist bombings," writes columnist Stephen Green about the incidents. He argues that the allegations made by Motamer, as well as evidence uncovered by Argentine and British authorities investigating the incidents, provide overwhelming circumstantial links to Iran. According to Green, "As the investigation proceeds, the evidence of Iranian involvement keeps accumulating."

Defending his country against such charges of terrorism, Kamal Kharrazi, Iran's ambassador to the United Nations, contends, "There is no evidence that Iran has been involved in terrorist activities. In fact, ['terrorist' is] a label, used by America against Iran to humiliate them, to put pressure on them." Kharrazi accuses the United States of creating an imaginary threat from Iran, making the country a scapegoat for the problem of international terrorism. The United States has accused Iran of terrorism because it opposes the religious revolution there, according to Kharrazi, though Iran has been a peaceful nation. He asserts, "Despite the labeling and stereotyping, Muslims are not terrorists."

According to official U.S. policy, expressed by Patrick Theros of the U.S. Department of State, "Iran remains the most dangerous sponsor and the greatest source of concern" for international terrorism. The viewpoints in the following chapter debate whether the Islamic Republic of Iran is involved in terrorism as well as whether Islam is a motivating factor in acts of terrorism.

*"[The culprits in the World Trade Center bombing] were united by a zealous Islamic fundamentalist ideology—a bitter hatred of the West."*

# Political Islam Promotes Terrorism

Steven Emerson

On February 26, 1993, a bomb exploded in the World Trade Center in New York City, killing six people and injuring many others—the most deadly act of terrorism ever carried out within the United States. The subsequent investigation by the Federal Bureau of Investigation led to the arrest of Sheik Omar Abd al-Rahman, a blind Islamic cleric also accused of a number of acts of terrorism by the government of Egypt. In the following viewpoint, Steven Emerson argues that though Iran and Iraq have in the past sponsored acts of international terrorism, a new trend is beginning. Random acts of terrorism are being carried out by loosely organized groups incited by the sermons and teachings of radical Islamic clerics like Abd al-Rahman. Emerson is a free-lance investigative reporter in Washington, D.C., and author of *The Fall of Pan Am 103: Inside the Lockerbie Investigation.*

As you read, consider the following questions:

1. How does Emerson define the Islamic ideology of the accused World Trade Center bombers?
2. What evidence does the author present that Iran sponsors terrorism?
3. If attacks "are not the work of sophisticated or organized terrorist cells," as Emerson states, who commits these attacks?

Steven Emerson, "Islamic Fundamentalism's Terrible Threat to the West," *San Diego Union-Tribune*, June 27, 1993, and "The Accidental Tourist," *The Washington Post*, June 13, 1993. Reprinted with the author's permission.

In January 1993, one of Germany's highest-ranking intelligence officials visited Washington, D.C., where he warned his Federal Bureau of Investigation (FBI) counterparts that radical Islamic fundamentalists had relocated to the West and now constituted a major new terrorist threat to the United States and Europe.

Although the German official did not possess any specific information about any imminent act of terrorism, his message, according to an official present at the talks, was "very clear in warning that the West was now confronting a radically new type of situation which was unambiguously different from the traditional terrorism threat faced by the West."

The official FBI reaction to the German warning? Thank you very much for your concern, but here in the United States we've got things well under control.

The response was remarkably similar to the FBI's reaction to an earlier Israeli warning about the presence in America of militant fundamentalists belonging to such radical fundamentalist groups as Hamas.

## The World Trade Center Bombing Conspiracy

Some two months later, the FBI's self-confidence was rudely shattered by the largest and most deadly act of Middle East–connected terrorism ever carried out on American soil. Six people were killed and more than 1,000 wounded in the bombing of the World Trade Center in New York City on February 26, 1993.

And in June 1993 eight Muslim fundamentalists were arrested in a surprise FBI raid in New York. They were reportedly planning bombings targeting the United Nations headquarters, FBI offices, and the Holland and Lincoln tunnels [in New York City], as well as several assassinations.

Both the June 1993 raid and the World Trade Center case, where the first of six alleged culprits behind the bombing was arrested within days, were remarkable demonstrations of brilliant detective work by American law enforcement agencies.

Yet, for the FBI and the Central Intelligence Agency (CIA), as well as Western intelligence agencies, the most critical question remains the most enduring and profound mystery: Was any foreign agency or government behind the conspiracies?

Was the World Trade Center bombing "state-sponsored" terrorism, which traditionally has been responsible for more than 80 percent of international terrorism? Or, was it conceived of and carried out purely by individuals acting on their own, united only by their militant Islamic rejection of the West and hatred of Israel?

The only definitive details known about the backgrounds of the suspected culprits are that they were united by a zealous Islamic fundamentalist ideology—a bitter hatred of the West and

158

its perceived surrogates such as Western-allied Arab regimes and Israel. Under the ideology of militant Islamic fundamentalists, not only is the West's separation of church and state viewed as blasphemous, the West by its very existence is deemed hostile.

" THE GOVERNMENT UNDOUBTEDLY HAS EVERYTHING WELL IN HAND, DON'T YOU THINK ? "

Reprinted by permission: Tribune Media Services.

"Islamicists," says Khalid Duran, a Muslim professor who is an expert in Islamic fundamentalist affairs, "wholly reject non-Islamic political systems and entities as intrinsically bellicose to Islam. And for followers of Sheik Omar Abd Al-Rahman [who was arrested in June 1993 in connection with the World Trade Center bombing conspiracy], it is the duty of a 'devout' Muslim to confront or attack the West or its agents."

Indeed, most of those arrested in the World Trade Center bombing prayed together at the mosque of Abd Al-Rahman, now considered the spiritual father of the Egyptian fundamentalist movement.

From his base in the United States, Abd Al-Rahman—according to hundreds of audio and video cassettes now in the hands of the FBI—has routinely preached that the United States is a "den of evil and fornication" and regularly called upon Moslems to annihilate their enemies.

In 1992, for example, Abd Al-Rahman said that "Moslems must kill the enemies of Allah, in every way and everywhere in order to liberate themselves from the grandchildren of the pigs and apes who are educated at the table of Zionists, the communists and the imperialists."

Besides praying at Abd Al-Rahman's mosques, at least three of the World Trade Center suspects had been to Afghanistan and Pakistan where they worked alongside thousands of *mujahedeen* (holy warriors) who had been recruited to overthrow the communist regime in Kabul and who have now refocused their *jihad* against Western Arab regimes.

As for evidence suggesting state sponsorship of the World Trade Center bombing, the most tantalizing evidence thus far points to an Iranian link, which according to the 1992 annual State Department survey on terrorism [*Patterns of Global Terrorism: 1992*] was "the most dangerous state sponsor of terrorism in 1992" and was the "principal sponsor of extremist Islamic and Palestinian groups."

According to Robert Oakley, former ambassador to Pakistan during the time of the massive Afghan resistance program, Iran was "certainly a contributor" to Sheik Omar Abd Al-Rahman's group, one of many *mujahedeen* in Afghanistan. Most important, as disclosed by Ralph Blumenthal of the *New York Times*, as much as $100,000 from Iran had been wired to several of the suspects in the months before the bombing.

Iraq, too, remains a possibility insofar as one of the top suspects—and now the only remaining fugitive—came to the United States in the fall of 1992 on an Iraqi passport to help carry out the conspiracy.

## No Specific Evidence of State Terrorism

Yet, according to CIA and FBI officials as well as Egyptian and Israeli intelligence officials, there is no specific evidence or intelligence linking the governments of Iran or Iraq to the bombing.

Nevertheless, a book released in June 1993, *Target America: Terrorism in the U.S. Today* by Yossef Bodansky, head of the Republican Task Force on Terrorism and Unconventional Warfare, asserts that Iranian intelligence officials personally directed the World Trade Center bombing as well as the shooting in January 1993 of two CIA employees outside CIA headquarters by Mir Amir Kansi, a Pakistani who has since fled to Pakistan.

To be sure, Iran's fingerprints can be found in much of the international terrorism taking place today. In September 1992, four Kurdish leaders were brutally machine-gunned to death in a Berlin restaurant. German police soon discovered that the attack was carried out by [Lebanon-based Shiite fundamentalist]

160

Hezbollah members in Germany acting under orders from Iranian intelligence.

Iranian hit squads have routinely carried out dozens of assassinations of political opponents abroad in recent years. The CIA has concluded that the Hezbollah carried out the devastating car bombing of the Israeli embassy in Buenos Aires [Argentina] in March 1992 that killed 29 people.

Yet, a radical shift is now occurring in the intelligence world's view of Iran and Islamic terrorism. Traditionally, international terror groups have been organized very much like the Mafia or even like a large corporation—pyramidally and linearly. That made fighting terrorism relatively easy.

## Loosely Organized Groups

[There is a] new face of violent Islamic radicalism in Israel and Egypt and across the Middle East—a swelling wave of grass-roots movements that are improvised in their military operations, modest in budgetary requirements, diffuse in organization and committed to radical pan-Islamic ideology.

From Tel Aviv to Cairo to New York, a frustrated alliance of pro-Western governments is struggling to unravel the insurgents' intricate structures and their sources of financial and material support—all in the hope of containing the radicals' political and military power. But because the radicals are so loosely organized, the effort has proven immensely difficult.

Steve Coll and David Hoffman, *The Washington Post National Weekly Edition*, August 9-15, 1993.

In the past, Western law enforcement and intelligence agencies (such as Germany's BfV, Israel's Mossad and Great Britain's MI-5) have been able to contain, for the most part, international terrorism by such groups as the Palestine Liberation Organization (PLO) by targeting both senior commanders and low-rung operatives and infiltrating up or down. But the rules—and structure—are changing.

For the intelligence and law enforcement communities, the changes raise stark challenges. Xavier Raufer, France's leading terrorism expert, likens the situation to the changing constellations in the universe. "At any given time, you can take a picture of the worldwide Islamic terrorist infrastructure—but two hours later, the entire constellation will appear radically different."

In Israel and Egypt, many of the brutal attacks carried out by Islamic fundamentalists are not the work of sophisticated or organized terrorist cells but rather local, self-generated attacks that flow from what is known as the *dawa*, Islam's political indoctrination arm.

In Israel, according to Israeli military intelligence tabulations, at least half of the more than 150 brutal stabbings and axe attacks against Israeli citizens carried out by Islamic fundamentalists between 1990 and 1993 were by militants who had no instructions from any group. "Some of the killers simply decided on the spur of the moment to kill Jews as a result of the religious sermons they had heard repeatedly in local mosques and schools," says Yigal Carmon, Israel's recently retired counterterrorism chief.

One of Israel's top military intelligence officials, whose name cannot be used, recently told me: "The enemy is identified by Iranian leaders and other radical fundamentalist leaders. And from their identification, local fundamentalists take it upon themselves to do their best in fighting the enemy. Everyone does whatever they can. They do not operate under a particular commander's control as some in the West would like to believe but rather feel themselves under God's command at all times."

## A Wake-Up Call for the West

For the West, the World Trade Center bombing has served as a wake-up call to the FBI in signaling the change in terrorism. Yet the handwriting has long been on the wall. For example, FBI agents now say it is clear that the 1990 killing of Jewish extremist Meir Kahane in New York was motivated by radical Islamic fundamentalist teachings. In their search of El Sayid Nossair's apartment, the man arrested in the killing, FBI officials confiscated scores of publications printed in both Arabic and English, as well as personal letters, expressing Islamic hatred of the West and sermons by Islamic leaders calling for a revolt against "Zionists and infidels in the United States." Diagrams of U.S. military facilities were found, as were hundreds of rounds of ammunition.

In recent years, hundreds of thousands of new Moslem fundamentalist immigrants have made their way to the United States to take advantage of the political and religious freedoms curtailed in their home countries. Islam is now the fastest-growing religion in the United States. While the overwhelming majority of these new immigrants do not condone violence, it is also a fact that there is a substantial volume of Islamic fundamentalist literature, videocassettes and publications disseminated in these communities that contain virulent attacks on Jews, Zionists, Christians and the entire Western political system.

In various mosques in Dearborn, Michigan, for example, home to a large transplanted Lebanese Shiite community, the Hezbollah's military attacks have been championed in sermons in mosques and in weekly publications as well as local television.

And according to intelligence collected by German, Israeli and

French agencies, senior Hamas, Moslem Brotherhood, Hezbollah, Palestine Islamic Jihad and Algerian Islamic Salvation Front leaders routinely visit—and in a growing number of cases, actually live—in the United States and Europe to organize terror attacks back in their home countries. In 1990, according to the confession of a Hamas terrorist arrested in Israel in 1993, Hamas officials organized a workshop in Chicago where Hamas inductees were taught how to assemble car bombs.

## The Future Looks Bleak

Can the United States and European law enforcement and intelligence agencies get a handle on the problem?

The prospects are not very good, it seems. The Department of Defense Office of Special Operations and Low Intensity Conflict in June 1993 sponsored an international conference on combating terrorism. In attendance were hundreds of intelligence and military representing the Pentagon, CIA, FBI, Secret Service, Federal Aviation Authority, State Department, Army, Air Force, Navy and Marines as well as senior intelligence officials from Canada, Germany, Israel, India, Great Britain and other countries. The primary "briefers" were senior FBI and Defense Intelligence Agency officials who gave classified briefings.

Yet the most surprising revelations did not come from the "secret" sessions but rather the "open" non-classified briefings provided by analysts and academicians. The most common frustration expressed was the very lack of hard information made available.

The absence of hard information is not the only problem. Western law enforcement officials have a genuine problem in grasping or accepting the notion that a religion different from theirs could be abused by Islamic militants and may actually serve as an organizational framework for violence in the name of God.

Said Oliver Revell, FBI special agent in charge of the Dallas division who had previously been in charge of FBI counterterrorism in Washington for many years, "There is no doubt that like other U.S.-based religious extremists who cloak themselves in religious dogma, violent Islamic fundamentalists, particularly because they are unstructured and ad hoc, are exceptionally difficult to track. And yet we have to make sure that immigrant and ethnic communities do not feel they are being targeted or harassed simply because of their religion.

"This means that unless we find absolute evidence of a conspiracy to commit an illegal act, law enforcement will end up reacting to terrorist acts after the event. Unless we get a handle ultimately on how to stop illegal immigration or to exclude people once they are here, the problem is going to get worse."

*"The notion of 'Islamic terrorism' is largely an invention on the part of the Israelis, their supporters in the First World and various Western 'experts.'"*

# Terrorism Is a Response to Western Hypocrisy

Michael Jansen

In June 1993, Sheik Omar Abd al-Rahman, a blind Egyptian cleric residing in the United States, was arrested, along with a number of the members of a New Jersey mosque where he preached, and charged with conspiring to commit acts of terrorism within the United States. In the following viewpoint, Michael Jansen argues that these charges and the extensive media coverage they received were the latest attack by the West in a long war between Christianity and Islam. If Muslims carry out acts of terrorism against the West, argues Jansen, it is because the West has been inconsistent in its stance on democracy, economic development, and human rights. Jansen is a journalist who covers the Middle East for the Gemini News Service.

As you read, consider the following questions:

1. According to Jansen, how does the United States' foreign policy create "the impression of an evil Islamic empire"?
2. Why have Western experts not presented a motive for Muslim involvement in the World Trade Center bombing, according to the author?
3. On what basis does Jansen accuse the West (or the First World) of hypocrisy regarding free elections?

Michael Jansen, "At War with Islam," *Toward Freedom*, April/May 1993. Reprinted by permission of Gemini News Service (News-Scan International Ltd.), London.

The arrest of Muslim Palestinians in connection with the February 26, 1993, bombing of New York City's World Trade Center threatens to transform a Third World power struggle between secularists and Islamists into a global confrontation between North and South.

Even if the accused bombers had been acquitted and Muslims' complicity disproved, the U.S. media and government authorities would have reinforced the link in many minds between Islam and terrorism.

## The "Evil Islamic Empire"

Islam, a 1400-year-old religion with some one billion adherents worldwide, is being demonized in much the same way that communists, socialists and anarchists were crudely caricatured by the fabricators of U.S. political culture. For years, several Muslim countries of the Middle East have been branded terrorist states by Washington. Sudan [has been added] and Pakistan may soon be added to a State Department list that already includes Syria, Libya, Iran and Iraq. And shortly after the Trade Center attack, the United States broke off diplomatic contact with the Palestinian Islamist movement known as Hamas.

Further buttressing the impression of an evil Islamic empire, the United States has sent military forces into four mainly Muslim countries during the past decade. Beginning in 1983, Lebanon, Libya, Iraq and Somalia have all been targeted for intervention. And a few years earlier, military units were assigned a walk-on role in the long-running geopolitical psychodrama that pitted Islamist revolutionaries in Iran against a group of U.S. hostages. [In November 1979, Iranian militants seized the U.S. embassy in Tehran and held 51 people hostage for 444 days.] That traumatic confrontation between militant Islamists and the nation that had propped up the shah's tyranny continues to serve as the paradigm for U.S. attitudes toward an undifferentiated "Muslim world."

In September 1992, a Republican congressional task force issued a report on Islamist terrorism that portrayed Bosnian Muslims as aggressors rather than as victims of Christian Serbian genocide. The report, subsequently repudiated by the task force's chairman in the House of Representatives, also suggested ominously that Muslims may soon account for 25 percent of Europe's total population.

Although the U.S. media seldom analyzes the conflict in this way, it is clear that the fighting in Bosnia results mainly from the Serbs' view of themselves as a Christian bulwark preventing Europe from being overrun by Muslim hordes. In the Serbian psyche, the key historical event shaping the national identity was the Battle of Kosovo Fields in 1389. Turkish Muslim forces defeated a Serbian Christian prince, leading to 500 years of Ottoman rule over Serbia.

Today, Serbian propagandists draw an analogy between the war in Bosnia and the Battle of Kosovo. Bosnia's Muslim leaders are painted as religious fanatics determined to impose Islam on Christian Serbs. Some Muslims in other countries meanwhile conclude that the United States and its European allies, by failing to stop the Serbian onslaught, are in effect siding with the Christians in a war against Islam.

---

### The World Trade Center Bombing and the Press

One need only glance at a headline run by the *Washington Times* a week after the explosion—"Muslim arrested in NYC bombing"—to realize that media reports are not being quite that objective. The press added impetus to the hysteria gripping the public when it began promoting the notion that an international Islamic terrorist network had finally landed its tentacles on U.S. soil. Soon, profiles of Islamists were printed in connection with the attack. The press refused to acknowledge the denial by *al-Jama'a al-Islamiyyah*, or the Islamic Group, of any involvement. The Group, waging a violent economic war against the Egyptian government, declared that "it does not attack innocent people, whatever their religion."

Ahmad AbulJobain, *Radical Islamic Terrorism or Political Islam?*, June 1993.

---

Christians and Muslims are simultaneously engaged in bitter confrontations in a few Third World hotspots. In Sudan's civil war, for example, the Islamist-controlled central government is attempting to stamp out a rebellion by Christian and Animist forces in the country's south. Both sides have committed atrocities in that gruesome conflict. In neighboring Egypt, the Christian Coptic minority is coming under attack from Islamist groups which are also challenging the secular, pro-Western regime of President Hosni Mubarak. Tensions occasionally flare up in Nigeria, too, where segments of the non-Islamic population resent the political power of the country's Muslims.

While some Islamist activists have indeed displayed intolerance and initiated violence, the notion of "Islamic terrorism" is largely an invention on the part of the Israelis, their supporters in the First World and various Western "experts." Their aim is to make Israel's subjugation of the Palestinians appear to be part of a wider struggle against the general menace of militant Islam.

Having suggested an "Islamic connection" to the Trade Center bombing, U.S. authorities and terrorism experts have conspicuously refrained from suggesting a motive for Muslims' alleged involvement. To theorize in that regard might cause the U.S. public to discover that many of the world's Muslims have a long list of grievances which the First World has refused to address.

The most important of these is that the United States staunchly supports monarchical and authoritarian secular governments in Muslim countries that have failed to meet the economic and social needs of their peoples. The intensifying Islamist campaign to replace these governments with rule in accordance with the *Sharia*, or Koran-based law, can be seen as an extension of national liberation struggles in the Third World. Moreover, the conflict between Islam and the West involves a clash of Third and First World civilizations.

## A History of Conflict

Christianity and Islam have intermittently battled one another for 1200 years, beginning with the Crusades and the campaign to expel Muslims from southern Iberia. That bitter history has left in many Western minds a psychological residue of fear and hatred of Islam. Part of this anxiety stems from Islam's vitality in a post-Christian age.

The historical antagonism toward Islam is now being exploited by those eager to demonize Islam in order to justify repression of Muslim reformers and militants by politically bankrupt governments allied to the West. This process satisfies the need of many Westerners for an external enemy on whom resentment can be focused, now that the Soviet Union is no longer available for this purpose.

At the same time, today's devoutly Islamic governments have not demonstrated any more responsiveness to ordinary citizens than have the secular regimes. The governments of Saudi Arabia, Sudan and Pakistan have failed just as miserably as have those of Egypt and the Maghreb. After nearly fifteen years, the Islamic Republic of Iran has still not supplied its hard-pressed people with either clean or efficient rule.

Islamist militants meanwhile do not pose any immediate threat in countries where they actively seek to replace secularist rulers. In Algeria, for example, the armed forces quickly and easily repressed an Islamist movement after it had secured a majority of parliamentary seats in 1992 elections. The West's mild response to that attack on both democracy and Islamist aspirations is taken elsewhere in the region as a sign of First World hypocrisy regarding free elections and hostility toward any Islamist alternative to secular dictatorship.

It is worth noting in this regard that Jordanian Islamists stand as a refutation to critics who claim that Islam and democracy are inherently incompatible. Jordan is the only Middle Eastern

Muslim country where democratic forces are generally tolerated, and Islamists currently hold 32 of the 80 seats in the lower house of the nation's parliament. Islamists have also been part of Jordan's political establishment for the past forty-five years.

While Third World Muslims may occasionally carry out attacks on First World targets, such strikes would cease if the West consistently promoted democracy, economic development and respect for human rights in Muslim countries. Such a radically revised approach would also lead the West to compel Israel and Serbs to withdraw from occupied Muslim lands just as completely as Iraq was forced to withdraw from Kuwait. Muslims simply want equal treatment under the New World Order.

VIEWPOINT

*"Khomeini and his heirs can be considered the godfathers of terrorism."*

# The Islamic Republic of Iran Sponsors International Terrorism

Mohammad Mohaddessin

Mohammad Mohaddessin is a member of the People's Mojahedin Organization of Iran, an exiled group that seeks to overthrow the current Iranian government. In the following viewpoint, he details a long list of incidents of terrorism and argues that they were instigated at the highest levels of the Iranian government. Mohaddessin outlines Iran's international network for carrying out terrorist actions, including its connection to the Hezbollah (Party of God)—a Shiite Muslim faction in Lebanon that has been accused of a number of incidents of international terrorism.

As you read, consider the following questions:

1. According to the author, what are the 8 characteristics of Iranian terrorism?
2. How do Iranian mullahs (Muslim leaders trained in Islamic law and doctrine) legitimize acts of terrorism, according to Mohaddessin?
3. What two groups do Iranians target for assassination, according to Mohaddessin?

Excerpted from Mohammad Mohaddessin, *Islamic Fundamentalism*, ©1993 by Mohammad Mohaddessin. Reprinted by permission of Seven Locks Press, Carson, California.

> If for every Palestinian martyred by Israeli mercenaries, five American or French citizens are murdered, they would no longer commit such crimes. . . . The Palestinians might say, In that case the world will call us terrorists. I say, however, do they not label you already?
>
> — President of Iran Ali Akbar Hashemi-Rafsanjani, May 6, 1989

Terrorism has been one of the primary tools of the mullahs' [religious authorities'] regime to spread fundamentalism and expand Iran's influence.

Most of the images that have come to symbolize terrorism since the early 1980s are tied closely to the Tehran regime's mercenaries: The 1986 street bombings in Paris, the corpse of an "executed" passenger thrown from a hijacked Kuwaiti plane in Cyprus, and the grim videotaped faces of hostages appealing to their governments.

Although not new, terrorism has acquired qualitatively different dimensions since Ayatollah Ruhollah Khomeini and his Islamic fundamentalist government came to power in 1979. Indeed, today, Khomeini and his heirs can be considered the godfathers of terrorism.

## Inciting Terrorism

1. *State-sponsored terrorism.* Because terrorism has been one of the main instruments to advance the mullahs' foreign policy, decisions about terrorist operations have always been made at the highest levels of the regime. Before he died, all decisions were made by Khomeini, who enjoyed the active advice of Ayatollah Ali Khamenei, Rafsanjani, and other leaders.

In his letter of resignation to Khamenei in September 1988, Prime Minister Mir-Hussein Moussavi unequivocally stated that many terrorist activities were planned and carried out at the order of the highest echelons of the government and without his knowledge. After surrendering to the French Police, a Tunisian national by the name of Lutfi, one of the Iranian regime's terrorist operatives in France, revealed that the 1986 bombings in France had been suggested to Khomeini by Ali Khamenei, the president at the time; Hashemi-Rafsanjani, then the majlis [Iranian parliament] speaker; Mohsen Rafiqdoust, the head of the Foundation of the Deprived (at the time the minister of the Revolutionary Guards Corps); and Muhammad Muhammadi-Rayshahri, the then intelligence minister. The bombings of shops and a café killed twelve people and wounded scores more.

When Khomeini was alive, Rafsanjani acted as the coordinator of the ministries of Foreign Affairs, Intelligence, Islamic Culture and Guidance, and the Guards Corps' units involved in terrorist activities. After Khomeini's death, Rafsanjani, as the country's president and the chairman of the Supreme National Security Council, has continued to make the final decisions on terrorist plans.

During the mullahs' rule, unlimited financial resources have been devoted to exporting terrorism. Tehran has also formed specific terrorist organs and institutions, and the Ministry of Foreign Affairs has played a key role in sponsoring terrorist activities.

2. *Religious fanaticism.* The Tehran mullahs also exploit religion to legitimize acts of terror by calling them divine duties. The mullahs promise the perpetrators of such actions "a place in heaven." This religious factor generates intense hatred and catastrophic results. Some of the most devastating blows have been delivered through suicide missions. Shedding the blood of innocent people and ordinary citizens is easily justified as "a necessary price." In many cases, public places have been bombed at random—victimizing civilians and even children—merely to create fear. The fundamentalists' targets are determined by Tehran's political and propaganda interests.

## Targets of Terrorism

3. *Handpicked targets.* The Iranian-sponsored terrorism has targeted a wide spectrum of victims since the early 1980s.

4. *Hostage taking.* The 444-day occupation of the United States Embassy in Tehran, beginning on November 4, 1979, marked the start of the newly established clerical regime's experimentation with terrorism and provided a glimpse of what was yet to come.

In 1986, when the departure of an Iranian cargo ship from an Italian port was delayed for a few days because an Iranian sailor had requested political asylum, Tehran retaliated by preventing Italian nationals, including diplomats, from leaving Iran. Rafsanjani had this to say about the incident: "They delayed our ship. We spoke with them with humane language. It was to no avail. Yesterday we ordered several Italians not to leave Iran. [The authorities] returned them from the airport."

In March 1992, when relations between Berne and Tehran soured over the arrest of a top Iranian terrorist in Switzerland, a Swiss businessman disappeared in Tehran without any trace. Several days later, it became clear that the Swiss national had been taken hostage.

The tragic saga of the Western hostages [journalists and foreign embassy personnel, seven of whom were American] held captive by Tehran's proxies in Lebanon [during the 1975–1991 civil war] was the very essence of Iranian-sponsored terrorism. In the words of Rafsanjani, "If the oppressed people of Lebanon do not take hostages, then what else can they do?" Rafsanjani tried to delay the hostages' release to gain the maximum concessions. Sheikh Muhammad-Hussein Fadhlullah, a Hizbullah leader, acknowledged in March 1991 that holding the Western hostages had become a liability: "If it were left to us, we would release them this very day. But Rafsanjani believes that the Americans are not yet ready to step forward and accept Iran's demands." Consequently, Tehran agreed to the freedom of the Western hostages only when the region's political landscape had been totally reshaped in the aftermath of the Persian Gulf War.

Lurie's World ©1993 worldwide copyright by Cartoonews International Syndicate, New York City, USA. Reprinted with permission.

5. *Hijacking.* Another method often employed by the mullahs' regime in recent years has been the hijacking of passenger airliners. In August 1983, an Air France Boeing 737 was commandeered as it left Vienna and forced to go to Tehran. Its cockpit was blown up on the tarmac of Mehrabad Airport by the hijackers. In June 1985, a TWA Boeing 727 was hijacked while en route to Rome from Athens. An American navy diver was murdered while the plane was parked on the tarmac of Beirut Airport. An Air Afrique DC-10 airliner was hijacked in July 1987 by Iranian-backed terrorists who killed a French passenger at the Geneva Airport. The Swiss president revealed in an interview at the time that the government of Iran was responsible for the affair. On April 5, 1988, a Kuwaiti airliner 747 jumbo jet was hijacked in Bangkok and forced to land in the northeastern Iranian city of Mashad. A leading Lebanese terrorist boarded the

172

plane to control the operation. After fifteen days, the episode ended in Algiers, but not before two passengers were murdered by the terrorists.

## Bombings

6. *Bombings in public places.* In September 1986 a wave of bombings shook Paris. Fuad Ali Saleh, accused of killing twelve people and injuring hundreds in these incidents, was arrested while carrying explosives into a car in Paris in March 1987. A student of theology in Qom, Saleh confessed that he had been commissioned by Tehran. Bomb blasts in two beach-side restaurants in Kuwait City in 1985 left ten people dead and eighty wounded. During the 1989 hajj [pilgrimage] in Mecca [Saudi Arabia], three bombs went off around the Grand Mosque, injuring scores of pilgrims. Terrorist agents who claimed responsibility for the explosions were captured and stated in their confessions several months later that they had been trained by the Iranian regime. In August 1986, a number of Iranian diplomat-terrorists were arrested in Jiddah Airport [Saudi Arabia] carrying large quantities of explosives.

7. *Suicide missions, car and truck bombs.* In April 1983, a bomb-laden truck exploded in front of the American Embassy in Beirut, killing 61 and wounding 120 persons. The Emir of Kuwait was wounded in a suicide attack on his motorcade in May 1985 that was linked to Iran. Car bombs were used to assassinate Saudi diplomats in Turkey and Thailand. In March 1992, a powerful bomb exploded in the Argentine capital, Buenos Aires, destroying the Israeli Embassy. Two months later, a senior official at the U.S. State Department said, "The United States has uncovered strong indications that Iranian diplomats helped plan the March 17 bombing." According to these reports, several other foreign embassies in Latin American countries had been identified for similar terrorist attacks.

Rafsanjani and other senior Iranian officials have repeatedly and officially accepted the responsibility for terrorist actions by their operatives in Lebanon and elsewhere. Three years after the explosion of the U.S. Marine barracks near Beirut, Rafsanjani said, "They hold us accountable for the blow the Americans received and the humiliation they suffered in Lebanon. We are indeed responsible [for it.]" Brigadier General Mohsen Rafiqdoust, the former Guards Corps minister and Rafsanjani's brother-in-law, stated, "Both the TNT and the ideology which in one blast sent to hell 400 officers, NCOs, and soldiers at the Marine Headquarters had been provided by Iran."

8. *Assassinations of foreign nationals and Iranian oppositionists.* The most publicized example of the mullahs' terrorism against foreign nationals was Khomeini's decree in 1989 ordering the execution of the Indian-born British author Salman Rushdie.

Despite a wave of international condemnation and appeals to annul the decree, Rafsanjani and other high-ranking officials have stressed its irrevocability. In reply to a question on the subject, Rafsanjani said:

> The fact that the entire power of the Arrogant West is defeated in relation to a blasphemous book provides a clear path to materialize the Imam's [Khomeini's] thoughts. The Imam's decree on the execution of Salman Rushdie is the decree of Islam; it remains in force and will be subject to no changes.

In November 1992, mullah Hassan Sane'i, a top cleric and the head of the state-run Panzdah Khordad Foundation, issued a statement, confirming an increase in the $2 million reward for killing Salman Rushdie. In a January 31, 1993, press conference in Tehran, Rafsanjani told foreign journalists, "Nothing can change this [the verdict] because the leader [Khomeini] is dead. . . ." The following month, Khamenei added, "The Imam [Khomeini] fired an arrow toward this brazen apostate. The arrow has left the bow and is moving toward its target and will sooner or later strike it. This sentence must definitely be carried out and it will be carried out."

---

## Iran's Support for Terrorism

It has been over fifteen years since the shah was toppled. The record since 1979 of Iranian behavior—to its own people and abroad—is appalling. At home, repression, violence and terror. Abroad, efforts to undermine the states in the Persian Gulf, to derail the peace process, and to support Hezbollah and other terrorist organizations and groups operating today from Algeria to Tajikistan.

The Iranian government . . . does everything within its power to strengthen the hand of extremist forces, to increase the carnage, and to upset any progress toward political reconciliation. Iran's most important client, Lebanese Hezbollah, has killed more Americans than any other terrorist group and receives support, training and arms from Tehran.

Central Intelligence Agency director R. James Woolsey, quoted by Harry Summers, *The Washington Times*, December 20, 1994.

---

In addition, the mullahs' terrorists have so far set several libraries and bookstores on fire for carrying Rushdie's book. They also wounded the Italian translator of the book and murdered its Japanese translator.

In March 1990, a famous Turkish journalist working for the

daily *Hurriyet* and his driver were shot and killed in Istanbul. According to *Hurriyet*, the police concluded that the murderers had received their orders from Iran. An Iranian diplomat named Aqiqi, who is also a member of the Intelligence Ministry, was involved in the murder. He is now [1993] working at the Iranian Embassy in Vienna. On January 15, 1992, Mustapha Geha, a Shi'ite Lebanese author who had written anti-Khomeini commentaries in Beirut's newspapers, was murdered in the Sabtiyeh district of Beirut.

On January 24, 1993, Ugur Mumcu, a renowned Turkish journalist, was killed as a powerful bomb exploded in the car he was driving in Istanbul. He was a staunch critic of the mullahs' fundamentalism. In a related development, a prominent Turkish industrialist escaped assassination on January 27, when his bodyguards exchanged gunfire with four armed men who stopped his car as he was driving to work.

## Assassination of Opponents

The clearest evidence of the terrorist nature of the mullahs' regime, however, is its extensive and vigorous campaign to assassinate its Iranian opponents abroad. A glance at the list of such victims indicates that during Rafsanjani's first four years as president, and despite his "moderate" reputation, the number of Iranian dissidents murdered by Tehran's terrorist squads exceeded the number of those assassinated during Khomeini's rule.

The most notable of these assassinations was the murder of Professor Kazem Rajavi, the elder brother of the Iranian Resistance's leader, Massoud Rajavi. Ordered by Rafsanjani, it required enormous resources, extensive planning, and coordination among several of the regime's organizations. On April 24, 1990, a terrorist squad killed Rajavi, the representative of the National Council of Resistance of Iran to the United Nations and Switzerland, near his home in a Geneva suburb. Because of his international endeavors to defend human rights in Iran, Rajavi was a distinguished personality. Sirous Nasseri, Tehran's ambassador to the United Nations Office in Geneva, on two occasions personally threatened to murder him. After extensive investigations, Roland Chatelain, the Swiss magistrate in charge of the case, and Swiss judicial and police officials confirmed the role of Rafsanjani's government and the participation of thirteen official agents of the Iranian regime who had used "service passports" to enter Switzerland for their plot.

On July 13, 1989, Abdul-Rahman Qassemlou, the secretary general of the Democratic Party of Iranian Kurdistan; Abdullah Qaderi, a member of the Party's Central Committee; and a Kurdish middleman were gunned down by a team from the Revolutionary Guards Corps who were negotiating with them in

Vienna on behalf of the mullahs' regime. The person commanding the attack was Muhammad-Ja'far Sahraroudi, chief of the Intelligence Directorate of the Guard Corps Qods Force. Police arrested Sahraroudi, who had gone to Austria under the assumed name of Rahimi, but released him quickly, enabling him to return to Iran at once. On August 6, 1991, Shapour Bakhtiar, the shah's last prime minister, and his personal secretary, Soroush Katibeh, were stabbed to death in Paris by the mullahs' terrorists.

On September 17, 1992, Farsi-speaking gunmen charged into a Greek restaurant in Berlin and murdered Sadegh Sharafkandi and two other Iranian Kurdish nationals. Sharafkandi had succeeded Abdul-Rahman Qassemlou, the leader of the Iranian Kurdish Democratic Party.

Prior to the killings in Berlin, Iranian agents stabbed to death Fereidoon Farrokhzad, an Iranian entertainer, at his home in Bonn in August 1992.

## An International Terrorist Network

To carry out bombings, hijackings, and assassinations, the Iranian clerics have established a vast network of agents and centers throughout the world [e.g., in Switzerland, Germany, France, Turkey, Cyprus, Kuwait, and Pakistan, as well as in Lebanon]. . . .

*Lebanon.* Because of its large Shi'ite population and its proximity to Israel, Lebanon has been one of the regime's prime targets for the export of fundamentalism and terrorism since the beginning of Khomeini's rule. In mid-1982, the Guards Corps' Muhammad Rasulullah brigade was dispatched to Lebanon. Two thousand Revolutionary Guards stayed in Lebanon when the brigade returned to Iran. In addition, the Guards Corps' organization was restructured to include a "Lebanon Corps," to provide manpower, training, and logistical support to the regime's forces in Lebanon. The Guards Corps based its forces in the city of Baalbek in the Bekaa Valley in eastern Lebanon, where a large enclave of Shi'ites live. Baalbek thus became the center where the Guards and the Khomeini regime's indigenous supporters were settled, trained, and subsequently dispatched on terrorist missions. The Guards Corps has many bases in the Bekaa Valley. The Sheikh Abdullah or Sakaneh Imam Ali base (also known as the Baalbek base) is the largest of these bases and plays a central role in such activities. The Guards Corps has also established many bases in townships around Baalbek to exert control over the area it holds. In 1992 senior Iranian government officials reportedly ordered their terrorist units in Lebanon to prepare for major operations all over the Middle East. They expanded command, control, and communications systems and sent personnel to sites in Sudan. According to one expert, "Sudan is an ideal position for launching attacks on Egypt, Israel, and Saudi Arabia." . . .

## Prospects

The long arm of Iran's terrorists stretches to Turkey, Pakistan, and India in Asia; Lebanon, Saudi Arabia, and Kuwait in the Middle East; Belgium, France, Austria, Sweden, Italy, Cyprus, Spain, Germany, Switzerland, the United Kingdom, and Greece in Europe; and Argentina in Latin America. The extent to which the mullahs enjoy a free rein to maneuver and operate—whether in the framework of diplomatic institutions or business facilities or other suitable cover in any given country—is directly correlated to the frequency and the number of terrorist activities in those countries. One can certainly say that the mullahs' regime is neither inclined nor able to abandon terrorism as one of the primary instruments of its foreign policy. One Tehran-based foreign diplomat noted, "The difference between now and before is that they do not want to get caught." The mullahs may try to exercise more caution in pursuing their terrorism, but terrorism will remain intertwined with the mullahs' foreign policy.

"*Accusations are always ready, so that whenever [some act of terrorism] happens the United States accuses Iran or Hezbollah.*"

# Iran and Hezbollah Do Not Sponsor International Terrorism

Sayyed Fadlallah, interviewed by George A. Nader

Sayyed Fadlallah is considered the spiritual leader (ayatollah) of the Shiite Muslim Hezbollah (Party of God) faction of Lebanon. In the following viewpoint, Fadlallah, interviewed by George A. Nader, counters charges that Iran and Hezbollah are behind incidents of international terrorism. He discusses several incidents, such as the taking of Western hostages during the 1975–1991 Lebanese civil war, and argues that such acts were not terrorism but a response to the violence perpetrated by undemocratic Middle East regimes and by Western countries. Fadlallah also contends that the political Islamic groups do not use terrorism, and that Western accusations are not backed by reliable proof. Nader is a staff writer for *Middle East Insight*, based in Washington, D.C.

As you read, consider the following questions:

1. Where did Islamic groups learn to use kidnapping and terrorism, according to Fadlallah?
2. According to Fadlallah, what is the "one battle in Lebanon" being waged against?

From "Give Islamists Their Right to Participate in the Political Process: An Interview with Ayatollah Sayyed Fadlallah" by George A. Nader, *Middle East Insight*, September/October 1994, ©1994 by International Insight, Inc. Reprinted with permission.

$M$iddle East Insight: *In light of the current debate in the West over the role of Islam and the responsibility of various militant groups for recent violent acts, do you see a difference between moderate and extremist Islam? If so, what characterizes the line between moderate and extremist?*

Fadlallah: I do not think there are two Islams: an extremist Islam and a moderate Islam. This is what the Western media in general has been trying to instill in world public opinion. This term has stemmed from the desire of the active Islamists to restore Islam as a concept and as a *sharia* (Islamic law) to governance and their attempt to direct the political tendencies in accordance with Islamic concepts. They believe that Islam is not only a religion of rituals but a religion carrying a civic message particularly with its legalistic view of the daily life of humans. Its laws cover the private and public domains of the individual. Similar to any intellectual force, it contains a political, economic and social paradigm.

## Islamists Are Not Extremists

We think Westerners have confused the common understanding of religion through the historical experience of Christianity and the Islamic understanding of religion. I think all Muslims share the same understanding. They all refer to the rulings of the *sharia* in their individual and social life, even without going back to the state. Therefore, considering the Islamists as extremists because they want to implement the *sharia* and restore Islam to their daily life is tantamount to considering anybody who advocates unfamiliar ideas as an extremist. We could possibly consider the Marxists, socialists, or anybody else who advocates ideas that differ from Western, democratic, and capitalist thinking as extremists.

We are similar to other people who have values that differ from the West and its perception of life. We as Islamists have no problem with dialogue or engaging in a discussion of our concepts and those of others. When we study the Glorious Quran we find that it has eternalized the criticisms that were directed against it during the first phase of the call to Islam, even the criticism that was directed against the Prophet himself, with regard to his state of mind, the content of his message, or similar issues. We do not fear any intellectual challenges because we are confident of confronting them.

On the other hand, we in our movement and in accordance with our political and social program do not think of imposing Islam on people. We try to follow every political and peaceful means to introduce our thought to the people in a civilized way as the Quran has taught us. "Invite (all) to the Way of thy Lord with wisdom and beautiful preaching; and argue with them in ways that are best and most gracious." So that people would be convinced about what we advocate, and when they are convinced, they will carry us to power. If we fail to convince them, we, like others who uphold different ideas from the ongoing conditions in this or that country, will continue our march to achieve our goals, or fail to do so, to prove our intellectual and political presence. We are not unique or different from the rest of the people in this respect. In this vein, we refuse to be extremists either in terms of our thinking or practices.

## Algerian Elections and the West

It might happen in some cases that other people put forceful pressures on our freedoms, as was exactly the case in Algeria [where a military coup prevented the completion of democratic elections]. Despite our differences with some intellectual and practical aspects of the Islamic movement in Algeria, either the Islamic Front for Salvation (FIS) or other parties, we believe that the Islamists in Algeria followed democratic means to reach power there, and gained the majority in clean and free elections [in 1990–91] as was recognized by most countries. The problem is that many Western countries are willing to accept democracy when it produces a regime of like-minded people who are willing to protect their interests. But when democracy produces people who are different in orientation and do not share the same political programs, we find these Western countries trying by every means through the incumbent regimes in the Third World to thwart the democratic experience under any shallow and meaningless pretext. We would like to put this negative point on the record of the Western policy, either American or European, in the Third World. This policy supports the most brutal and autocratic regimes in the Third World because they achieve the interests of the West and submit to its political programs.

The Islamists do not impose themselves on the people, but it is the regimes in the Third World—be it Arab, Muslim or other—that are allied with the United States and Europe and persecute their peoples and confiscate their freedom. We wonder about the Arab regimes that are the closest to the United States, such as Egypt, in which democracy proceeds on the concept of 99.99% [inflated government claims of popular support], and the United States knows that. Does that indicate a respect for democracy or the people? The same applies when we talk about the rest of these regimes. We think that the Islamists currently believe they should reach power by the people's votes. If some reached power, as in the case of the Sudan, through a coup d'état, remember most regimes in the Third World came to power through the same means, and then were transformed into civil ones. If the Islamic regime in the Sudan is criticized because it reached power through a coup d'état—it must be remembered that the Egyptian regime took power by the same way. In fact most of the regimes with which the United States is allied have reached power through the same means. So these regimes are no better than that of the Sudan.

## Terrorism and Kidnapping in Lebanon

With regards to the issue of violence and terrorism, the Westerners hold against the Muslims that the latter have kidnapped Westerners in Lebanon. I think that examining the Lebanese situation during the civil war [1975-1991] indicates that it was indeed insane. The Lebanese did not invent the act of kidnapping. The Lebanese, during their conflict amongst each other, adopted this act as a means of pressure and a means of war. We saw Christians kidnapping Muslims, Muslims kidnapping Christians, or one party kidnapping a member of the opposing party. This issue has not come as a result of Islamic terrorism, but emerged out of the crazy tactics the Lebanese war witnessed.

We think the Lebanese Muslims and Christians learned this act from the West. Lebanon, which has had close relations with France, learned this act from the French themselves, who kidnapped Mehdi Ben Baraka, the Moroccan opposition leader. They also kidnapped the airplane that carried Ben Bella [Algerian president 1963-65] and his comrades. We found that this act happens in the West in more than one way. It was carried out in Italy by the Red Brigades, and we might even find it in the United States and Britain in the form of kidnapping somebody for ransom. The issue of kidnapping as a means of pressure, to obtain money or for political purposes, was not invented by the Islamists. The Islamists, like others, found this means practiced around the world and resorted to it on the basis of the idea that was common during the Lebanese conflict that if you cannot directly pressure your adversary, you might try to pressure him indirectly. We observed Israel doing that when it kidnapped many Germans and accused them of being behind the tragedies of the Jews in Germany [during World War II].

The issue is not regarding the extent of the legality of kidnapping this or that person, but the issue is that kidnapping was not an Islamic act: it was found everywhere else and practiced by many countries in the world. We even think that Islamists, like others in the East, learned it from the West. We had not practiced this means in the East in the past in order to settle our political differences. We therefore wonder why the West raises the issue of kidnapping Westerners in Lebanon under the label of Islamic terrorism at a time we find Italian terrorism and British terrorism and American terrorism with regards to this point in particular, notwithstanding the different vocabulary often used.

The principle is the same in this respect.

Referring to the issue of terrorism and the confrontation between the Muslims and some Arab regimes, such as Egypt, Algeria, Tunisia, Iraq in the past, or others, we do not think that violence in these cases emerged as a result of an Islamic initiative. We believe the violence is a response to the violence of these regimes. The regime in Algeria that used force against the Islamists after their success in securing the majority of the votes, and the regime in Egypt, which has prevented the Islamists from participating in the political process and detained them, have contributed to the response of the Islamists who have been denied their basic human, political and natural rights. It is natural that when a conflict arises between the regime and any opposition force, it develops according to the generated atmosphere of violence and counter-violence.

---

## Inflated Claims of Popular Support

Hosni Mubarak's administration and his ruling National Democratic party have suffered a remarkable erosion of public confidence since the 1991 Persian Gulf War. Increasingly, Egyptians express anger over the arrogance, insensitivity, incompetence, and alleged corruption of a government they say has been too long in power. This disaffection was most apparent during the October 1993 referendum on a third term for Mubarak. The state-run media's adulation of the 65-year-old president came close to resembling the Iraqi press's notoriously obsequious acclaim of Saddam Hussein. This, and the patently absurd official results of the vote (an 84.2 percent turnout and a 96.3 percent "yes" vote) were viewed with open contempt by many Egyptians. Some said they felt "insulted."

Caryle Murphy, *Current History*, February 1994.

---

I say, and bear all the responsibility: Give the Islamists in Egypt, Algeria, Tunisia, and other Muslim countries their right to participate in the political process, and you will never find an Islamist carrying a weapon to kill anybody. If civilians are dying in this confrontation, it is not the Muslims who are killing civilians, but the regime, trying through different means to kill civilians and accuse the Islamists of such acts.

When war erupts in crazy conditions like those in the Third World, all the cards are confused. It becomes difficult to distinguish between fair means and unfair ones. Everyone, either the regime or the opposition, tries to justify and legitimate killing. We condemn many of the practices allegedly done by the Islamists or the regime, such as the killing of foreigners. We believe that when any foreigner comes to a Muslim country and tries to help improve the conditions and provide technical expertise, the entire country is responsible for that person's safety and protection. We condemn the killing of foreigners under any pretext, unless a foreigner is working on harming the security and safety of this country.

We say that this problem turns into an insane condition, particularly with the statements of some officials in big countries. For example, when we read the statements of the French Interior Minister Charles Pasqua when he says that we have two alternatives, either we support the Algerian regime in suppressing the fundamentalists, or we let radical fundamentalists take over power; and when he talks about a plan to crush the fundamentalists in coordination with the Algerian regime, what would you expect the response of the Islamists to be after France entered as a party in this internal conflict? It is natural that anybody who enters as a party in this war would bear the consequences of the war and should not complain when this war generates problems for him, regardless whether this is right or not.

I claim that the Islamists are not terrorists. They do exactly as others would. We think the United States and Europe support the opposition in the Third World when it attempts to overthrow a regime not agreeable to Western interests. We know the Central Intelligence Agency has assisted, in combat and terrorist acts, opposition forces allied with the United States in many parts of the Third World in their attempt to reach power. We can refer to Afghanistan, Rwanda, Poland, and other countries. The United States does not act as a bystander in front of the regimes that oppose its interests and policy. It supports the opposition forces in this case even when they resort to violence. Therefore, when we want to examine these issues in an objective manner, we find that the Islamists are the least violent in the face of the international violence inflicted through the intelligence or through other means by which the United States can pressure the United Nations Security Council in order to secure its interests by combating this or that regime.

## State-Sponsored Terrorism

*There have been a number of terrorist acts in Argentina, Britain, and Panama and these have been blamed on Islamic groups like the Hezbollah and also linked directly to Iran. What are your views on these incidents and the possibilities of state-sponsored global terrorism?*

Let us examine these issues. The political system in Iran makes it the most democratic in the region. Iran is described as a clergy state. When the elections took place, some clergymen lost the election in the Tehran district to an Iranian Muslim woman. No government can receive a consensus. The *shura* [consultative] council questions every minister and his policies, such as practiced in the United States to some extent. There is freedom of the press, which criticizes the *Wali el-Faqih* [Ayatollah Khamenei] and the President of the Republic without facing imprisonment. We think that in Iran there is a voting process that is more credible than many other countries in the Third World that are allied with the United States.

## Ready-made Accusations by the United States

Regarding Hezbollah, as an Islamic party, Hezbollah is very open to political realism, rationalism, and objectivity. Though it objected to the Lebanese system and considered it non-Islamic, the party participated in the elections like the others and practiced its right of criticizing policies and increasing political awareness in a normal fashion. It also entered more than once into a direct dialogue with the Christians in an objective way.

Accusing Iran and Hezbollah of [the bombing of the Israeli embassy in Argentina in March 1992], we notice that the United States and Israel rushed to accuse Iran and Hezbollah immediately after the explosions took place without even trying to know what happened. This makes us believe that such accusations are always ready, so that whenever something happens the United States accuses Iran or Hezbollah. We still insist that the United States present accurate legal evidence for this accusation. The United States, Israel, and even Argentina have not yet been able to present any evidence. When the Iranian diplomats were accused of the bombing, we find that the Argentinean courts relied on the statements of an Iranian individual who had applied for asylum claiming to be a former Iranian diplomat, which he was not, or that he was an official in the Ministry of Guidance, which he was not either. The media referred to him as a defector. He is an untrustworthy and discredited person. How could they base the accusation on the testimony of that person, given the fact he did not have any access to such issues, which are usually planned and are only known to very few people?

It is also noteworthy that Iran informed the Argentinean investigators and court that these four diplomats had already left Argentina several years ago and presented undisputable documents attesting to this fact. We have also heard the statement of the British government that it does not have a single shred of evidence against Iran. We think the United States was not fair nor politically prudent in accusing Iran and Hezbollah because it does not possess any evidence, but only allegations, claims, and guesses. What if we in return, and on the basis of claims and allegations, say that Israel was behind all of this because

184

Israel benefits from such acts, even if they took place against some of its people, in order to gain the sympathy of the world. Israel has an interest whereas Iran does not. Iran would be hurt by such acts as its image would be even more damaged and it would become further besieged. . . .

## Israel vs. Hezbollah

*But couldn't these acts have been a Hezbollah retaliation for the Israeli bombing of their camps in Lebanon [in February 1992] and the kidnapping of Mustafa al-Dirani [in May 1994]? Is it possible that the bombings were part of a larger war between Israel and the Hezbollah?*

It is possible that this environment generates some kind of guessing and impressions, but it does not produce any kind of legal evidence. I would like to comment on one example. Why has the United States not condemned the kidnapping of Mustafa al-Dirani or the killing of children in the bombings? Does the United States think that Israel owns the Lebanese skies? Lebanon is a member state in the United Nations. We wonder why the United States even justifies Israel's mistakes and crimes, while not justifying others' rights of self-defense and resistance against the occupation of their country. We ask the American public: Is the Israeli presence in Lebanon an occupation or not? If it is not an occupation, what is then the meaning of an occupation? Any country could then occupy another under the pretext of defending its own security.

We therefore think that the United States does not apply fairness in its relations with other countries. We wish the American public would see the destruction Israel inflicted on southern Lebanon and western Beka'a so that they can get to know what kind of civilization Israel represents and the civilization the Lebanese people represent—this people that rose to the level of a martyred population defending itself even in a situation in which it possesses very little means of defense. We do not think that there is a global war between Israel and the Islamists, but we believe that when Israel attempts to besiege the Islamists in the world, it is natural that this would generate a reaction. The Islamists do not initiate a confrontation with the Israelis all over the world and harm global security. . . .

## Lebanon and the United States

*A travel embargo continues to be imposed on Lebanon by the United States. Recently the unsettled environment in Lebanon has raised fears of a return to the wanton kidnappings of previous years. Do you think that this renewed fear of kidnappings of Americans is justified?*

I can absolutely confirm from my experience with the Islamic situation in Lebanon that there is no intention whatsoever on the part of any Islamic party to kidnap anybody of American, European, or other nationality. These acts were part of the Lebanese war, and I think the Islamists, like the rest of the Lebanese, are preserving the national peace and wish for anyone who enters Lebanon in peace for any purpose to be able to do so in safety and security.

I can confirm that Islamists in general do not contemplate, do not even have the faintest idea, of repeating the kidnappings under any circumstances or context. There is only one battle in Lebanon, and that is against the Israeli occupation. We might differ politically with the United States, but we confront it through political means. We respect the American people who come to our country as guests and we think they deserve from us all respect as guests open to the issues of the people in this country. We see Arab-Americans come to their country, Lebanon.

I would like to stress two points I frequently talk about: We respect the security of any country in which Muslims reside either for the purposes of work, education, or to escape political repression in their original countries. We believe that Muslims, even those considered by the West as extremists, find more and complete freedom in the United States to express their views and serve their intellectual and political stands than any Arab country. Hence, we always advise all the Muslims who go to the United States or Europe—on the level of *fatwa* [binding legal opinion]—not to harm the security of their host country under any circumstances. We even prohibit committing any act of bombing, as was the case in New York [at the World Trade Center in February 1993]. From the view of the Islamic *sharia*, we legally prohibit this. We say this to all Muslims who go to the West as a *fatwa*. You could go back to the cassette tapes that we send there in which we urge Muslims to respect the laws of the host country and practice their freedom only in ways that are guaranteed by the laws of these countries and not to act against the system under any condition.

I just wanted to reconfirm this point, because we respect the American people and respect our presence there. And as we find the American administration and people respect this presence, we have to reciprocate and respect them as well. Our difference with the policy of the US administration does not mean that we differ with the American people.

# Periodical Bibliography

The following articles have been selected to supplement the diverse views presented in this chapter.

| | |
|---|---|
| Fouad Ajami | "Have Sermon, Will Travel," *U.S. News & World Report*, July 12, 1993. |
| Yonah Alexander | "Superterrorism: A Global Threat," *The World & I*, June 1993. Available from 3600 New York Ave. NE, Washington, DC 20002. |
| Noam Chomsky | "Terrorism Strikes Home," *Z Magazine*, May 1993. |
| Alexander Cockburn | "Beat the Devil," *The Nation*, December 23, 1991. |
| Steve Coll and David Hoffman | "Islam's Violent Improvisers," *The Washington Post National Weekly Edition*, August 9–15, 1993. Available from 1150 15th St. NW, Washington, DC 20071. |
| Brian Duffy | "What Kind of Terror Network?" *U.S. News & World Report*, July 5, 1993. |
| Rachel Ehrenfeld | "Follow the Money," *National Review*, November 1, 1993. |
| Jack Epstein | "Partisans of Terror," *U.S. News & World Report*, August 8, 1994. |
| Kamal Kharrazi | "Iran and Islamic Revivalism," *Middle East Insight*, May/June 1993. Available from 1200 18th St. NW, Suite 305, Washington, DC 20036. |
| Martin Kramer | "Islam and the West (Including Manhattan)," *Commentary*, October 1993. |
| Martin Kramer | "The Jihad Against the Jews," *Commentary*, October 1994. |
| Tom Morganthau | "The New Terrorism," *Newsweek*, July 5, 1993. |
| *The Nation* | "Terror City," March 29, 1993. |
| Don Oberdorfer | "The Iranian Hostage Connection," *The Washington Post National Weekly Edition*, January 27–February 2, 1992. |
| Giandomenico Picco | "Can There Be Peace Without an Enemy?" *New Perspectives Quarterly*, Summer 1993. |
| Thomas Sancton | "The Tehran Connection," *Time*, March 21, 1994. |
| Jill Smolowe | "A Voice of Holy War," *Time*, March 15, 1993. |
| James M. Wall | "The Media's Dark Side," *The Christian Century*, March 24–31, 1993. |
| Tim Weiner | "Blowback from the Afghan Battlefield," *The New York Times Magazine*, March 13, 1994. |

# Is the Islamic World a Threat to the West?

**Islam**

# Chapter Preface

Some Western observers of political Islam see it as a growing threat to the West, likening it to the threat presented by the Soviet Union during the cold war. Among them, Peter W. Rodman, author of *More Precious than Peace: The Cold War and the Struggle for the Developing World*, declares, "As the Islamic political virus spreads . . . the West now confronts a principal strategic challenge of the post–cold war era." In his analysis, groups that espouse political Islam oppose the integration of their countries into the world community because they believe that community is dominated by the West. According to Rodman, "Islamic radicalism's . . . proclaimed goal is a transformation of the [Middle East], if not the world, to diminish the West's influence and undermine the West's friends."

Others dispute the assertion that political Islam will present a threat to the West. According to John L. Esposito, author of *The Islamic Threat: Myth or Reality?*, "The politics of the Middle East refutes theories of a monolithic threat." Even if Islamically oriented states resent Western cultural dominance, he argues, they are unlikely to unite in opposition to the West. In Esposito's opinion, "Despite a common 'Islamic' orientation, the governments of the region reveal little unity of purpose in interstate or international relations." Islam is unlikely to challenge the West because Islamic countries are too busy challenging each other, in Esposito's analysis.

Mark Juergensmeyer, author of *The New Cold War?*, warns that Islamic states "hold the potential of making common cause against the secular West, in what might evolve into a new Cold War." Others in the West warn against creating a new cold war where none exists. The viewpoints in the following chapter debate the likelihood of this potential confrontation as well as what policies the West should pursue in the Islamic world.

---

*"Americans know an opponent when they see him."*

---

# Political Islam Is a Threat to the West

Daniel Pipes

Since the end of the cold war, liberals and conservatives have debated whether the West should fight a new cold war against Islamic fundamentalism. In the following viewpoint, Daniel Pipes compares the new debate between liberals and conservatives on the threat of fundamentalist Islam with old debates on the threat of communism. He finds that the new arguments mirror the old arguments to a great extent, and contends that like communism during the cold war, Islam is a threat to the West. Pipes is the editor of the journal *Middle East Quarterly* and author of *In the Path of God: Islam and Political Power*.

As you read, consider the following questions:

1. How does Pipes define fundamentalism? What distinguishes Islam from fundamentalism, according to the author?
2. What is the difference between the threat to the West of communism and that of fundamentalism, according to Pipes?

The Western confrontation with fundamentalist Islam has in some ways come to resemble the great ideological battle of the twentieth century, that between Marxism-Leninism and liberal democracy. Not only do Americans frame the discussion about Iran and Algeria much as they did the earlier one about the Soviet Union and China, but they also differ among themselves on the question of fundamentalist Islam roughly along the same lines as they did on the Cold War. Liberals say: Co-opt the radicals. Conservatives say: Confront them. As usual, the conservatives are right.

At first glance, how to deal with fundamentalist Islam appears to be a discussion unrelated to anything that has come before. Islam is a religion, not an ideology, so how can the U.S. Government formulate a policy toward it? A closer look reveals that while Islam is indeed a faith, its fundamentalist variant is a form of political ideology. Fundamentalists may be defined, most simply, as those Muslims who agree with the slogan: "Islam is the solution." When it comes to politics, they say that Islam has all the answers. The Malaysian leader Anwar Ibrahim spoke for fundamentalist Muslims everywhere when he asserted some years ago that "we are not socialist, we are not capitalist, we are Islamic." For the fundamentalists, Islam is primarily an "ism," a belief system about ordering power and wealth.

Much distinguishes fundamentalism from Islam as it was traditionally practiced, including its emphasis on public life (rather than faith and personal piety); its leadership by schoolteachers and engineers (rather than religious scholars); and its Westernized quality (e.g., whereas Muslims traditionally did not consider Friday a Sabbath, fundamentalists have turned it into precisely that, imitating the Jewish Saturday and Christian Sunday). In brief, fundamentalism represents a thoroughly modern effort to come to terms with the challenges of modernization.

The great majority of Muslims disagree with the premises of fundamentalist Islam, and a small number do so vocally. A few, such as Salman Rushdie and Taslima Nasrin, have acquired global reputations, but most toil more obscurely. When a newly elected deputy to the Jordanian parliament in fall 1993 called fundamentalist Islam "one of the greatest dangers facing our society" and compared it to "a cancer" that "has to be surgically removed," she spoke for many Muslims.

Americans can in good conscience join them in criticizing fundamentalism. As an ideology, fundamentalist Islam can claim none of the sanctity that Islam the religion enjoys.

## Battle Lines

In responding to fundamentalist Islam, Americans tend, as I have suggested, to divide along familiar liberal and conservative

191

lines. More striking yet, the same people hold roughly the same positions they held vis-à-vis that other quasi-religious ideology, Marxism-Leninism. A left-wing Democrat like George McGovern advocates a soft line, now as then. A right-wing Republican like Jesse Helms argues for a tough line, now as then. Consider the following parallels:

*Causes.* The Left, in keeping with its materialist outlook, sees Communist or fundamentalist Islamic ideology as a cover for some other motivation, probably an economic one. The Russian Revolution expressed deep-seated class grievances; fundamentalist violence in Algeria, the U.S. State Department tells us, expresses "frustration arising from political exclusion and economic misery." In contrast, the Right sees radical utopian ideology as a powerful force in itself, not just as an expression of socio-economic woes. Ideas and ambitions count at least as much as the price of wheat; visions of a new order go far toward accounting for the revolutions of 1917 [in Russia] and 1979 [in Iran].

---

## A New Strategic Threat

More than a dozen years after the Iranian revolution, it is now clear that Islamic fundamentalism has spread to the Sunni world as well as the Shiite, and is a growing factor in regions far afield, from North Africa to the Israeli-occupied West Bank to Afghanistan to the Muslim republics of the former Soviet Union. It is filling the vacuum left by the discrediting of other outlets for popular frustration, such as Pan-Arabism, nationalism, and Arab "socialism." On its face, the Islamic trend looks to replace those "isms" as the main strategic threat to moderate or pro-Western governments in these regions.

It is, of course, an ironic turn. With the end of the cold war, our values have triumphed. We won not only a geopolitical victory over the Soviet Union but a victory in a two-hundred-year struggle of ideas in Western thought, between theories of collective will dating to the French Revolution and theories of individual liberty dating to the American. Yet now the West finds itself challenged from outside by a militant, atavistic force driven by hatred of *all* Western political thought, harking back to age-old grievances against Christendom.

Peter W. Rodman, *National Review*, May 11, 1992.

---

*Solutions.* If misery causes radicalism, as the Left argues, then the antidote lies in economic growth and social equity. The West can help in these areas through aid, trade, and open lines of communication. But if, as the Right believes, ambitious intellectuals are the problem, then they must be battled and defeated. In both cases, liberals look to cooperation, conservatives to confrontation.

*The West's responsibility.* The Left sees Western hostility as a leading reason why things have gone wrong. According to one journalist, the West "made its own sizable contribution" to the current crisis in Algeria. [Close to 4,000 people have been killed in violence between the Algerian military and militant Islamic groups since the military overturned elections in January 1992.] It's the old "blame America first" attitude: just as Americans were responsible for every Soviet trespass from the Gulag to the arms race, so they are now answerable for the appearance of the Ayatollah Khomeini (due to U.S. support for the Shah) and for the many Arab fundamentalist movements (due to U.S. support for Israel). The Right adamantly denies Western culpability in both cases, for that would absolve tyrants of their crimes. We made mistakes, to be sure, but that's because we find it hard to contend with radical utopian movements. Along these lines, Arnold Beichman argues that "we are at the beginning of what promises to be a long war in which new moral complexities . . . will present themselves as once they did in the days of Soviet Communism."

*A single source.* When the State Department disclaims "monolithic international control being exercised over the various Islamic movements," it uses almost the same words it once used to speak of Marxism-Leninism. For decades, American "progressives" insisted that Communist organizations around the world had indigenous sources and did not owe anything to Moscow (a claim easier to make so long as Moscow's archives remained closed). To which conservatives typically replied: Of course there's no "monolithic international control," but there is an awful lot of funding and influence. Teheran administers a network akin to an Islamist Comintern, making its role today not that different from Moscow's then.

## Opposition to Fundamentalism

*The antis.* For many decades, the Left saw those Russians, Chinese, and Cubans whose firsthand experience turned them into anti-Communists as marginal elements. In similar fashion, the Left today looks at anti-fundamentalist Muslims as inauthentic. Churches are among the worst offenders here. For example, in one recent analysis, a German priest presented the extremist element as the Muslim community per se. The Right wholeheartedly celebrates the new antis, like the old, as brave individuals bringing advance word of the terrors that result from efforts radically to remake society.

*Do moderates exist?* The Left distinguishes between those ideologues willing to work within the system (deemed acceptable) and those who rely on violence and sabotage (deemed unacceptable). The Right acknowledges differences in tactics but perceives no major difference in goals. Accordingly, it tends to lump most Communists or fundamentalists together.

*Motives.* When the other side strikes out aggressively, the Left often excuses its acts by explaining how they are defensive. Invasions by Napoleon and Hitler explain the Soviet presence in Angola; a legacy of colonial oppression accounts for the depths of fundamentalist rage. The Right concludes from events like the September 1983 downing of a Korean Airlines flight or the February 1993 World Trade Center bombing that the other side has offensive intentions, and it listens to no excuses.

*Fighting words.* The two sides draw contrary conclusions from aggressive speech. Liberals dismiss the barrage of threats against the West (Muslim prisoner in a French court: "We Muslims should kill every last one of you [Westerners]") as mere rhetoric. Conservatives listen carefully and conclude that the West needs to protect itself (French Interior Minister Charles Pasqua: fundamentalist groups "represent a threat to us").

### A More Profound Challenge

*Threat to the West.* If they are approached with respect, says the Left, Marxist-Leninists and fundamentalist Muslims will leave us alone. Don't treat them as enemies and they won't hurt us. The Right disagrees, holding that all revolutionaries, no matter what their particular outlook (Communist, Fascist, fundamentalist), are deeply anti-Western and invariably target the West. Their weaponry ranges from ICBMs [intercontinental ballistic missiles] to truck bombs, but their purpose is the same: to challenge the predominance of modern, Western civilization.

And if truck bombs are less threatening than missiles, it should be noted that fundamentalists challenge the West more profoundly than Communists did and do. The latter disagree with our politics but not with our whole view of the world (how could they, as they pay homage to Dead White Males like Marx and Engels?). In contrast, fundamentalist Muslims despise our whole way of life, including the way we dress, mate, and pray. They admire little more than our military and medical technologies. To appease Communists means changing the political and economic spheres; to appease fundamentalists would mean forcing women to wear the veil, scuttling nearly every form of diversion, and overhauling the judicial system.

*Future prospects.* In the 1950s, the Left portrayed Marxism-Leninism as the wave of the future; today, it ascribes the same brilliant prospect to fundamentalist Islam. In other words, these radical ideologies are an unstoppable force; stand in their way, and you'll not only get run over, you might even spur them on.

But conservatives see utopianism enjoying only a temporary surge. The effort to remake mankind, they say, cannot work; like Communism, fundamentalism has to end up in the dustbin of history.

## Conciliation or Containment?

Summing up, the Left is more sanguine than the Right about both Communism and fundamentalist Islam. It's hard to imagine a conservative calling the Ayatollah Khomeini "some kind of saint," as did Jimmy Carter's ambassador to the United Nations, Andrew Young. It's about as uncommon to hear a liberal warning, along with France's Defense Minister François Léotard, that "Islamic nationalism in its terrorist version is as dangerous today as National Socialism was in the past." On the scholarly level, a liberal Democrat like John Esposito publishes a book titled *The Islamic Threat: Myth or Reality?*, in which he concludes that the threat is but a myth. In sharp contrast, Walter McDougall, the Pulitzer Prize–winning historian and sometime assistant to Richard Nixon, sees Russia helping the West in "holding the frontier of Christendom against its common enemy," the Muslim world.

These contrary analyses lead, naturally, to very different prescriptions for U.S. policy. The Left believes that dialogue with the other side, whether Communists or fundamentalist Muslims, has several advantages: it helps us understand their legitimate concerns, signals that we mean them no harm, and reduces mutual hostility. Beyond dialogue, the West can show goodwill by reducing or even eliminating our military capabilities. Roughly speaking, this is the Clinton Administration's position. In Algeria, for instance, the administration hopes to defuse a potential explosion by urging the [military] regime to bring in fundamentalist leaders who reject terrorism, thereby isolating the violent extremists.

The Right has little use for dialogue and unilateral disarmament. Communists and fundamentalists being invariably hostile to us, we should show not empathy but resolve, not goodwill but will power. And what better way to display these intentions than with armed strength? Now as then, conservatives think in terms of containment and rollback. For conservatives, Algeria's regime fits into the tradition of friendly tyrants—states where the rulers treat their own population badly but help the United States fend off a radical ideology. It makes sense to stand by Algiers [capital of Algeria] (or Cairo), just as it earlier made sense to stick by Ky in Saigon or Pinochet in Chile.

## Interests, Ideology, and U.S. Policy

Of course, the schemas presented here do not align perfectly. The Reagan Administration searched for "moderates" in Iran (an effort led by none other than Oliver North), and the Bush Administration enunciated a soft policy toward fundamentalism. The Clinton Administration, in contrast, has pursued a quite resolute policy toward Iran.

Interests sometimes count for more than ideology. Circumstance on occasion compels the U.S. Government to aid one enemy against another; thus, we have recently helped fundamentalist Afghans against Communist ones, and Communist Palestinians against fundamentalist ones. The liberal Clinton Administration speaks out against a crackdown on fundamentalists in Algeria, where the stakes are low for Americans, but accepts tough measures in Egypt, where the United States has substantial interests. The conservative French government bemoans the crackdown in Egypt (not so important for it) but encourages tough measures in Algeria (very important).

Still, the basic pattern is clear. And as the lines of debate sort themselves out, the two sides are likely to stick more consistently to their characteristic positions. This suggests that while Marxism-Leninism and fundamentalist Islam are very different phenomena, Westerners respond in similar ways to ideological challenges.

They do so because of a profound divide in outlook. American liberals believe that mankind is by nature peaceful and cooperative; when confronted with aggression and violence, they tend to assume it is motivated by a just cause, such as socio-economic deprivation or exploitation by foreigners. Anger cannot be false, especially if accompanied by high-minded goals. Less naïvely, conservatives know the evil that lurks in men's hearts. They understand the important roles of fanaticism and hatred. Just because an ideology has utopian aims does not mean that its adherents have lofty motives or generous ambitions.

The Left's soft approach to fundamentalist Islam predominates in Washington, and in the universities, the churches, and the media. Indeed, to recall one of the Left's favorite phrases, it has become the hegemonic discourse in the United States. On the other side stand nothing but a handful of scholars, some commentators and politicians, and the great common sense of the American people. Americans know an opponent when they see him, and they are not fooled by the Left's fancy arguments. That common sense prevailed in the Cold War and no doubt will suffice yet again to overcome the follies of the New Class.

2

---

*"Neither Islam nor Islamic fundamentalism is by definition 'anti-Western.'"*

---

# Political Islam Is Not a Threat to the West

Leon T. Hadar

With the cold war rivalry between the West and the Soviet Union ended, some foreign policy experts have said that Islam is the next rival of the West. In the following viewpoint, Leon T. Hadar contends that Middle Eastern and Central Asian countries that benefited from U.S. and Soviet aid during the cold war have been playing up the threat of Islamic fundamentalism in order to receive aid from the United States. Islamic movements in the Middle East are quite varied, according to Hadar, and some are even democratic. He argues that a U.S. policy that blindly opposes Islam is likely to be harmful to U.S. interests. Hadar is an adjunct scholar at the Cato Institute in Washington, D.C., and author of *Quagmire: America in the Middle East*.

As you read, consider the following questions:

1. Why is the alleged threat to the West from militant Islam different from the threat from Saddam Hussein, according to Hadar?
2. What policies do the leaders of Algeria's Islamic Salvation Front (FIS) advocate, according to the author?

From Leon T. Hadar, "The 'Green Peril': Creating the Islamic Fundamentalist Threat," *Cato Institute Policy Analysis*, August 27, 1992. Reprinted by permission of the Cato Institute, Washington, D.C.

Now that the Cold War is becoming a memory, America's foreign policy establishment has begun searching for new enemies. Possible new villains include "instability" in Europe—ranging from German resurgence to new Russian imperialism—the "vanishing" ozone layer, nuclear proliferation, and narcoterrorism. Topping the list of potential new global bogeymen, however, are the Yellow Peril, the alleged threat to American economic security emanating from East Asia, and the so-called Green Peril (green is the color of Islam). That peril is symbolized by the Middle Eastern Moslem fundamentalist—the "Fundie," to use a term coined by *The Economist*—a Khomeini-like creature, armed with a radical ideology, equipped with nuclear weapons, and intent on launching a violent jihad against Western civilization.

George Will even suggested that the 1,000-year battle between Christendom and Islam might be breaking out once more when he asked, "Could it be that twenty years from now we will be saying, not that they're at the gates of Vienna again, but that, in fact, the birth of Mohammed is at least as important as the birth of Christ, that Islamic vitality could be one of the big stories of the next generations?"

## A New Cold War?

Indeed, "a new specter is haunting America, one that some Americans consider more sinister than Marxism-Leninism," according to Douglas E. Streusand. "That specter is Islam." The rise of political Islam in North Africa, especially the recent electoral strength of anti-liberal Islamic fundamentalist groups in Algeria; the birth of several independent Moslem republics in Central Asia whose political orientation is unclear; and the regional and international ties fostered by Islamic governments in Iran and Sudan are all producing, as *Washington Post* columnist Jim Hoagland put it, an "urge to identify Islam as an inherently anti-democratic force that is America's new global enemy now that the Cold War is over."

"Islamic fundamentalism is an aggressive revolutionary movement as militant and violent as the Bolshevik, Fascist, and Nazi movements of the past," according to Amos Perlmutter. It is "authoritarian, anti-democratic, anti-secular," and cannot be reconciled with the "Christian-secular universe," and its goal is the establishment of a "totalitarian Islamic state" in the Middle East, he argued, suggesting that the United States should make sure the movement is "stifled at birth."

## The Gulf War and the Green Peril

The Islam vs. West paradigm, reflected in such observations, is beginning to infect Washington. That development recalls the efforts by some of Washington's iron triangles [interest groups] as well as by foreign players during the months leading up to the 1990–91 Persian Gulf crisis. Their use of the media succeeded in building up Saddam Hussein as the "most dangerous man in the world" and as one of America's first new post–Cold War bogeymen. Those efforts, including allegations that Iraq had plans to dominate the Middle East, helped to condition the American public and elites for the U.S. intervention in the gulf.

---

### Islam: A New Global Enemy

The Cold War has barely ended, but already the search seems to be on for a new global, universal enemy—around which the United States can orient its foreign policy. . . . Topping the global-threat list has been our all-too-reliable nemesis: fundamentalist Islam.

Islam seems in many ways to fit the bill, enemy-wise: It's big; it's scary; it's anti-Western; it feeds on poverty and discontent; it spreads across vast swaths of the globe that can be colored green on the television maps in the same way that Communist countries used to be colored red.

Already, strategists are invoking familiar Cold War concepts: "containment" of Iranian influence in Central Asia; the drawing of "red lines" for the Muslim fundamentalist leaders of Sudan, warning them against any export of terrorism or revolution; an "iron fist" military coup in Algeria in 1992 to prevent Muslims from winning elections there.

David Ignatius, *The Washington Post National Weekly Edition*, March 16-22, 1992.

---

There is a major difference between the Saddam-the-bogeyman caricature and the Green Peril. Notwithstanding the Saddam-is-Hitler rhetoric, the Iraqi leader was perceived as merely a dangerous "thug" who broke the rules of the game and whom Washington could suppress by military force. Saddam's Iraq was a threat to a regional balance of power, not to the American way of life.

The alleged threat from Iran and militant Islam is different. The struggle between that force and the West is portrayed as a zero-sum game that can end only in the defeat of one of the sides. The Iranian ayatollahs and their allies—"revolutionary," "fanatic," and "suicidal" people that they are—cannot be co-opted into balance-of-power arrangements by rewards and are even seen as immune to military and diplomatic threats. One can reach a tactical compromise with them—such as the agreement with Lebanese Shi'ite groups to release the American hostages—but on the strategic level the expectation is for a long, drawn-out battle.

199

Indeed, like the Red Menace of the Cold War era, the Green Peril is perceived as a cancer spreading around the globe, undermining the legitimacy of Western values and political systems. The cosmic importance of the confrontation would make it necessary for Washington to adopt a long-term diplomatic and military strategy; to forge new and solid alliances; to prepare the American people for a never-ending struggle that will test their resolve; and to develop new containment policies, new doctrines, and a new foreign policy elite with its "wise men" and "experts."

## Islam Replaces Communism

There are dangerous signs that the process of creating a monolithic threat out of isolated events and trends in the Moslem world is already beginning. The Green Peril thesis is now being used to explain diverse and unrelated events in that region, with Tehran replacing Moscow as the center of ideological subversion and military expansionism and Islam substituting for the spiritual energy of communism.

Islam does seem to fit the bill as the ideal post–Cold War villain. "It's big; it's scary; it's anti-Western; it feeds on poverty and discontent," wrote David Ignatius, adding that Islam "spreads across vast swaths of the globe that can be colored green on the television maps in the same way that communist countries used to be colored red."

Foreign policy experts are already using the familiar Cold War jargon to describe the coming struggle with Islam. There is talk about the need to "contain" Iranian influence around the globe, especially in Central Asia, which seemed to be the main reason for Secretary of State James A. Baker III's February 1992 stop in that region. Strategists are beginning to draw a "red line" for the fundamentalist leaders of Sudan, as evidenced by a U.S. diplomat's statement in November 1991 warning Khartoum to refrain from "exporting" revolution and terrorism. Washington's policymakers even applauded the January 1992 Algerian "iron fist" military coup that prevented an Islamic group from winning the elections. The notion that we have to stop the fundamentalists somewhere echoes the Cold War's domino theory.

"Geopolitically, Iran's targets are four—the Central Asian republics, the Maghreb or North Africa, Egypt and other neighboring Arab countries, and the Persian Gulf states," explained Hoover Institution senior fellow Arnold Beichman, who is raising the Moslem alarm. Beichman suggested that "the first major target" for radical Iran and its militant strategy would be "oil-rich, militarily weak Saudi Arabia, keeper of Islam's holy places and OPEC's decisionmaker on world oil prices." If the West does not meet that challenge, a Green Curtain will be drawn across the crescent of instability, and "the Middle East and the once Soviet Central Asian republics could become in a few years the cultural and political dependencies of the most expansionist militarized regime in the world today, a regime for which terrorism is a governing norm," he warned.

## The Making of a "Peril"

The Islamic threat argument is becoming increasingly popular with some segments of the American foreign policy establishment. They are encouraged by foreign governments who, for reasons of self-interest, want to see Washington embroiled in the coming West vs. Islam confrontation. The result is the construction of the new peril, a process that does not reflect any grand conspiracy but that nevertheless has its own logic, rules and timetables.

The creation of a peril usually starts with mysterious "sources" and unnamed officials who leak information, float trial balloons, and warn about the coming threat. Those sources reflect debates and discussions taking place within government. Their information is then augmented by colorful intelligence reports that finger exotic and conspiratorial terrorists and military advisers. Journalists then search for the named and other villains. The media end up finding corroboration from foreign sources who form an informal coalition with the sources in the U.S. government and help the press uncover further information substantiating the threat coming from the new bad guys.

In addition, think tank studies and op-ed pieces add momentum to the official spin. Their publication is followed by congressional hearings, policy conferences, and public press briefings. A governmental policy debate ensues, producing studies, working papers, and eventually doctrines and policies that become part of the media's spin. The new villain is now ready to be integrated into the popular culture to help to mobilize public support for a new crusade. In the case of the Green Peril, that process has been under way since October 1991.

A series of leaks, signals, and trial balloons is already beginning to shape U.S. agenda and policy. . . . The Bush administration tried to devise policies and establish new alliances to counter Iranian influence: building up Islamic but secular and pro-Western Turkey as a countervailing force in Central Asia, expanding U.S. commitments to Saudi Arabia, warning Sudan that it faces grave consequences as a result of its policies, and even shoring up a socialist military dictatorship in Algeria.

Not surprisingly, foreign governments, including those of Turkey, Saudi Arabia, Egypt, Israel, India, and Pakistan, have reacted to the evidence of U.S. fear. With the end of the Cold War they are concerned about a continued U.S. commitment to them and are trying to exploit the menace of Islamic fundamentalism to secure military support, economic aid, and political backing from Washington as well as to advance their own domestic and regional agendas. The Gulf War has already provided the Turks, Saudis, Egyptians, and Israelis with an opportunity to revive the American engagement in the Middle East and their own roles as Washington's regional surrogates. Now that the Iraqi danger has been diminished, the Islamic fundamentalist threat is a new vehicle for achieving those goals.

## Regional Powers Exploit U.S. Fears

Pakistan, which lost its strategic value to the United States as a conduit of military aid to the guerrillas in Afghanistan, and India, whose Cold War Soviet ally has disintegrated, are both competing for American favors by using the Islamic card in their struggle for power in Southwest Asia. That struggle involves such issues as the Kashmir problem [the dispute between India and neighboring Pakistan over ownership of Kashmir] and an accelerating nuclear arms race.

Even such disparate entities as Australia and the Iranian Mojahedin opposition forces are conducting public relations and lobbying efforts in the United States based on the Islamic fundamentalist threat. Colin Rubenstein in February 1992 discussed the need to maintain an American military presence in Asia to contain the power of the Moslem government in Malaysia, which according to him has adopted increasingly repressive measures at home and has been developing military ties with Libya as part of a strategy to spread its radical Islamic message in Asia. If Washington refuses to project its diplomatic and military power to contain the Malaysian-produced Islamic threat in Asia, there is a danger that the United States and Australia will soon face anti-American and anti-Israeli blocs, Rubenstein insisted.

The Iranian opposition group, which in the past has subscribed to socialist and anti-American positions, is now interested in maintaining U.S. pressure on the government of President Hashemi Rafsanjani and in winning Western public support. To achieve those goals it is playing up the possibility of a Tehran-led political terrorist campaign aimed at creating an "Islamic bloc" in Central Asia, the Middle East, and North Africa and suggesting that to avoid such a campaign Washington should back the Mojahedin in Tehran.

Even Washington's long-time nemesis—the hard-core Marxist and former Soviet ally, former president Mohammad Najibullah of Afghanistan, against whom the United States helped sponsor Pakistani-directed guerrilla warfare—a few days before his ouster from power offered his services in the new struggle against the radical Islamic threat. "We have a common task, Afghanistan, the United States of America, and the civilized world, to launch a joint struggle against fundamentalism," he explained. Najibullah warned Washington that unless he was kept in power, Islamic fundamentalists would take over Afghanistan and turn it into a "center of world smuggling for narcotic drugs" and a "center for terrorism.". . .

## Is Political Islam a Threat?

There is no easy answer to the question of whether Islam and democracy are compatible. As John L. Esposito and James P. Piscatori put it, "History has shown that nations and religious traditions are capable of having multiple and major ideological interpretations or reorientations." The transformation of European principalities, whose rule was justified by divine right, into modern Western democratic states was accompanied by religious reform. Christian tradition, which once supported political absolutism, was reinterpreted to accept the democratic ideal.

Islam also lends itself to various interpretations and has been used to support democracy, dictatorship, republicanism, and monarchy. Some leaders of Islamic movements have adopted a negative attitude toward democracy as an expression of their rejection of European colonial influence and, more recently, of U.S. intervention in the Middle East.

Islamic fundamentalism should not be considered "a disease that spreads willy-nilly to infect whole populations." Like Protestant fundamentalism, argues David Ignatius, it is a "religious response to the confusion and contradictions of the modern world." It is not inconceivable that the new Islamic force will play the same constructive political role that the Protestant reformation played in Europe.

In most Middle Eastern countries, including Algeria and Iran, Islamic fundamentalism is already sweeping away the corrupt old political order of the Arab world. Indeed, according to Ignatius, "support for the fundamentalists in Algeria, as in Iran, has come in part from the bazaar, from the merchants and small businessmen who have been ignited by the statist regime."

One question that troubles many analysts is whether the Islamic movement will tolerate diversity when in power or try to impose an intolerant monolithic order on society. The record of the Islamic experiments in Iran, Pakistan, and Sudan is mixed. Those governments have used power to discriminate against minorities and women and to repress dissidents. But their record has not been worse—and in some cases it has been better—than that of secular regimes or more traditional monarchies.

"Based on the record thus far," wrote Esposito and Piscatori, "one can expect that where Islamic movements come to power in the Middle East, they will have problems similar to those of secular governments in the region." That is especially true where democratic institutions are weak and political pluralism and human rights remain sources of tension and conflict.

The danger for the Western nations, in particular the United States, is that misperceptions will cloud their judgment of and produce counterproductive policies toward Islam and the Middle East. Instead of viewing Islam as a monolithic force, Western analysts and policymakers should recognize that it is a diverse civilization, divided along cultural, ideological, religious, ethnic, and national lines. Even the term "Islamic fundamentalism" should perhaps be modified to reflect the different movements and groups that are lumped into that category.

Moreover, neither Islam nor Islamic fundamentalism is by definition "anti-Western." As noted, the anti-American attitudes of Islamic groups and movements in the Middle East are not directed against Christianity or Western civilization per se. They are instead a reaction to U.S. policies, especially Washington's support for authoritarian regimes and the long history of U.S. military intervention.

American policies that stem from political, economic, and military interests are bound to lead to more incidents that pit the United States against the forces of political and economic change in the Middle East. Political players in both the United States and the Middle East fan the fear of the Green Peril as a way of maintaining public support for policies that serve their self-interest. The interests of the iron triangles are, however, not necessarily synonymous with those of the American nation.

Although it is not in America's interest to launch a crusade for democracy, neither is it in her interest to be perceived as the guarantor of the status quo and the major obstacle to reform. Now that the Cold War is over, Washington should not be searching for a new enemy; instead, it should view regional conflicts with detachment, realizing that they will rarely pose a danger to America's security.

*"Islam has bloody borders."*

# Islamic Civilization Will Clash with Western Civilization

Samuel P. Huntington

In the following viewpoint, Samuel P. Huntington argues that future international conflicts will occur along the lines that divide the Western, Islamic, Slavic-Orthodox Christian, and other civilizations. Although economic modernization and social change are weakening local, tribal, and national identities, Huntington contends, civilization-consciousness is stronger and is being enhanced. Because the Islamic world is unable to compete economically, according to Huntington, it is likely that military conflict will occur between the Islamic civilization and its neighbors. Huntington is director of the Olin Institute for Strategic Studies at Harvard University and is author of *The Third Wave: Democratization in the Late Twentieth Century.*

As you read, consider the following questions:

1. How does Huntington define civilization?
2. According to Huntington, how do economic modernization and social change affect people's identities?
3. How long has the West been in conflict with Islamic civilization, according to the author?

World politics is entering a new phase, and intellectuals have not hesitated to proliferate visions of what it will be—the end of history, the return of traditional rivalries between nation states, and the decline of the nation state from the conflicting pulls of tribalism and globalism, among others. Each of these visions catches aspects of the emerging reality. Yet they all miss a crucial, indeed a central, aspect of what global politics is likely to be in the coming years.

It is my hypothesis that the fundamental source of conflict in this new world will not be primarily ideological or primarily economic. The great divisions among humankind and the dominating source of conflict will be cultural. Nation states will remain the most powerful actors in world affairs, but the principal conflicts of global politics will occur between nations and groups of different civilizations. The clash of civilizations will dominate global politics. The fault lines between civilizations will be the battle lines of the future. . . .

## The Nature of Civilizations

During the Cold War the world was divided into the First, Second and Third Worlds. Those divisions are no longer relevant. It is far more meaningful now to group countries not in terms of their political or economic systems or in terms of their level of economic development but rather in terms of their culture and civilization.

What do we mean when we talk of a civilization? A civilization is a cultural entity. Villages, regions, ethnic groups, nationalities, religious groups, all have distinct cultures at different levels of cultural heterogeneity. The culture of a village in southern Italy may be different from that of a village in northern Italy, but both will share in a common Italian culture that distinguishes them from German villages. European communities, in turn, will share cultural features that distinguish them from Arab or Chinese communities. Arabs, Chinese and Westerners, however, are not part of any broader cultural entity. They constitute civilizations. A civilization is thus the highest cultural grouping of people and the broadest level of cultural identity people have short of that which distinguishes humans from other species. It is defined both by common objective elements, such as language, history, religion, customs, institutions, and by the subjective self-identification of people. People have levels of identity: a resident of Rome may define himself with varying degrees of intensity as a Roman, an Italian, a Catholic, a Christian, a European, a Westerner. The civilization to which he belongs is the broadest level of identification with which he intensely identifies. . . .

Civilization identity will be increasingly important in the future, and the world will be shaped in large measure by the interactions among seven or eight major civilizations. These include Western, Confucian, Japanese, Islamic, Hindu, Slavic-Orthodox, Latin American and possibly African civilization. The most important conflicts of the future will occur along the cultural fault lines separating these civilizations from one another.

## The Islamic World

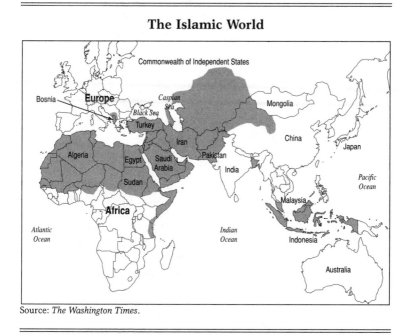

Source: *The Washington Times.*

Why will this be the case?

First, differences among civilizations are not only real; they are basic. Civilizations are differentiated from each other by history, language, culture, tradition and, most important, religion. The people of different civilizations have different views on the relations between God and man, the individual and the group, the citizen and the state, parents and children, husband and wife, as well as differing views of the relative importance of rights and responsibilities, liberty and authority, equality and hierarchy. These differences are the product of centuries. They will not soon disappear. They are far more fundamental than differences among political ideologies and political regimes. Differences do not necessarily mean conflict, and conflict does not necessarily mean violence. Over the centuries, however, differences among civilizations have generated the most prolonged and the most violent conflicts.

Second, the world is becoming a smaller place. The interactions between peoples of different civilizations are increasing; these increasing interactions intensify civilization-consciousness and awareness of differences between civilizations and commonalities within civilizations. North African immigration to France generates hostility among Frenchmen and at the same time increased receptivity to immigration by "good" European Catholic Poles. Americans react far more negatively to Japanese investment than to larger investments from Canada and European countries. Similarly, as Donald Horowitz has pointed out, "An Ibo may be . . . an Owerri Ibo or an Onitsha Ibo in what was the Eastern region of Nigeria. In Lagos, he is simply an Ibo. In London, he is a Nigerian. In New York, he is an African." The interactions among peoples of different civilizations enhance the civilization-consciousness of people that, in turn, invigorates differences and animosities stretching or thought to stretch back deep into history.

## The Revival of Religion and Culture

Third, the processes of economic modernization and social change throughout the world are separating people from long-standing local identities. They also weaken the nation state as a source of identity. In much of the world religion has moved in to fill this gap, often in the form of movements that are labeled "fundamentalist." Such movements are found in Western Christianity, Judaism, Buddhism and Hinduism, as well as in Islam. In most countries and most religions the people active in fundamentalist movements are young, college-educated, middle-class technicians, professionals and business persons. The "unsecularization of the world," George Weigel has remarked, "is one of the dominant social facts of life in the late twentieth century." The revival of religion, "la revanche de Dieu," as Gilles Kepel labeled it, provides a basis for identity and commitment that transcends national boundaries and unites civilizations.

Fourth, the growth of civilization-consciousness is enhanced by the dual role of the West. On the one hand, the West is at a peak of power. At the same time, however, and perhaps as a result, a return to the roots phenomenon is occurring among non-Western civilizations. Increasingly one hears references to trends toward a turning inward and "Asianization" in Japan, the end of the Nehru legacy and the "Hinduization" of India, the failure of Western ideas of socialism and nationalism and hence "re-Islamization" of the Middle East, and now a debate over Westernization versus Russianization in Boris Yeltsin's country. A West at the peak of its power confronts non-Wests that increasingly have the desire, the will and the resources to shape the world in non-Western ways.

In the past, the elites of non-Western societies were usually the people who were most involved with the West, had been educated at Oxford, the Sorbonne or Sandhurst, and had absorbed Western attitudes and values. At the same time, the populace in non-Western countries often remained deeply imbued with the indigenous culture. Now, however, these relationships are being reversed. A de-Westernization and indigenization of elites is occurring in many non-Western countries at the same time that Western, usually American, cultures, styles and habits become more popular among the mass of the people.

## Cultural Differences

Fifth, cultural characteristics and differences are less mutable and hence less easily compromised and resolved than political and economic ones. In the former Soviet Union, communists can become democrats, the rich can become poor and the poor rich, but Russians cannot become Estonians and Azeris cannot become Armenians. In class and ideological conflicts, the key question was "Which side are you on?" and people could and did choose sides and change sides. In conflicts between civilizations, the question is "What are you?" That is a given that cannot be changed. And as we know, from Bosnia to the Caucasus to the Sudan, the wrong answer to that question can mean a bullet in the head. Even more than ethnicity, religion discriminates sharply and exclusively among people. A person can be half-French and half-Arab and simultaneously even a citizen of two countries. It is more difficult to be half-Catholic and half-Muslim. . . .

As people define their identity in ethnic and religious terms, they are likely to see an "us" versus "them" relation existing between themselves and people of different ethnicity or religion. The end of ideologically defined states in Eastern Europe and the former Soviet Union permits traditional ethnic identities and animosities to come to the fore. Differences in culture and religion create differences over policy issues, ranging from human rights to immigration to trade and commerce to the environment. Geographical propinquity gives rise to conflicting territorial claims from Bosnia to Mindanao. Most important, the efforts of the West to promote its values of democracy and liberalism as universal values, to maintain its military predominance and to advance its economic interests engender countering responses from other civilizations. Decreasingly able to mobilize support and form coalitions on the basis of ideology, governments and groups will increasingly attempt to mobilize support by appealing to common religion and civilization identity.

The clash of civilizations thus occurs at two levels. At the microlevel, adjacent groups along the fault lines between civilizations struggle, often violently, over the control of territory and each other. At the macro-level, states from different civilizations compete for relative military and economic power, struggle over the control of international institutions and third parties, and competitively promote their particular political and religious values. . . .

## The Fault Lines Between Civilizations

Conflict along the fault line between Western and Islamic civilizations has been going on for 1,300 years. After the founding of Islam, the Arab and Moorish surge west and north only ended at Tours in 732. From the eleventh to the thirteenth century the Crusaders attempted with temporary success to bring Christianity and Christian rule to the Holy Land. From the fourteenth to the seventeenth century, the Ottoman Turks reversed the balance, extended their sway over the Middle East and the Balkans, captured Constantinople, and twice laid siege to Vienna. In the nineteenth and early twentieth centuries as Ottoman power declined Britain, France, and Italy established Western control over most of North Africa and the Middle East.

After World War II, the West, in turn, began to retreat; the colonial empires disappeared; first Arab nationalism and then Islamic fundamentalism manifested themselves; the West became heavily dependent on the Persian Gulf countries for its energy; the oil-rich Muslim countries became money-rich and, when they wished to, weapons-rich. Several wars occurred between Arabs and Israel (created by the West). France fought a bloody and ruthless war in Algeria for most of the 1950s; British and French forces invaded Egypt in 1956; American forces went into Lebanon in 1958; subsequently American forces returned to Lebanon, attacked Libya, and engaged in various military encounters with Iran; Arab and Islamic terrorists, supported by at least three Middle Eastern governments, employed the weapon of the weak and bombed Western planes and installations and seized Western hostages. This warfare between Arabs and the West culminated in 1990, when the United States sent a massive army to the Persian Gulf to defend some Arab countries against aggression by another. In its aftermath North Atlantic Treaty Organization (NATO) planning is increasingly directed to potential threats and instability along its "southern tier."

## Democracy and Demography Complicate Relations

This centuries-old military interaction between the West and Islam is unlikely to decline. It could become more virulent. The Gulf War left some Arabs feeling proud that Saddam Hussein had attacked Israel and stood up to the West. It also left many feeling humiliated and resentful of the West's military presence in the Persian Gulf, the West's overwhelming military dominance, and their apparent inability to shape their own destiny. Many Arab countries, in addition to the oil exporters, are reaching levels of economic and social development where autocratic forms of government become inappropriate and efforts to introduce democracy become stronger. Some openings in Arab political systems have already occurred. The principal beneficiaries of these openings have been Islamist movements. In the Arab world, in short, Western democracy strengthens anti-Western political forces. This may be a passing phenomenon, but it surely complicates relations between Islamic countries and the West.

Those relations are also complicated by demography. The spectacular population growth in Arab countries, particularly in North Africa, has led to increased migration to Western Europe. The movement within Western Europe toward minimizing internal boundaries has sharpened political sensitivities with respect to this development. In Italy, France and Germany, racism is increasingly open, and political reactions and violence against Arab and Turkish migrants have become more intense and more widespread since 1990.

On both sides the interaction between Islam and the West is seen as a clash of civilizations. The West's "next confrontation," observes M.J. Akbar, an Indian Muslim author, "is definitely going to come from the Muslim world. It is in the sweep of the Islamic nations from the Maghreb to Pakistan that the struggle for a new world order will begin." Bernard Lewis comes to a similar conclusion:

> We are facing a mood and a movement far transcending the level of issues and policies and the governments that pursue them. This is no less than a clash of civilizations—the perhaps irrational but surely historic reaction of an ancient rival against our Judeo-Christian heritage, our secular present, and the worldwide expansion of both. . . .

## Conflicts on Islam's Borders

On the northern border of Islam, conflict has increasingly erupted between Orthodox and Muslim peoples, including the carnage of Bosnia and Sarajevo, the simmering violence between Serb and Albanian, the tenuous relations between Bulgarians and their Turkish minority, the violence between Ossetians and Ingush, the unremitting slaughter of each other by Armenians and Azeris, the tense relations between Russians and Muslims in Central Asia, and the deployment of Russian troops to protect Russian interests in the Caucasus and Central Asia. Religion reinforces the revival of ethnic identities and restimulates Russian fears about the security of their southern borders. This concern is well captured by Archie Roosevelt:

> Much of Russian history concerns the struggle between the Slavs and the Turkic peoples on their borders, which dates back to the foundation of the Russian state more than a thousand

years ago. In the Slavs' millennium-long confrontation with their eastern neighbors lies the key to an understanding not only of Russian history, but Russian character. To understand Russian realities today one has to have a concept of the great Turkic ethnic group that has preoccupied Russians through the centuries.

. . . The interactions between civilizations vary greatly in the extent to which they are likely to be characterized by violence. Economic competition clearly predominates between the American and European subcivilizations of the West and between both of them and Japan. On the Eurasian continent, however, the proliferation of ethnic conflict, epitomized at the extreme in "ethnic cleansing," has not been totally random. It has been most frequent and most violent between groups belonging to different civilizations. In Eurasia the great historic fault lines between civilizations are once more aflame. This is particularly true along the boundaries of the crescent-shaped Islamic bloc of nations from the bulge of Africa to central Asia. Violence also occurs between Muslims, on the one hand, and Orthodox Serbs in the Balkans, Jews in Israel, Hindus in India, Buddhists in Burma and Catholics in the Philippines. Islam has bloody borders.

*"We may be on the threshold of a new, mutually beneficial relationship between Islam and the West."*

# Islamic Civilization Need Not Clash with Western Civilization

Rachid Gannouchi

In the following viewpoint, translated by Ahmad AbulJobain, Rachid Gannouchi argues that the confrontation between Islam and the West must be understood in light of the history of Western cultural and political domination of the Islamic world. There are two paths that the relationship of Islam and the West can take in the future, according to Gannouchi: The West can continue its confrontational course, promoting development and democracy only where that serves its interests; or the West can cooperate with the political development furthered by the Islamic political movements, which represent real democracy and an end to colonialism. Gannouchi, a founding member of Tunisia's outlawed al-Nahda, or Renaissance Movement, lives in exile in England.

As you read, consider the following questions:

1. What is the double standard of the Western agenda toward Eastern Europe and the Muslim world, according to the author?
2. What are the four indicators of a positive relationship between Islam and the West that Gannouchi points out?

Excerpted from Rachid Gannouchi, "Islam and the West: Realities and Potentialities," in *The Politics of Islamic Resurgence: Through Western Eyes* by Ahmad Bin Yousef and Ahmad AbulJobain, published by the United Association for Studies and Research, Inc., 1992. Reprinted with permission.

The manner in which Islam's relationship to the West is addressed will be an essential determinant of the future—whether peace and prosperity will reign or the world will succumb to wars and devastation. To evaluate the years to come, one must study the past and evaluate the relationship that has existed thus far. Once such retrospection has occurred, determining the possible ramifications for the future becomes an easier objective.

Realistically, one is compelled to resort to simplification when tackling the arduous task of distinguishing between two civilizations—particularly those that have preserved their inherent characteristics in spite of a number of socio-political upheavals. The endeavor is substantially more difficult when trying to reconcile the differences between the Islamic and Western civilizations.

## Defining Islamic and Western Civilization

The Islamic civilization's history is less problematic to define. The intrinsic qualities of Muslim culture, evolving nearly fifteen centuries ago in the Arabian Peninsula, were formed concurrently with the message of Islam. They flourished through trade, conquest, and propagation. Physically, towns and states ensued; and intellectually, literature, the sciences, and humanities developed. Battles were won and lost, as were the spoils of conquest. Although the infrastructure created by decades of progress, and at times decadence, did not last long, it instilled within a global Muslim *ummah*, or community, an undeniable allegiance and affinity to its ideals. It has been a unifying force, bonding disparate peoples—who adhere to the same religious authorities— on the basis of a mutual history and theology. The principles of Islam have maintained the concept of one *ummah* throughout the past, and continue to link divergent cultures. No contemporary political or ideological platform can boast similar achievements.

Thus, when discussing Islam within its socio-cultural context—one based purely on ideological factors and ignoring the barriers normally raised by color, race and language—the issues are defined with relative ease. The West, however, emanates from a vastly different background and must be broken down into its distinct units to be understood. Whereas Muslim cultural development was based on the values, lessons, and standards set by Islamic ideals, Western civilization has been profoundly affected by several societal structures that were empires in and of themselves.

The West evolved from rich and vibrant Greek roots. It was then enriched and expanded by the Roman influence. Once it embraced Christianity, it fluctuated between progress and regress. As the Islamic empire reached its apogee, Western nations had fallen into a state of debauchery and decadence characterized by religious wars, feudalism, intolerance, intellectual repression, and moral regression. Nevertheless, with the advent of religious reform, scientific discovery, liberalization, and industrialization, the two civilizations exchanged positions. The Middle Ages gave way to the eventual domination of the world by Western powers.

## Western Cultural Imperialism

This ascendancy, dating back two centuries, did not seek justification in the righteous conversion of heathens native to the Americas, Africa, and Asia as did the original Christian missionaries. Rather, the concept of scientific fundamentalism (*intégrisme scientiste*)—the transfer of secular, scientific values to the primitive nations who lived under the hegemony of the theological age (*age théologique*)—underscored the colonial expansion. The tenets of such ideologies were defined by several European thinkers, among whom were John Stuart Mill and August Comte.

The export of knowledge, however, was not predicated on a desire for mutual cooperation or understanding. Western civilization was being implicitly forced upon the colonized nations. Jules Ferry, a French official, addressed parliament averring: "Upper races have a practical right over the lesser races." He continued, "[the Human Rights Declaration] was not written to serve blacks in tropical Africa." This was the colonial philosophy that accentuated the supremacy of the West over other nations. The unwritten law, therefore, was that human rights were inapplicable to non-White, unchristian peoples.

This inherent desire to dominate motivated the 1990–91 Western campaign in the Gulf [the Persian Gulf war]. International law was a convenient tool, rather than a universal dictum to be applied evenhandedly. Apparently, enforcement of these legal doctrines is dependent on the geo-political nature of the countries involved, i.e. whether they are Western or Third World. The Gulf campaign objectives were three-fold: 1) control of oil resources, 2) protection of Israel, and 3) the attainment of U.S. hegemony, not only over the Middle East, but also over the Western world. . . .

## Possibilities for the Future West-Islam Relationship

When Islam comes to power, a reality likely to occur fairly soon, what are the prospects for the development of a relationship between it and the West? Simply put, there are two possible paths to follow.

First, a perpetuation of the general Western mode of tarnishing the image of political Islam can continue. This has traditionally taken the form of portraying the Islamic trend as the antithesis of humanity's achievements—democracy, freedom, women's rights, the arts, tolerance, progress, and plurality. Such nega-

tivism is manifest in the pejorative use of terms such as fundamentalism, radicalism, and extremism, which embody the mis-
perception of an Islamic threat. Many Western observers believe
the Middle East to be incapable of embracing freedom and prosperity. This static view dictates that the region will always be an
enemy of, rather than a partner to, progress.

## U.S. Policy Toward Islam

The U.S. government does not view Islam as the next "ism" confronting the West or threatening world peace. That is an overly
simplistic response to a complex reality.

The Cold War is not being replaced with a new competition between Islam and the West. It is evident that the Crusades have
been over for a long time . . . Americans recognize Islam as one of
the world's great faiths. It is practiced on every continent. It counts
among its adherents millions of citizens of the U.S. As Westerners
we acknowledge Islam as a historic civilizing force among the
many that have influenced and enriched our culture. . . .

In countries throughout the Middle East and North Africa, we
thus see groups or movements seeking to reform their societies in
keeping with Islamic ideals. There is considerable diversity in
how these ideals are expressed. We detect no monolithic or coor-
dinated international effort behind these movements. What we do
see are believers living in different countries placing renewed emphasis on Islamic principles and governments accommodating
Islamist political activity to varying degrees and in different ways.

Edward P. Djerejian, *New Perspectives Quarterly*, Summer 1993.

This attitude is nurtured and reinforced, in addition to the historic legacy, by a hostile media establishment, a determined
missionary effort, and prejudicial research centers and universities. Regrettably, it is also accentuated by the ignorance and reactionary actions of Muslims who express antagonism towards
the accomplishments of humanity in areas such as civil liberties, human rights, and so on. The Islamic image has also suffered considerably at the hands of despots who, seeking to legitimate the injustices perpetrated under their authoritarian rule,
invoke religion to whitewash their crimes.

Nevertheless, the West remains guilty of hypocrisy at the very
least. No example better serves my argument than the Bosnian
crisis. On the one hand, we find a sympathetic Western conscience responding to the televised Serbian atrocities by voicing
their abhorrence. On the other, however, Western decision-
makers have remained mute to the uproar reverberating among

their people. In fact, politicians have issued a barrage of statements designed to give the appearance of forthcoming action and to conceal resolute inaction. The London Conference [proposing a division of Bosnia to end the civil war] clearly demonstrated these reprehensible tactics. It revealed two realities: 1) the maxim that interests supersede principles and 2) the apparent revulsion to the notion of a national, Muslim entity within the European geo-political sphere.

Furthermore Bosnia, unlike Kuwait, does not contain precious oil wells that demand immediate, decisive Western acts of bravery. Since no tangible spoils will be gained, the neo-fascist Serbian genocide of the Muslims will find no "lines drawn in the sand." International law is apparently inapplicable to the Bosnian slaughterhouse, where intervention is confined to token declarations of being "deeply disturbed" by events. . . . The tragedy of Bosnia echoes the afflictions of Africans, Native Americans, Andalusians, Palestinians, and many others.

## The Western Agenda as Seen by Muslims

Events in Bosnia underscore the international, political agendas set by Western powers regarding weaker nations. First, the pretentious declaration of universal human rights and principles is selective. And second, less powerful nations that pose the slightest obstacle to Western goals are doomed. To be sure, Bosnia has leveled the hopes of all those who, particularly during the Gulf crisis, saw a just peace emerging from the American version of a New World Order. The post–Cold War era, far from initiating justice based on truth rather than power-politics, has furthered suspicions within the Muslim *ummah* that the international legal system, embodied in the United Nations' charter, is aimed at their subjugation rather than their emancipation.

The Western agenda—ratified repeatedly by policy-makers for centuries—has sought the stagnation of Muslim productivity. It prevents the Muslim world from reentering the global community as an equal partner. The concept of a Muslim entity embracing modernity, on its own terms, seems to be a reality held in the highest contempt by Western powers. One example is the blind eye, and discreet assistance, accorded India in its drive for nuclearization. Pakistan, however, as a Muslim state is chastised for its efforts, which are actively opposed. On an intranational basis, tyrannies are pampered while opponents are persecuted.

The justification proffered is the threat of extremism—a tide emphatically rejected by the mainstream of political Islam. Thus, what becomes evident to us is that the West is not motivated by the desire for democracy, modernism, human rights, international legitimacy, or even the spread of Christianity. The overwhelming evidence points towards preservation of interests,

217

which necessitate domination of the world by controlling its resources and hampering its growth. Islam and its people, territory, culture, and civilization have traditionally been deemed
obstacles to the colonial tendencies of the West—erstwhile phys-
ical masters and currently ideological expansionists, aided by
force when necessary.

This overall desire for hegemony has caused world wars, civil
wars, and battles fought on the soil of others. It has shattered
the socio-cultural structures that unify people and demeaned the
communal values that maintain high standards of conscience.
Man has been reduced to an isolated being in densely populated
regions, which has led to the miseries associated with disunity,
conflict, materialism, individualism, selfishness, and hypocrisy.

## The Double Standards of the West

The double-standards are clearest when two revolutionary
trends, occurring simultaneously in Eastern Europe and the
Muslim world, are treated with a markedly bipolar attitude. The
democratic drive was given full support in the former—not due
to its sacredness, but because it was politically prudent in combating the spread of socialism by fragmenting it. Conversely,
democracy in the Muslim world would unify its people, topple
autocratic regimes, and ignite an irreversible trend of progress.
Such a synthesis would pose, by Western definition, serious obstacles to their interests, which are tied to the current dictatorships. For this reason, the falsification of elections and mass, far-
cical trials in Tunisia, as well as the theft and oppression of the
Algerian freedom of choice, are met with insincere objections.

It is amazing that the West, a pioneer in the fields of espionage and intelligence, acted as though Saddam Hussein's
despotism was a revelation that materialized on August 2, 1990.
Was he a democrat when he received an abundance of military
and economic aid from the West? The atrocious crimes committed against the Iraqi people did not precede the Gulf crisis by
days; they had been in full force for years. And what of Kuwait?
Did the monarchy present a beacon of democratic ideals that attracted over thirty nations to intervene on its behalf?

And so, when the Muslim people lose faith in Western values
(wanting instead to revive their own) and express the agonies that
riddle their psyches due to so much injustice, how can they be
blamed? I often remind myself of the tortured slave, Epictetus.
When subjected to the humiliation and abuse of his Roman master, he resolved to endure the pain no matter how excruciating it
became. And when, at one point, he heard his legs break, he
turned with dignity to the Roman and said: "Master, my legs have
broken and I am in pain." And so must I, and the Muslim *ummah*,
suffer our burdens yet make our grievances known with dignity,

and not reaction.

There is, however, as I mentioned earlier, another path, positive in tone, which the Western-Islamic relationship could conceivably follow. Several indicators have highlighted the possibility of such a development.

First are the unprecedented statements made by Edward P. Djerejian, Assistant Secretary of State for Near Eastern and South Asian Affairs during 1992. He clarified the American government's position by stating: "We do not view Islam as the next 'ism' confronting the West or threatening world peace. That is an overly simplistic reaction to a complex reality. It is evident that the Crusades have been over for a long time." Even prior to this speech, he had noted the immense contributions made to civilization by the rich, Islamic heritage. He also pointed out that millions of American citizens adhere to Islamic principles, which was proof in itself that the Islamic trend was not a monolithic entity. Djerejian asserted that the United States was against extremism in any form, regardless of the ideology behind it.

## A New Relationship?

In light of such positive remarks, we may be on the threshold of a new, mutually beneficial relationship between Islam and the West. Many Western scholars have also contributed immensely to bridging the ideological divide, such as Francois Burgat in France and John L. Esposito in the United States.

Second, elements of the Western media have been far more receptive to the afflictions of the Muslim world in recent years than in the past. Broad coverage of the heartbreaking famine consuming Somalia; the frequent, detailed reports of the Bosnian tragedy; and the objective, if not frequent, news of the Palestinian *intifada* (uprising) have all earned the media recognition for their drive towards accurate reporting in their profession.

Third, the resolute efforts of human rights organizations, political parties, and diplomats are a testament to the fact that the West, like the Islamic revival, is not a monolithic entity with a singular philosophy of subjugation. These groups have exerted sincere efforts to expose the inhumane politics implemented by despots in the Muslim world, particularly in North Africa. The Islamists are grateful to these people who operate from France, the United Kingdom, and the United States. In the case of Tunisia, the results of their intervention, be it direct or otherwise, have saved many of the Islamists' lives who were slated for execution, but whose sentences were commuted to life imprisonment.

The final indicator stems from the relatively new phenomenon of Muslim communities in Western cities, as well as the rapid conversion of many believers to Islam. . . . Today Islam is recognized as the second largest religious community in many Western nations, with some exceptions such as Belgium. Mosques are plentiful and generally accepted as part of the cities in which they stand. . . .

As far as the dictates of Islam regarding other faiths are concerned, there can be no doubts. Islam recognizes fully the rights of others to coexist peacefully with Muslims. Islamic law prohibits compulsion in religion and, as a result, no non-Muslims should be fearful of persecution in an Islamic polity. . . .

### Confronting Extremism

I do not deny the existence of extreme, radical elements within certain Muslim circles. As Roger Garaudy, the prominent, French Muslim thinker, said: "This phenomenon poses a paramount threat to Islam. Fanaticism, in general, is one of the most detrimental factors facing the world community."

The abundance of antagonists in the Third World, however, did not materialize without provocation. They emerged as a reaction to the legacy of oppression, degradation, and injustice which accompanied Europe's Renaissance. They rebelled against the "White Man's Burden," which preached civility but sought conquest and the paralysis of Third World development.

Nevertheless, extremes are inexcusable and must be confronted. However, confrontation does not connote violence. The most lethal weapon available to sap radicalism of its strength incorporates the promotion of dialogue, freedom, and respect for human rights. These elements, applied without prejudice, will constitute an impregnable barrier to the spread of intolerance.

Technological progress has converted disparate nations into a world community. Regional conflicts, no matter how seemingly isolated, have assumed universal dimensions by virtue of widespread transportation and communication capabilities. Therefore, contemporary conflicts represent a precarious situation for the global community. If dialogue, mutual cooperation, and farsighted planning for the future are not achieved, then humanity will plummet towards self-destruction.

I have neither the resources of human rights activists and environmental activists, nor do I produce the enormous amount of literature prepared by learned men, nor are my admonishments as well-known as those of many philosophers. Yet I can rely on one source, next to which these others pale, to concisely instruct humanity on the imperative of coexistence and cooperation rather than blind hatred and senseless violence.

None can hope to equal Qur'anic verses, including the one advising Man: "We created you from a single (pair) of male and female, and made you into nations and tribes, that you may know each other (not that you may despise each other). Verily the most honoured of you in the sight of Allah is (he who is) the most righteous of you."

Were people to study such verses and look deeper, without prejudice, into the dynamics of Islam, the perceived threat would dissipate. The extensive research and magnanimous comments made by several Western intellectuals have signaled a reversal of the ancient egocentricism, born either of self-interests or of inherited misperceptions, regarding Muslims. In addition, contemporary scholarly activity is also tempered with a knowledge of Arabic, enhancing the appreciation of Islamic culture.

Once these efforts are complemented in diplomatic circles, the walls dividing the two civilizations will become bridges. Recent history witnessed the ignorance of politicians whose knowledge of Islamic language, both literal and metaphysical, was limited to colonial tales and not experience.

It is our sincere hope that the trend towards an unbiased quest for knowledge and the increased awareness of Islam will result in a better understanding of the Muslims and an added respect for their faith. It is upon the common principles we share that Muslims and Westerners can establish a mutually beneficial relationship. There can be no escaping the reality that the destinies of our respective civilizations are intertwined.

*"You don't always get what you want when you have a democracy."*

# Democratization in the Middle East Does Not Threaten the West

R. Scott Appleby

In December 1991, the Islamic Salvation Front (FIS) won a near-majority of parliamentary seats in Algeria's first democratic election. In the following viewpoint, R. Scott Appleby argues that the Islamic party's electoral success, although it was subsequently nullified by a military coup, reveals that Islamic fundamentalism is gaining popular appeal in the Middle East. Appleby contends that the West is wrong to perceive this growth of Islamic fundamentalism as antithetical to democracy and a threat to the West. He concludes that the West should promote democratization in the Middle East—even if it brings fundamentalists to power—or risk inflaming anti-Western sentiments within Muslim countries. Appleby is associate director of the Fundamentalism Project of the American Academy of Arts and Sciences and coeditor of *Fundamentalisms Observed*.

As you read, consider the following questions:

1. According to Appleby, are Algerian supporters of the FIS interested in democracy? Explain.
2. How does the author define "the Arab problem"?
3. What are some of the secular problems that an Islamic party would have to solve in Algeria, according to Appleby?

From R. Scott Appleby, "The Arab Problem and the Islamic Solution." Copyright 1992, Christian Century Foundation. Reprinted, by permission, from the February 19, 1992, issue of *The Christian Century*.

Lest the Western allies become drunk on their apparent invincibility, what with the instant victory over the forces of Saddam Hussein and the protracted but no less successful resolution of the cold war, the Muslims of the Middle East and North Africa have served notice that they have their own ideas about the design of the "new world order." It is unwise to generalize about the various Islamic fundamentalisms spanning an arc from Morocco to the gulf emirates; the diverse Muslim responses to the gulf crisis dispelled any lingering notions of a monolithic "political Islam." Nonetheless, one may expect that in the future "the Islamic current" will gain prominence in shaping the social and political order in the Middle East.

## The Algerian Elections

Several events of 1992 suggest as much. Most dramatic is the situation in Algeria, where the fundamentalist Islamic Salvation Front (FIS) was poised to assume a commanding majority in parliament until President Chadli Benjedid of the ruling National Liberation Front resigned on January 11, delivering the government into the hands of the military and effectively ending Algeria's three-year experiment in democracy. By winning 180 of 231 contested seats in the first free national election since Algeria gained independence from France in 1962, the Islamists surprised even the most pessimistic of their secular opponents, none of whom had predicted that the Islamists would win more than one-third of the popular vote. Exploiting widespread disgust with the National Liberation Front, the Marxist party that has controlled Algeria for thirty years despite a record of inefficiency and corruption, the Islamists mobilized the disgruntled and the zealous alike, including thousands of veiled Algerian women clad in traditional Islamic garb.

The government version of events leading up to the December 1991 election, uncritically absorbed by the Western media, held that the Islamists would falter as a result of voter dissatisfaction with their incompetent administration of the municipalities they had won in local elections in June 1990. Yet the voters seemed not to notice; the FIS was better organized and much more popular than the 40 other alternatives, including the Front for Socialist Forces, which took a mere 25 seats in December. Apparently the electorate was willing to be patient with the Islamists. Even the government's predictable charges of vote tampering and electioneering could not overturn the mandate awarded them.

Thus Benjedid and the ruling establishment, with close ties to the military, found themselves in a no-win situation in the wake of the first round of elections. With more than 200 additional seats in parliament to be decided in the January 16 election, the

Islamists were only 28 seats short of a simple majority, and well within reach of the two-thirds majority that would allow them to rewrite Algeria's constitution on the model of an Islamic republic.

The government's initial response was to try to preserve the trappings of democracy. A government-appointed Constitutional Council began investigating "voting irregularities" involving at least 70 of the National Assembly seats won by the FIS, and establishment figures launched a campaign to arouse antifundamentalist Algerians, 200,000 of whom staged massive protests in the weeks following the election. But this strategy proved futile. In resigning, Benjedid bemoaned the fact that the democratization process he had inaugurated under intense pressure in 1988 had become "riddled with irregularities and cannot be quashed safely"—a phrasing that suggested an imperfect understanding of what genuine democratization is all about. Tanks and armored vehicles took up positions around government buildings, television and radio stations, and telephone exchanges in order, Premier Sid Ahmed Ghozali explained, "to protect public security." Three days later a High Security Council composed of military and civilian leaders canceled the second round of elections and announced the creation of a five-man body, the High State Council, to rule the country into 1993. Described as a "junta" by FIS spokesmen, this ruling body is headed by a founding member of the National Liberation Front and dominated by army officials.

The cancellation of the Arab world's first full-fledged experiment in democracy has been followed by a thoroughgoing crackdown on the FIS. Hundreds of Islamic fundamentalists, along with Arab-language journalists who had criticized the military or printed fundamentalists' communiqués, have been arrested. The ruling body banned rallies and other political activities at mosques, a move widely interpreted as intended to taunt and provoke the poor and jobless young men who constitute the inner cell of FIS supporters. Indeed, confrontations with the army ensued, and on February 9, 1992, the government imposed a state of emergency and moved to dissolve the FIS.

## Western Media Views of Islam

In covering these developments the (secular) Western media perceived the crisis through lenses similar to those held by the (secular) Algerian government. The January 13, 1992, issue of *Time* was typical of much of the reporting: "An Alarming No Vote: The fundamentalists' big gain is more a protest against socialist rule than a mandate for an Islamic republic." Not only does this judgment run contrary to the evidence as well as to common sense, it also contains the questionable supposition that no rational voter would choose an Islamic party on its own merits, but would do so only if coerced or deceived. For who in her right mind would choose a party that wishes to impose "the chilling penal law known as Shari'a"? Evidently lost on the *Time* reporter was the fact that Islam's penal code, including the *huddud* punishments for adultery, theft and other crimes, makes up only a small portion of the Shari'a—the body of sacred law drawn from the Qur'an, the Traditions of the Prophet, and revered commentary on both.

## The United States Should Tolerate Political Islam

The United States should not in principle object to the involvement of Islamic activists in government if they have been duly elected. Islamically oriented politicians and groups should be evaluated by the same criteria as any other potential leaders or opposition parties. While some are rejectionists, most will be critical and selective in their relations with the United States, generally operating on the basis of national interests and showing a flexibility that reflects understanding of the globally interdependent world. The United States should demonstrate by word and action its belief that the right to self-determination and representative government extends to an Islamically oriented state and society, if these reflect the popular will and do not directly threaten United States interests. American policy should accept the ideological differences between the West and Islam to the greatest extent possible, or at least tolerate them.

John L. Esposito, *Current History*, January 1994.

By the logic that prevailed in much of the media analysis, Algerian voters were either unaware of the dozens of alternatives to the Islamic party, were duped by the Islamists, or were simply irrational and hopelessly backward. American University political scientist Amos Perlmutter, writing in the *Washington Post*, sounded the alarm bell loudest. For Perlmutter, no distinctions need be made among Islamic movements around the world. "Islamic fundamentalism of the Sunni or Shia variety in Iran, Iraq, Egypt, Jordan, the West Bank and Gaza, the Maghreb and also Algeria is not merely resistant to democracy but wholly contemptuous of and hostile to the entire democratic political culture." It is "an aggressive revolutionary movement as militant and violent as the Bolshevik, Fascist, and Nazi movements of the past." Perlmutter tipped his hand by asserting in the same editorial that the world's 800 million Muslims should be viewed as one monolithic force. "The issue is not democracy but the true nature of Islam," he wrote. "Is Islam, fundamentalist or otherwise, compatible with liberal, human-rights oriented Western-style representative democracy? The answer is an emphatic 'no.'"

Of course, there is no mistaking the scandalous aspect of the recent manifestations of fundamentalism in the Sudan and in Iran, two quite different regimes but comparable in their disregard for Western standards of human rights. Also disconcerting are reports suggesting that the Sudan has inherited Lebanon's role as the home for international terrorists, including Shi'ite cadres financed by Iran. (This development may indicate that barriers to pan-Islamic fundamentalist collaboration have fallen in the wake of the gulf war, the collapse of the Soviet Union and the loose talk of a new world order, which Islamic radicals interpret as a code for a return of Western control of Arab resources.) Neither does an outsider find reassurance in 100,000 Algerians chanting at a rally on election eve, "We recognize no constitution and no laws but the laws of God and Islam," nor in calls for the veiling of women and their retreat from the workplace.

Nonetheless, Perlmutter's diatribe against Islamic politics obscures rather than clarifies matters. It is possible and even likely that the Algerian supporters of the FIS are motivated more by a passion for Islam than for democracy, and are not preoccupied with working out a long-term alliance between the two. But such an alliance is not out of the question. The Qur'an and the Shari'a provide a sociomoral framework rather than a detailed blueprint for the political order, and they allow a measure of adaptation and flexibility in state-building, as Islam's history demonstrates. Islamic fundamentalists have made great demands on their governments without yet developing coherent and sophisticated alternative economic and social policies. Up to this point they have stressed cultural and political authenticity and self-reliance. But the quest for sovereignty and self-reliance does not rule out a gradual process of incorporation and "Islamization" of Western structures and mechanisms, including mass participation in democratic procedures. Indeed, this pattern marks the Islamists' appropriation of Western science and technology. The incorporation of these tools into Islamic culture is described as an act of "repossession" of a mode of discourse and production that originated, the Islamists claim, in the golden age of Islamic civilization.

## The Islamic Salvation Front and Democracy

Abdelqader Hachani, the acting president of the FIS before his arrest on January 23, 1992, insists that Islamic political rule in Algeria will be different from the theocracy in Iran or the military rule in the Sudan. "We guarantee freedom of opinion in Algeria. Our purpose is to persuade, not to oblige people into doing what we say. We have won control of over 800 municipalities in elections of over a year ago. We have a record of tolerance that no one can deny. This is the essence of Islam." Notwithstanding questions about Hachani's sincerity, one can only wonder at the Western media's rush to judgment, especially considering the alternatives to Islamic rule in Algeria—namely, a martial-law regime or more of the same governmental mismanagement that led to a 100 percent inflation rate and a 30 percent unemployment rate. The fundamentalists may well be capable of surpassing even this formidable record of incompetence, but, as *Le Monde* argued: "To minimize the existence of an Islamic current that traverses all classes of Algerian society without a doubt is more dangerous than betting on the Islamic Front's evolution into a more moderate force."

Precisely because Islamic fundamentalism is not monolithic, we may hope that its every manifestation will not repeat the experiences of revolutionary Iran and the Sudan. Certainly the Algerian case, which is linked to an inchoate process of democratization, offers the possibility that the fundamentalists will in this instance retrieve and even develop Islam's traditional practice of respecting the rights of non-Muslims in an Islamic society. Hachani, an engineer employed by the state oil firm Sonatrach, was among the FIS leaders disavowing violence as a response to the "coup" by the High State Council. "The FIS has achieved a legitimacy that nothing and no one can take away from it," he was quoted as saying after the cancellation of the January 16 election. "The FIS will not permit violence, despite the incitements of the junta.". . .

## Defining "the Arab Problem"

Two seismic shifts in the political terrain of the Arab world—the display of Arab disunity during the gulf crisis and the dismantling of the Soviet patron state—have placed "the Arab problem" in bold relief. By "the Arab problem" I refer to the situation confronting the secularized elites who have ruled the Arab nations for decades through the apparatuses of a modern security state. With Marxist socialism in ruins, discredited finally and fully not only in Algeria but in its very birthplace; with the myth of Arab nationalism given the lie by the policies of Egypt [which joined the Western alliance against Iraq] during the gulf crisis; with the Ba'th party spent as a pan-Arab unifying force beyond the borders of Syria or Iraq—with such developments these rulers, whose power is based exclusively on military might, find themselves bereft of authenticating ideologies to bolster their sagging regimes.

In what seems to some observers little more than a last-ditch effort to retain control of civil society, and also a response to pressure from the West and from internal opponents, the ruling elites in Egypt and Algeria (and, haltingly, even in Kuwait, which in early January 1992 reportedly ended government censorship of newspapers) embarked cautiously on a perilous road of reform touted as "liberalization" or "democratization." As the developments in Algeria suggest, that road has many detours and dead ends. One possibility is that fundamentalists will prove adaptive enough to succeed in democratic politics.

Every major war in the Middle East has occasioned an inward-turning, a time of repentance and soul-searching on the part of the vanquished. After the gulf war, this spirit has gripped not the religious radicals but the Arab secular intellectuals who were hoping to reconstitute a regional political order fragmented by the demise of the Ottoman empire. But shared ethnicity and language could not transcend national self-interest; neither could the now exhausted utopian secular political philosophies. This is, of course, what the Islamists have been predicting all along. Naturally, they feel (not for the first time this century) that prophecy is fulfilled and the moment come for the rebirth of the one indigenous glory of their homelands, Islam. For the Islamists, Islam is the only force capable of transcending ethnic, linguistic and cultural barriers to unify the disparate peoples of the worldwide Islamic community (umma). In Algeria, Tunisia, Morocco, Egypt and Kuwait, Islamists press demands with a re-newed vigor and sense of purpose.

### Lessons for the Islamists

Yet the Islamists are learning that a divine mandate to rule does not make the social and economic problems of the umma less intractable. The mantle of political power has not seemed to fit comfortably over the mantle of the Prophet in Iran, where Shi'ite (and Persian) militancy was and is more purely consolidated than in Sunni Islam; or in the Sudan, where a makeshift Islam is a thin and unconvincing embellishment of despotic rule. If "Islam is the solution" in Algeria, it must be prepared to tackle a $25 billion foreign debt, a 30 percent unemployment rate, and severe short-ages of health services and housing. And it must do so while avoiding charging riba (interest) and dealing with the International Monetary Fund [IMF] and the World Bank—Western institutions that do not honor the economic prescriptions and proscriptions of Islamic law. Comparative studies of "Islamic economics" in the four nations in which Islamists have striven to implement the Shari'a—Iran, Pakistan, the Sudan and Saudi Arabia—demonstrate a wide and often inconsistent variety of practices in fulfillment of the religiously mandated zakat (voluntary tax system) and the reli-giously proscribed charging of interest.

Should they come to power in Egypt and Northern Africa, a region with a rapidly growing population and a shortage of food, the Islamists may find it impossible to resist the temptation to make accommodations with the industrialized West. After the

IMF recognized Egypt's achievement of the short-term reforms it had demanded, including the painful accelerated privatization of the public sector, accompanied by rising interest rates and consumer prices, the IMF signed an agreement with Egypt in May 1991 awarding Cairo $400 million in aid. In conjunction with forgiving $10 billion in foreign debt to the Western allies, the IMF agreement underscored the irrefutable material advantages to Arab nations of an alliance with the West.

## U.S. Support for Democracy in Islamic Countries

So far, the U.S. government has not publicly demanded that the Algerian elections be reinstated. State Department officials and policy analysts seem ambivalent. "If the fundamentalists eventually win, we will be identified with a regime hostile to our interests, like we were in Iran," said Henry Schuler of the Center for Strategic and International Studies in Washington. "You don't always get what you want when you have a democracy. We'll have to learn to live with what we get or back away from our ideals."

To dismiss the results of the Algerian election would imply that we continue to misunderstand and thus to underestimate the appeal of Islamic fundamentalism to Muslims—even as we overestimate what we see as its unenlightened, buffoonish and predatory qualities. (We certainly know by now that what appears buffoonish to our eyes may well appear poised and sensible to others; what appears predatory to us may appear responsibly protective to others.) American policymakers' reluctance to ride the Islamic current in Algeria may produce its own unintended consequences, not the least of which is an increase in the appeal of Islamic radicals who are already claiming that the lackluster American reaction to the military coup confirms the perception that the "democratization" process is a farce. "The people of Algeria have said loudly and clearly that they want an Islamic government," Hachani proclaimed after the December election. Their frustration in reaping the fruits of that electoral victory could lead to an abandonment of hope in the possibility of playing the Western game at all.

It may well be that the very elasticity of Islamic fundamentalism will keep Algeria, Egypt, Jordan and other Arab nations within its orbit for some time to come. The dramatically different outcomes of the Islamization programs in countries as ethnically and linguistically diverse as Pakistan, Iran, Saudi Arabia and the Sudan suggest that the history, social outlook and cultural patterns of the peoples who follow the Shari'a contribute at least as much as the law itself to the character and direction of an Islamic society. If this is so, then "the Arab problem" may eventually admit of several "Islamic solutions."

*"The Islamic world brings into question Washington's easy assumption that the promotion of democracy is inevitably in the national interests of the United States."*

# Rapid Democratization in the Middle East Could Threaten the West

Jonathan S. Paris

Continuing the policies of previous administrations, the Clinton administration has declared support for democratization in the Middle East. In the following viewpoint, Jonathan S. Paris argues that democratization in the Middle East may bring to power Islamic fundamentalist groups that could threaten U.S. interests in the region. Paris rejects the arguments of those who support rapid democratization in favor of those of confrontationists, who believe that the United States should confront and contain the Islamic fundamentalists. Democratization should be encouraged at different paces for different countries, he contends. Paris is a visiting fellow at the Yale Center for International and Area Studies.

As you read, consider the following questions:

1. What are the three reasons, in the view of non-interventionists cited by Paris, why the triumph of Islamic fundamentalists would not threaten the West?
2. What are the three interests of the United States in the Middle East, according to the author?

Excerpted from Jonathan S. Paris, "When to Worry in the Middle East." This article originally appeared in the Fall 1993 issue of *Orbis: A Journal of World Affairs*, published by JAI Press, and is reprinted by permission of the Foreign Policy Research Institute, Philadelphia.

In a May 1993 speech, Martin Indyk, national security advisor for Near East and South Asia, stated that the United States should "help the people and governments of the Middle East to confront this emerging threat [of radical Islamic fundamentalism], in part by pursuing peace with vigor, in part by containing extremism throughout the region, and in part by holding out an alternative vision of democratic political development and free market economic development." It is important to consider the Islamic fundamentalist threat, the arguments for accommodating and confronting radical Islam, and the potential conflict in U.S. policy that might occur by encouraging democracy in the Arab world on the one hand, and containing radical Islamic fundamentalism and promoting the Arab-Israeli peace process on the other. The Islamic world brings into question Washington's easy assumption that the promotion of democracy is inevitably in the national interests of the United States. In some countries, the risks of democratization may be worthwhile, but, in several Arab countries, where the United States has other vital interests, fast-track democratization may undermine those interests.

## The Islamist Appeal

Islamic fundamentalism has emerged in several Middle East countries as a significant social and cultural force, and, most recently, as a political movement. The violent assault by radical Islamists against state authority can be distinguished from Islamic fundamentalism's benign form: the health, education, and welfare aspects of community-oriented activities, and heightened religiosity and observances of the strictures of the Koran. While some argue that the mosque–community service activities provide a legal cover for fundraising and planning of violent activities, resulting in a division of labor scheme for destroying the state, most observers agree that the degree of militancy emanating from the mosque is proportionate to the shortcomings of the existing government in meeting the expectations of its citizens. The emerging consensus, therefore, is that Islamic fundamentalist movements in the Arab world tend to be indigenous, homegrown responses to the socioeconomic and political circumstances in those countries.

The ideology of the militant Islamists is well illustrated by the writings of Sayyid Qutb, an Egyptian intellectual who rediscovered Islam after being repulsed by America's materialistic culture while touring the United States in the early 1950s. Qutb led the Muslim Brotherhood's split in 1954 from Nasser's secular socialist revolution, and, consequently, spent most of his remaining life writing and proselytizing in prison, until he was executed in 1966.

Qutb attributes the failures of the Arabs in successive wars and the growing poverty, anomie, and disillusionment within Arab societies to the apostasy of Arab leaders who have abandoned Islam. Seduced by Western political intrigue and culture, Arab leaders have led the people backwards into the pre-Islamic age of ignorance. Qutb's prescription is *takfir*, or the elimination of pseudo-Muslim leaders who the Koran says are worse than non-believers and must be killed. Just about anyone who is in power and does not meet the Islamist test of a pure Muslim is seen as illegitimate in the eyes of Islamic fundamentalists. Cleanse society of these false Muslims, and God will be with the Muslims again. The Islamists take great pride in the Afghan war, where, with God on the side of the true Muslims, the Islamic *mujahidin* defeated that great infidel Russia. The current weakness of Arab states, by contrast, can be attributed to their being ruled by apostate Muslims. In formulating a strategy for meeting the Islamist challenge, remember that the priority of *takfir* is the replacement of existing nominally Muslim governments with authentic Islamic rule, and only then waging war against the forces of unbelief—Zionism, the Great Satan, the Christian 'crusaders,' communists, and so forth.

### The Case for Accommodation

Those who urge that the Islamists be accommodated offer several reasons. First, the Islamic revival is not a threat but a healthy grassroots response to the failure of sclerotic Arab governments to tackle growing socioeconomic problems. This view dismisses the militant Islamists as marginal and on the fringes of a predominantly cultural and religious movement.

A second school acknowledges that Islamists pose a political threat to Arab regimes, but allows that the regimes can keep the Islamists on the defensive not through repression, but by co-opting the more moderate Islamists into the political system. The legalization of the Muslim Brotherhood under Mubarak's Egypt has, at least until recently, splintered the fundamentalist movement. In Jordan, King Husayn has adroitly bowed to public disaffection by changing ministers and engaging the Muslim Brotherhood in parliamentary elections where their electoral success may not pose a threat to Hashemite legitimacy. The advantage of co-optation is that by empowering the Islamists, albeit within limits, they are made more accountable to the electorate and are not merely a magnet for the protest vote.

Those who advocate fast-track democratization would go further by allowing all political factions, including the formerly suppressed leftists, to compete for legislative and executive power. The victor would then be able to claim true popular legitimacy, and the people's frustration at the corruption, injustice, and economic failures of the incumbent regime would at last be vented.

If the Islamists win at the ballot box, as happened in Algeria in December 1991, this school of thought would have allowed the Islamists to rule Algeria in the sanguine view that popular constraints, such as the need to be re-elected, would inject a dose of pragmatism and moderation in the Islamist program.

A non-interventionist school of accommodation, directed in particular at policy makers in the West, argues that even if Arab states ultimately succumb to the Islamists, the triumph of the Islamists does not pose a threat to Western interests. No amount of outside economic aid or political engineering can abate the tensions within Arab society between the intellectual inquisitiveness of Arab modernists, who creatively reinterpret the Koran, and the prevailing orthodoxy's resistance to tampering with the word of God since the decision of Sunni religious authorities in the tenth century to close the door to interpretation.

## Support Friendly Governments

The West should be wary of pushing friendly governments into risky experiments. Traditional governments in the Middle East, often tribally based, may well have their own social contract and their own accountability even if they don't observe all the Western electoral forms. Western conservatives can appreciate how difficult it is to meld tradition and modernization while preserving social stability. As with the Shah's Iran, it is a mistake to accelerate the delegitimization of governments that seem not to meet our standards, only to have them replaced by something infinitely worse. We should approach with a certain humility the dilemmas of moderate governments that choose to react sternly against forces determined to destroy them.

Peter W. Rodman, *National Review*, May 11, 1992.

According to the non-interventionist view, there are three reasons why this civil war within Arab society should not threaten the West. First, the Islamists, even if victorious, do not share the modern approach that fosters innovation and technological success, which is the major buttress of state power. Secondly, the fundamentalist groups, if triumphant, are likely to fragment at the top, as in Afghanistan today. And thirdly, as may be happening within Iran in the post-Khomeini era, the population will ultimately tire of Islamic rigidity and lose their zeal for militancy. Since Islamic unity is a mirage, the Islamists cannot unite into a pan-Islamic hegemony that might dominate the Persian Gulf or wage Jihad against Israel.

Non-interventionists try to minimize Islamic fundamentalism

as much as possible. An activist U.S. policy, they warn, will not defeat fundamentalism but will accelerate it by turning a simmering civil war between Muslim secularists and fundamentalists into a clash between the West and Islam. Besieged by another Western crusade, the Islamists will gain support from those in the Arab world who are susceptible to the conspiratorial view that the West is the root cause of their problems, and who detest the West more than they fear the tyranny of an Islamist regime. It should be remembered, however, that the predicted ill-effects of a confrontationalist policy have failed to materialize in the past. In the autumn of 1990, non-interventionists warned that a strident U.S. confrontation with Saddam would turn an inter-Arab territorial dispute into an eruption of the Arab masses against the West. In fact, Saddam continues to remain isolated and bereft of meaningful Arab support as a result of unrelenting Western confrontation. The question underlying the current debate between accommodation and confrontation is whether Western confrontation is more likely to accelerate or contain the Islamic surge.

### The Case for Confrontation

Samuel Huntington implies the futility of Western accommodation of Islamic civilization when he writes that

> Western ideas of individualism, liberalism, constitutionalism, human rights, equality, liberty, the rule of law, democracy, free markets, the separation of church and state, often have little resonance in Islamic [and several other] . . . cultures. Western efforts to propagate such ideas produce instead a reaction against 'human rights imperialism' and a reaffirmation of indigenous values, as can be seen in the support for religious fundamentalism by the younger generation in non-Western cultures.

The clash between Islam and the West is not over territory or economic domination, but over values. The West cannot mollify the Islamic world by promoting democratic ideals because there is no convergence of values between the two cultures. We are simply talking a different language. If the United States wishes to accommodate President Hafiz al-Asad of Syria, who does not appear to be a prisoner of the Islamic culture described above, it might offer credits and remove Syria from the terrorist list in return for Syrian peace with Israel. How does the United States reach out to the militant Islamists who reject the very carrots, such as economic development, that the United States might offer as an inducement to compromise on other issues?

On a policy level, confrontationalists argue that as unstylish and undemocratic as Arab authoritarian governments are today, the Islamist alternative might be worse, as Khomeini's Islamic revolution was far more problematic than the shah of Iran. The

234

United States has warned that Islamist success at the ballot box may result in non-democratic, ideological, authoritarian regimes. Islamist ideologues like Hasan Turabi, head of the National Islamic Front of Sudan, disdain the factionalism of party politics and refuse to accept the corollary of majority rule, that is, protecting the rights of the minority opposition. Behind the pithy phrase "one man, one vote, once," real lives and issues are at stake. Do Arab regimes allow the Islamists to win at the ballot box when Islamist leaders have indicated they will not tolerate political opposition or cultural diversity, or that Coptic Christians may be persecuted, and women may forfeit the gains they have made under the benign authoritarian regimes currently in power?

The confrontationalists do not believe the Arab world is ready for democracy and would guard against opening up the praetorian system too fast too soon without an institutionalized rule of law to safeguard minority rights. They point to Algeria, where the National Liberation Front (FLN)–Benjedid government, facing an unexpectedly severe food riot in 1988, panicked and abruptly legalized political parties. The result was the defeat of the FLN, the unpopular incumbent governing party, by the better organized Islamic National Front (FIS). Nearly every time there is an election, the fundamentalists win, in part because the secular oppositions in Arab societies have failed to articulate the democratic pluralistic alternative. If the Islamists gain power through the ballot box, they will have succeeded in taking over the government without having to defeat that bastion of secularism, the army.

Democracy has worked in countries that have achieved prior economic development, industrialization, and an urban middle class, whose private-sector behavior stimulates accommodation and compromise so that more can benefit from the expanding economic pie. Although a few poor countries, like India, Gambia, Mauritius, and Costa Rica have democratized, more economic development in Algeria, Egypt, and several other Arab countries would increase the chances of successful democratization. Also, the political legitimacy of Arab states is weak, and a rule of law that tolerates loyal political opposition does not yet appear. Any winner-take-all election is likely to result in majority rule without minority rights. Victory by the Islamists complicates democratization further because of the contradictions between the authoritative law of God, whose word is final, and the desire of an electorate to change its mind through periodic exercise of the vote. . . .

## Balancing U.S. Interests

U.S. interests in the Middle East are threefold. First, the United States seeks a successful outcome to the peace process, by which Israel and its Arab neighbors would move beyond the current non-war status based on Israeli deterrence and toward a collaborative political, social, and economic relationship. In such a full peace, Israel might justify its sacrifice of some strategic advantages because "full peace" means that it no longer must rely solely on deterrence.

The second U.S. interest is the dual containment of Iran and Iraq and the maintenance of a network of pro-U.S. states in the Persian Gulf to ensure unimpeded Western access to oil. A strong U.S.-Saudi relationship, cemented by the successful precedent of Desert Storm, helps deter Iraq or Iran from pursuing hegemony over the Persian Gulf.

A third U.S. interest is expanding the political participation of Arab people in their governments so as to increase the political legitimacy and stability of Arab states and their capacity to withstand assault by extremist movements. Democratization is a proven method of increasing popular participation and strengthening the legitimacy of the nation-state. Although the promotion of democracy by the United States in the Middle East may emanate from idealistic and humanitarian concerns, democracy may also help promote Arab state stability and contain Islamic extremism. A careful balancing of U.S. vital interests is needed to determine how much risk to take in promoting ballot-box democracy among Arab countries before the desirable accompanying conditions of political liberalism and free market economic development have taken full root.

## Democracy: A Threat to Peace?

If the choice facing U.S. policy makers was merely between Arab authoritarian regimes and emerging liberal democratic oppositions, there is little doubt that the United States would support the latter vigorously, as demonstrated by the State Department's negative reaction to the recent cancellation of electoral results by the ruling military regime in largely Muslim Nigeria. The militant Islamists are the wild card in the Middle East game. The West must be careful not to promote a fast-track ballot-box democratization that may lead to the replacement of unpleasant dictatorships, who are at least constrained in varying degrees by public opinion and the international order, with revolutionary Islamists, who are committed first to radically remolding public thought, and then to challenging the regional and international order. In the case of Indonesia, the most populous Muslim country in the world, the failure of its benign authoritarian regime to democratize more quickly is not as bad as the irreparable social, economic, and international harm that might result from its army panicking at the onslaught of populist pressure and resorting to wanton violence similar to the anticommunist bloodbath of the late Sukarno years [1960–66]. A gradual approach to democratization makes even more sense in those areas of the Middle East where the United States has other vital interests, as in the Arab-Israeli arena and the Persian Gulf. The pace at which the United States pushes democracy depends on the Arab country in question. . . .

It is not axiomatic that every democratic election in the Arab Middle East will result in an Islamist victory. . . . It is by no means clear that even if the Islamists win an election, U.S. interests in containing fundamentalism will fail in the long run. Had the FIS fundamentalists taken over a very distressed Algerian economy in 1992 [when elections were overturned by a military coup], they might have failed by now and discredited Islamist movements elsewhere. By being repressed, the FIS remains an unaccountable protest movement.

The United States cannot determine beforehand whether democratization will lead to a fundamentalist victory, but it can assess the likely collateral impact of democratization on other U.S. interests. In Egypt, fast-track democratization might cause so much instability as to interfere with Egypt's critical assistance to the peace process. It may make more sense to soft-pedal democratization and prod Egypt to strengthen its free-market sector and increase the population's stake in the system, thereby diminishing the appeal of anti-state Islamist movements.

The road to change from authoritarian regimes to democracies is likely to be chaotic, and the closer the chaos is to the Arab-Israeli sphere and the Gulf, the more troubling the likely ripple effects. Outside the Arab-Israeli and Gulf arenas, the primary risk to the United States is that democracy may unwittingly bring to the forefront a succession of charismatic Islamist leaders who might catalyze the fragmented pockets of Islamic militancy into a pan-Islamic movement that would sweep away neighboring secular dictators and monarchies alike. But such leaders may also emerge through a coup or a popular uprising against a repressive regime. In the absence of a crystal ball, U.S. policy makers might set a more modest objective of carefully calibrating the pace of democratization in the context of its other goals in the region.

# Periodical Bibliography

The following articles have been selected to supplement the diverse views presented in this chapter.

| | |
|---|---|
| Shlomo Avineri | "The Return to Islam," *Dissent*, Fall 1993. |
| Tariq Banuri | "Justice Is the Strife," *New Perspectives Quarterly*, Spring 1994. |
| Edward P. Djerejian | "One Man, One Vote, One Time?" *New Perspectives Quarterly*, Summer 1993. |
| John L. Esposito | "Political Islam: Beyond the Green Menace," *Current History*, January 1994. |
| Leon T. Hadar | "Islamic Fundamentalism Is Not a Threat to U.S. Security," *USA Today*, November 1993. |
| Leon T. Hadar | "What Green Peril?" *Foreign Affairs*, Spring 1993. |
| Pervez Hoodbhoy | "Myth-Building: The 'Islamic' Bomb," *The Bulletin of the Atomic Scientists*, June 1993. |
| David Ignatius | "The West's Next Crusade: Fighting Fundamentalist Islamic Rule," *The Washington Post National Weekly Edition*, March 16–22, 1992. Available from 1150 15th St. NW, Washington, DC 20071. |
| Josef Joffe and Chandra Muzaffar | "A Clash Between Civilizations—or Within Them?" *World Press Review*, February 1994. |
| Phebe Marr | "The Islamic Revival: Security Issues," *Mediterranean Quarterly*, Fall 1992. Available from Duke University Press, Box 90660, Durham, NC 27708. |
| Bradford R. McGuinn | "Should We Fear Islamic Fundamentalists?" *USA Today*, November 1993. |
| Bruce W. Nelan | "Bombs in the Name of Allah," *Time*, August 30, 1993. |
| George Perkovich | "Insecurity and Islam," *Tikkun*, May/June 1993. |
| B.A. Roberson | "Islam and Europe: An Enigma or a Myth?" *Middle East Journal*, Spring 1994. |
| Peter W. Rodman | "Co-opt or Confront Fundamentalist Islam?" *Middle East Quarterly*, December 1994. Available from 1920 Chestnut St., Suite 600, Philadelphia, PA 19103. |
| Peter W. Rodman | "Islam and Democracy," *National Review*, May 11, 1992. |
| Mortimer B. Zuckerman | "Beware of Religious Stalinists," *U.S. News & World Report*, March 22, 1993. |

# Is Islam Uniting
# the Islamic World?

**Islam**

# Chapter Preface

Since 1992, the Egyptian government has been battling Islamic militants who have carried out terrorist attacks on government officials and tourist destinations. Approximately 300 people—militants, police, bystanders, and tourists—were killed in 1992 and 1993 in violent clashes between Islamic militants and the Egyptian military and police.

Some Western reporters and academics believe the clashes are a sign that Egypt is on the verge of an Islamic revolution. According to Jeffrey Bartholet, a *Newsweek* magazine reporter, the danger of an Islamic revolution in Egypt is great. "A growing body of evidence suggests that [Islamic] terrorist groups have infiltrated the [Egyptian] army," he warns, as they did in 1981 when then-president Anwar Sadat was assassinated. An Islamic revolution in Egypt, he believes, could lead to a succession of Islamic revolutions in the Middle East and Central Asia. "If Egypt, the most populous country in the Arab world, were to fall into the hands of militant Islamists, the political psychology of the whole region would be transformed," Bartholet argues.

Other observers of the Middle East disagree that Egypt is in danger of an Islamic revolution. Edward W. Said, a professor of comparative literature at Columbia University in New York City, has traveled extensively in the Middle East and Egypt since 1992. "The more I read and saw," he says of his experience in Egypt, "the less probable was any sign of a mass Islamic uprising of the kind conjured up by Western reporters and sages." Nor is there a danger of an Islamic revolution sweeping the region, in Said's opinion. "Most of these societies—Egypt's certainly . . . —are still largely secular despite the clamorings and debates over Islamic government," he contends.

Robert D. Kaplan, contributing editor of the *Atlantic Monthly*, writes, "Political violence, though still of limited scale, may be a sign that Egypt is nearing crisis." The viewpoints in the following chapter debate whether such a crisis is occurring and whether events in Egypt signal a larger phenomenon, a worldwide Islamic revolution.

*"Iran is already immersed in a quest to transform both institutional Islam and Muslim societies as a whole into the resurrection of an Islamist empire led from Tehran."*

# Iran Is Fomenting a Worldwide Islamic Revolution

Yossef Bodansky

In 1979, Iran became the world's first Islamic republic. In the following viewpoint, Yossef Bodansky argues that Iran is now seeking to lead an Islamic revolution that will unite the Muslim countries of the Middle East, former Soviet Union, and Asia. Bodansky points to Iran's program of rearmament and its resumption of relations with other Muslim countries as signs that Iran is preparing for a clash, which it intends to lead, between the Muslim world and the West. Bodansky is director of the House Republican Research Committee Task Force on Terrorism and Unconventional Warfare.

As you read, consider the following questions:

1. What has been Iran's dual approach to foreign policy since the 1979 revolution, according to the author?
2. What is the main principle of Iran's strategy, according to Iran's Mussavi-Khoiniha, quoted by Bodansky?
3. From what country did Iran purchase nuclear weapons, according to Bodansky?

From Yossef Bodansky, "The Grand Strategy of Iran," *Global Affairs*, Fall 1993. Reprinted with permission.

Iran is already immersed in a quest to transform both institutional Islam and Muslim societies as a whole into the resurrection of an Islamist empire led from Tehran. If successful, it perhaps would be the most important surge of power in the Mideast region since the establishment of the Turkish Empire in 1453. Iran envisions that this new empire, essentially a loose federation of local socio-political entities, would then jointly confront the West in a fateful struggle for the soul and future of Islam.

Preposterous as such imperial aspirations might seem in the West—and conveniently vague as the global utopian portion of Tehran's vision is—the Mullahs' all-out commitment is genuine. Toward that end, Tehran is ready to sacrifice the wealth and well-being of Iran, launch a worldwide campaign of terrorism and subversion, and embark on a military buildup of major proportions, to the point of risking a major war. Moreover, in sharp contrast with the illusions of grandeur of the overall vision, Tehran's plans for consolidation of hegemony over the Near East, the first phase in the grand design, are pragmatic and sophisticated.

### Iran Seeks Influence Over the Near East

With a sense of urgency, Tehran's immediate objective is the establishment of a traditional regional sphere of influence. This hegemony—an Islamic Bloc stretching from North Africa to the Indian subcontinent and Central Asia—is already emerging as the establishment of Islamist regimes strongly influenced by Iran. Tehran is convinced that confrontation with the United States over access to the Near East, as well as the destruction of Israel, is inevitable and imminent. The launch of international terrorism into the United States is an integral and important component of this grand strategy.

Since her Islamic Revolution in 1979, Iranian strategy has been characterized by a dual approach combining aspirations for a global utopian Islamic empire and pragmatic regional objectives. Ayatollah Khomeini reconciled the two objectives when he determined his Islamic Revolution would concentrate on the Near East, and only then develop into a confrontation with the United States and its allies. "We are at war against infidels," Khomeini declared on January 14, 1980. "*Jihad* must triumph." Tehran's commitment to a confrontation with the United States further strengthened with the outbreak of the war with Iraq in 1980, which Tehran attributed to a U.S. conspiracy. Indeed, the relentless drive to acquire strategic capabilities Iran embarked on soon after the Revolution was optimized toward reviving regional military capabilities.

Once Khomeini was certain that the war with Iraq would not bring about the collapse of the Islamic Republic, he returned to urging a major regional confrontation with the United States as a strategic priority. In a sermon on July 16, 1982, Khomeini defined Iran's strategic tenet that the success of any Islamic global surge depended on consolidating regional dominance, and argued that "Muslims should unite and defeat America; they should know that they can do this, and they have many possibilities. America and the West's lifeline depends on this region's oil." Since the Persian Gulf was declared an area of American vital interest, Tehran was convinced that a confrontation with the United States over regional hegemony was not inconceivable.

Indeed, already in 1983, Tehran increased its traditional preoccupation with regional strategy even though the war with Iraq was still raging. Ali Akbar Hashemi-Rafsanjani, then Speaker of the *Majlis* [Parliament of Iran], stressed "the security of the Persian Gulf is more important to us than any other party, and we will strive to maintain the Gulf's [security] as much as we can." These objectives would soon dominate not only Iran's acquisition policies, but its strategic alliances and posture. . . .

## A Regional Strategy

In the aftermath of the 1991 Gulf War, although apprehensive about growing challenges, the Islamists were determined to capitalize on the upheaval. Shaykh Muhammad Hussayn Fadlallah explained that the Near East was providing incomparable conditions for the resurrection of the Islamic Revolution on a global scale: "The Middle East is the base of the Islamic fundamentalist movement. . . . No region other than the Middle East could enable the U.S. to control the world economy and political conditions and, therefore, control the world's security game."

Tehran's Institute of Strategic Studies under Hojjat-al-Islam Mussavi-Khoiniha was ordered to study Iran's future long-term grand strategy. At the conclusion in May 1991 of a major conference, Mussavi-Khoiniha emphasized that the American threat would increase since Iran was emerging as "the only center of national liberation movements in the world. . . . If we obtain the nuclear ability, the waves of Islamic Revolution will get a new power, and liberation movements throughout the world will look at the Islamic Republic as a new superpower with all its ideologic potentials." Mussavi-Khoiniha concluded it would enable Tehran to lead the entire radical movement worldwide to a confrontation with and in the United States. In October 1991, in a subsequent international conference devoted to long-term strategy to confront *Pax-Americana*, Ahmad Khomeini said: "We should realize that the world is hostile toward us only for [our commitment to] Islam. After the fall of Marxism, Islam replaced it, and as long as Islam exists, U.S. hostility exists, and as long as U.S. hostility exists, the struggle exists."

Thus, by the fall of 1991, Tehran defined a coherent grand

243

strategy and reached a major decision to implement it, convinced the United States directly threatens Islam. Tehran stresses that in order to prevail "under the present sensitive conditions, a state of unity must emerge among Muslim countries." Iran, "the upholder of the banner of unity the world over," is the key to triumph in such a confrontation, being "a major Islamic country which can help unite the Islamic World," according to Iranian official sources. The ensuing Islamic Bloc, Tehran believes, would compel the Arab World, and especially the Persian Gulf states, to gravitate under Iranian influence.

Tehran also joins the Beijing-led South bloc aimed at challenging the United States. Iranian Republican Guard Command (IRGC) Major General Muhsin Reza'i explained that "[I]f there is unity among Iran, Pakistan, and Afghanistan, this will strengthen Muslim solidarity and enable the peoples of Soviet Central Asia and Kashmir to join in. China would also welcome such a development." He urged an all-out mobilization to face Washington's "dangerous designs in the region, as America sees Islamic fundamentalism as a threat now after the collapse of Communism."

The Islamic Commonwealth (Bloc) is composed of Iran, Afghanistan, Pakistan, Kazakhstan, Turkmenistan, Kyrgizstan, Uzbekistan, Tajikistan, Azerbaijan and, ultimately, Turkey. Tehran believes that all of these countries will soon have some form of Islamist-oriented regime. By the end of 1991, Tehran already had signed treaties with all the former Soviet Central Asian states, promising extensive financial support for virtually any conceivable project, as well as massive Islamist educational efforts. "I think that the Central Asian states will follow whoever pays the most. A bulging purse will prove stronger than political sympathies and antipathies," acknowledged a Kyrgizstan Foreign Affairs Ministry high official.

## Iran's Relations with Sudan

By mid-1991, Tehran embarked on an audacious move to tighten the noose around the Arabian peninsula, as well as to rejuvenate terrorism and subversion worldwide, especially in the Muslim World. By the end of the year, Iran became the hegemonic power in Sudan. A year later Iran was capable of blocking the Red Sea and threatening the Hijaz (Western Saudi Arabia), as well as destabilizing segments of Africa and the Near East.

Ever since his rise to power in a military coup on June 30, 1989, Sudan's General Umar al-Bashir had tried to impose an Islamist regime he would define as "a twin of the Iranian Revolution." He repeatedly emphasized his support for pan-Arab causes and hoped for Arab support for designs in Africa and the Red Sea. Most important was the emergence of Shaykh Hassan al-Turabi as the spiritual leader of Sudan. In August 1989, he arranged for Sudan to become an Islamist "springboard to Arab and African countries" in return for substantial financial assistance from Islamists. Turabi considers the essence of the Sudanese foreign policy to be "a program for the Islamic Call" and the manifestation of "the policy of the Islamic Movement, which is national, or rather, cosmic and universal." In essence, Turabi was able to provide a crucial link between the Islamist militant Sunnis and the Shi'ite militants of Tehran.

## The United States Opposes Iranian Extremism

The American quarrel with Iran should not be misconstrued as a "clash of civilizations" or opposition to Iran as a theocratic state. Washington does not take issue with the "Islamic" dimension of the Islamic Republic of Iran. As President Clinton has said, America has a deep respect for the religion and culture of Islam. It is extremism, whether religious or secular, that we oppose. The United States is concerned with the actions and policies of the Tehran government. Iran is actively engaged in clandestine efforts to acquire nuclear and other unconventional weapons and long-range missile-delivery systems. It is the foremost sponsor of terrorism and assassination worldwide. It is violently and vitriolically opposed to the Arab-Israeli peace process. It seeks to subvert friendly governments across the Middle East and in parts of Africa. It is attempting to acquire offensive conventional capabilities to threaten its smaller gulf neighbors. Its record on treatment of its own citizens—especially women and religious minorities—is deeply disturbing.

Anthony Lake, *Foreign Affairs*, March/April 1994.

The consolidation that made Sudan Iran's fiefdom was completed in mid-December 1991 during the visit to Khartoum by a delegation of 157 senior officials led by Iranian president Hashemi-Rafsanjani to "boost relations between the two fraternal countries and widen horizons of cooperation and cohesion." Hashemi-Rafsanjani predicted that "the Islamic revolution in Sudan would undoubtedly seriously affect the entire Arab world, Africa, and the world of Islam. . . . [T]he two Islamic revolutions of Iran and Sudan, with regards to the strategic importance they enjoy in Asia, Africa, and the Middle East, undoubtedly can be the source of movement and revolution in the Islamic world." Sudanese Foreign Minister Ali Sahlul explained that Iran and Sudan "are facing the same threats" from the West.

Tehran moved quickly to take over and expand the strategic infrastructure in Sudan. The Sudanese armed forces, "under the complete control of the Islamic Front," were ripe for expediting the Iranian-Sudanese drive "on the Muslim North [Africa] and the Horn of Africa region," according to newspaper reports. Indeed, Dr. Mustafa Uthman Ismail, the secretary general of the Khartoum-based International People's Friendship Council, declared that "Sudan has become the strong man of Africa, and is a helping hand to its neighbors and friends." Strategically, all of this effort was aimed at Sudanese-Iranian presence in the Horn of Africa toward the transformation of the Red Sea into a "Green [Muslim] Lake.". . .

### Iran's Weapons Buildup

Another major aspect of the Iranian strategic surge was a massive military buildup with emphasis on strategic weapons. In late 1991, Iran purchased its first operational nuclear weapons from ex-Soviet Central Asia, primarily from Kazakhstan. Iran is known to have the following nuclear weapons: 1) Two warheads for a SCUD-type ballistic missile, that should fit on any SSM [surface-to-surface missile] that is a derivative of the basic SCUD, and are operational; 2) One aerial bomb of the type carried by a MiG-27 that is operational; and 3) One nuclear artillery shell that is at an unclear operational stage. These weapons reached initial operational status in late January 1993. In the fall of 1992, Iran signed a new deal with Kazakhstan to purchase four additional upgraded nuclear warheads. The new warheads are being adapted to fit advanced missiles purchased by Iran.

In the course of this buildup, Tehran absorbed the ex-Iraqi combat aircraft that landed during the Gulf War and concluded several major aircraft deals with Russia/Commonwealth of Independent States (CIS). Iran is rebuilding a modern air force with regional theater capabilities equipped with several hundred of the latest fighters, deep-strike aircraft and medium bombers optimized for anti-shipping strikes, as well as the latest air-launched anti-ship cruise missiles. Iran also purchased 100–150 additional combat aircraft and bombers from China. Tehran also embarked on comprehensive ballistic missile programs. In the near term, of strategic importance are the large-scale purchases from North Korea. (These come in addition to existing ambitious programs with China, North Korea, and Syria on development of indigenous missile and nuclear weapons. Impressive and strategically important as they are, those programs are out of the scope of this viewpoint.) In this procurement round alone, Iran received several hundred ballistic missiles, ranging from the basic NK-SCUD-B to the specially modified *Nodong-1* with a range of 1,300 kms and "capable of delivering nuclear warheads," according to news reports.

No less important is the rebuilding of the Iranian fleet by China and Russia including missile-equipped surface combatants, mainly with blue water capabilities, and attack submarines. Tehran stresses the importance of submarines, especially in preventing foreign task forces from approaching the Arabian Sea.

Altogether, since spring 1992, Tehran has embarked on a massive long-term rearmament program aimed at transforming it into the region's undisputed leading military power. By late September 1992, several additional Russian-Iranian weapons deals were completed after "months of secret negotiations" with strategic connotations, according to newspaper reports. These deals with Russia are a part of a comprehensive arrangement that includes agreements on joint hegemony over Central Asia, the containment of Western influence, especially in the Persian Gulf and South Asia, and extensive Iranian access to Russia's vast military scientific-technical resources in return for financing. In early September 1992 ". . . China agreed to help Iran in strengthening and expanding its Armed Forces under a 'strategic agreement' worth billions of dollars." The cooperation includes sharing military technologies, according to newspaper reports.

Back in mid-February 1992, with its nuclear weapons in initial operational status, Tehran intensified its active preparations for challenging the United States for the dominance over the Near East. President Ali Akbar Hashemi-Rafsanjani declared that Iran would lead the Muslim Bloc to become a "world power." Foreign Minister Ali Akbar Velayati declared that Iran "will attain a new strategic balance in the region" as head of the Bloc. The availability of nuclear weapons, irrespective of their operational capabilities, is considered by Tehran a key element. "Iran has learned from Iraq's experience in the Gulf War," explains Bahman Etemad. "It believes the West will think twice about a military confrontation if it has the bomb."

## Testing Iran's Gulf Capabilities

In summer 1992, Tehran embarked on the first real test of its capabilities. Ayatollah Ali Khamene'i explained that since the United States had emerged as "the leader of the anti-Islamic front of arrogance," all Muslims must form "a united, worthy and calculated stand to face it as soon as possible." Tehran was convinced that a crisis instigated by the United States was imminent and urged all local Arab governments to ignore their past enmities and rally behind Tehran. "In view of its superior military and economic capability, its peace-loving and enlightened diplomacy, and Islamic beliefs in common with its neighbors, the Islamic Republic of Iran is the best axis for ensuring such understanding and security in the region," said Khamene'i.

IRGC Commander Muhsin Reza'i attributed both the regional instability and Iran's military buildup to the U.S. presence. "If the Americans were to depart from the Islamic World and leave it to its own devices, we could find great conditions for security and political stability," he stressed. "Iran possesses excellent facilities for delivering an appropriate response to any possible aggression by Israel. These types of facilities may not be present in the entire region. We also have some practical possibilities insofar as [among] all the countries of the Islamic World, if the situation were to arise, we would deliver a suitable response."

Iran urged the region to recognize its supremacy and "if only a unified Islamic Bloc in the region covering the Central Asian states, Afghanistan, Pakistan, Bangladesh, Iran and Saudi Arabia could be established, all Western influence and especially that of the Great Satan could be staved off," according to an Iranian newspaper. The collapse of the USSR and the Gulf Crisis "tilted the regional balance" against the Arab and Muslim World, but newly acquired military capabilities now permit Iran to restore the strategic regional balance in favor of Islam.

By late July 1992, Iran saw imminence of a U.S. military clash in the Persian Gulf as a function of the U.S. election process. On August 23, 1992, Khamene'i chaired a significant strategy-formulating session of the entire Iranian leadership, including Hashemi-Rafsanjani, devoted to assessing the situation and to ensuring that "global arrogance will be cut to size." Tehran believed that if its initiative succeeds, "Islamic countries as a bloc have a unique and historic opportunity to produce the desired political changes in the global system," according to Radio Tehran. Khamene'i explained: "America and arrogant powers are sensitive to the presence of Islamic Iran in the Persian Gulf region and among several newly established Islamic states in the aftermath of the Soviet collapse." Khamene'i said he was optimistic about the outcome because "as long as we adhere to Islam and Islamic principles neither America nor other powers could harm our nation."

### Preparing for the U.S. Confrontation

In preparations for the confrontation, Tehran concluded it must have additional anti-shipping missile batteries to ensure simultaneous launches from several directions. Abu-Mussa Island, as well as the Greater and Lesser Tumb at the eastern mouth of the Strait of Hormuz, are the optimal sites for such launchers. During spring 1992 Iran had already reasserted its determination to hold the islands in accordance with the 1971 international agreement. In July, Iran began clandestinely building "a huge military airfield on the island, in addition to a naval and air observation and surveillance station," according to newspaper reports.

On August 25, 1992, Iran consolidated its hold over Abu-Mussa Island. Lt. Salim Mukarrab of the al-Shariqah police pointed out that "Iran now has a military base on the island. It includes speedboats, military vehicles and helicopters." Iranian diplomats presented the island's seizure as "a move to control the Strait of Hormuz, through which one fifth of the world oil exports pass" and thus a strategic move of global importance. Iranian sources acknowledged that Iran already had "started to build a group of huge military bases inside Abu-Mussa Island. . . . Under the plan being implemented the missiles unit belonging to the Iranian naval forces will set up five mobile missile bases underground for the Chinese-made Silkworm missiles." Several foreign military experts arrived on the island immediately after the Arab inhabitants had been evicted. Tehran reiterated Iranian sovereignty over the islands "has never been seriously doubted" and that "security of those islands is part of Iran's undeniable responsibility." It warned the Gulf states that they were "playing with fire" if they sought to evict Iran, according to official reports. . . .

Although the major crisis Tehran was anticipating did not break out in fall 1992, Tehran remained actively preparing hegemony over the Gulf. Additional military buildup, including improvement of the command and control elements, was completed in late November 1992. Most important is the establishment of a new national-level forward headquarters at Bandar Abbas.

Tehran's inflated confidence was first expressed by Hashemi-Rafsanjani: "Iran is surely stronger than the likes of you [Gulf Arab states]. To reach these islands one has to cross a sea of blood." Moreover, Tehran raised the ante, by declaring that it has the "right of sovereignty" over Bahrain. The Supreme National Security Council [SNSC] on December 26, 1992, resolved that "our brave nation will never hesitate to defend the sovereignty and safeguard the territorial integrity of Iran," and the warning that "no country will ever be able to covet even an inch of Iranian soil."

Examining the likely policies of the Clinton Administration, Tehran concluded that Washington was determined to pursue "a policy of 'blocking or deterring' Iran," and that once the U.S. maneuvers were completed, it would be "surrounded politically and militarily in every direction by the West, particularly the U.S." Tehran concluded that "there is possibility for maneuver by Iran in the two regions of the Persian Gulf and Central Asia, to guard its national security and at the same time to play a role in preserving stability and peace in the countries of these regions."

*"Pan-Islamism will never succeed because there can never be agreement on who would lead such a movement."*

# Iran Is Not Leading a Worldwide Islamic Revolution

Shireen T. Hunter

In July 1993, the United States articulated its policy of "dual containment" toward Iran and Iraq designed to prevent either country from expanding its influence. In the following viewpoint, Shireen T. Hunter argues that the Muslim republics of the former Soviet Union are unlikely to become part of an Islamic bloc that is opposed to the West. The Islamic movements are not like the Islamic revolutionary movement in Iran, Hunter contends, and Iran's influence in the region is limited because of historical, cultural, and religious differences. Hunter believes that a U.S. policy based on opposition to Iranian influence or so-called militant Islam would be a mistake. Hunter is deputy director of Middle East Studies at the Center for Strategic and International Studies, in Cambridge, Massachusetts.

As you read, consider the following questions:

1. What four reasons does Hunter give to support her assertion that the development of militant Islam in the Muslim republics of the former Soviet Union is unlikely?
2. According to Hunter, why is Iran feeling "hemmed in and threatened"?

From Shireen T. Hunter, "The Muslim Republics of the Former Soviet Union: Policy Challenges for the United States," *The Washington Quarterly*, vol. 15, no. 3, Summer 1992. Copyright ©1992 by The Center for Strategic and International Studies and The Massachusetts Institute of Technology. Reprinted by permission of The MIT Press.

If judged by the statements of Western officials and reports in the Western press, fear of the expansion of Islamic fundamentalism appears to be the most serious preoccupation of Western countries and the most important influence shaping their policy toward the new Muslim states [of the former Soviet Union in Central Asia]. Yet how serious is this threat and is the West justified in fashioning its policy toward these states on this basis? To answer the question, the following preliminary observations are necessary.

## How Serious Is the Threat of Fundamentalism?

The newly independent Muslim states are still governed by the same elites that ruled under the Soviet system, although most of them have now embraced nationalist themes. Moreover, although individual leaders may have different tendencies, the political, and more important, the bureaucratic infrastructures that support them and manage the country have not changed since Soviet times. Yet, with the discrediting of communism, which for nearly seventy years provided the ideological underpinnings of these states' political institutions and acted as the principal legitimizing factor of power, these countries are facing an ideological vacuum. In addition, they lack any experience of democracy, or even of other forms of governance apart from the Soviet system. This is because they went from a feudal-colonial system to a Communist-colonial system without any experience similar to the constitutional, anticolonial, and postcolonial movements and governments of other Third World nations. Of course, there were anti-Russian and anti-Communist movements and reformist intellectuals in these lands, and some of the current republics were briefly independent between the fall of the czarist regime and the consolidation of the Bolshevik government. But none of these phenomena was of a duration or magnitude to leave a lasting imprint, although a good deal of mythologization of these aspects of the past is now taking place.

In addition to these considerations, the important place that Islam holds in the cultural makeup of the new states, the reality of their being surrounded only by Muslim states (with the exception of Azerbaijan and Kazakhstan), and the increasing politicization of Islam in recent years, have led to widespread expectation and fear in the West that Islam would fill the ideological vacuum.

Moreover, the West legitimately fears that the brand of Islam involved would be of the extremist type reminiscent of the early days of the Islamic revolution in Iran. Indeed, the West sees Iran as the primary agent of the spread of this brand of Islam in the new republics.

What makes such a prospect even more alarming is the theory held by no negligible number of Western and other observers that such a development would lead to the consolidation of a pan-Islamic bloc, presumably under Iran's leadership, which potentially could have nuclear capability. It is further feared that this bloc would then proceed to threaten Western allies and interests in the Persian Gulf, the Middle East, and elsewhere. These fears account for the basic U.S. and Western strategy that has at its center the "containment" of Islamic and Iranian influence.

These are serious concerns that deserve serious consideration. The West, however, runs the risk of putting an exaggerated emphasis on these threats and overlooking others. No doubt, given that Islam is a vital part of their cultural makeup and the fact that for seventy years they were deprived of expressing their Islamic sentiments, Islam is bound to play a more prominent role in the social and political life of the ex-Soviet Muslim states as they begin to assert their cultural identity.

## The Development of Militant Islam Is Unlikely

Yet the likelihood of the development of the kind of militant Islamic ideology with strong anti-Western sentiments witnessed during the early years of the Islamic revolution or currently to be observed among certain militant movements in the Arab world is not very strong. The following reasons support this judgment.

First, the rise of militant Islam in Iran and in a number of Arab states was, and is, in large part related to two factors: the failure of the secular Western-oriented governments to meet their people's expectations for economic and social development; and the ideological vacuum created because of the growing popular disenchantment with both socialist and Western economic and political models. Given the identification of "establishment" Islam with the ruling elites, those who were searching for an alternative vehicle to express their frustration developed variants of a militant and unorthodox Islamic theory. The anti-Western dimension of these movements derived from the fact that Western powers were and are the dominant presence in most of the Islamic world, plus resentment generated by the perceived Western bias in favor of Israel and against Muslims.

None of these conditions prevails—at least to a degree to make it threatening—in the Muslim republics of the former Soviet Union. None of these states has experienced Western models of economic and social development, and thus they cannot experience the same feeling of disappointment as the Muslims who did. Quite the contrary, many of their people, and certainly their elites, view the Western model as the best road to economic prosperity and technological and scientific progress.

Second, none of these countries has experienced colonial or other types of domination by Western countries, and thus they do not harbor the same kind and degree of resentment evident among certain groups in the Middle East.

Third, the Arab-Israeli conflict and the baggage that goes with it are also less important for these states. Indeed, because anti-Israeli policies are identified with the old Communist system, they suffer from the general discredit now applied to all aspects of that system. This means that the anti-Westernism related to Western support for Israel is also far less important in these areas.

## Central Asian Republics of the Former Soviet Union

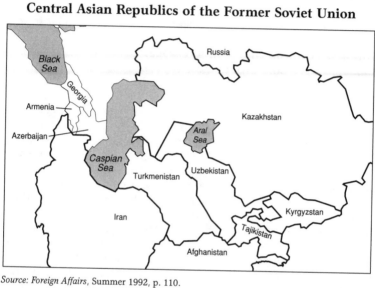

Source: *Foreign Affairs*, Summer 1992, p. 110.

Thus, even if they were to adopt a social and political system based on Islam, it is unlikely that the newly independent Muslim states would display the sort of anti-Western sentiments observed among groups in the Middle East. Moreover, there is a significant difference between, on the one hand, desiring a more prominent place for Islam and Islamic culture in the society and wanting to be included in the community of Islamic nations and, on the other, desiring to establish a government and polity based on a militant and extremist interpretation of Islam.

Fourth, the Islamic groups in these areas have not been influenced or financially supported in any significant degree by Iran. On the contrary, the most significant local influence has emanated from the Afghan mujahidin with Wahhabi [a strict Islamic sect] sympathies, Pakistan, and Saudi Arabia. Indeed, the overwhelmingly Sunni character of these republics makes them much less receptive to Iranian influence. Consequently, most of the Islamic groups in these countries are influenced by Wahhabism. In fact, Soviet publications often used to refer to them as "Wahhabis" and equated fundamentalism with Wahhabism.

## Iran's Influence Is Limited

The leaders of these groups also make it clear that despite their desire for an Islamic type of polity and society, they have no wish to emulate Iran. For example, one of the leaders of the Islamic movement in Tajikistan told a Western reporter that despite close cultural and linguistic links between Iran and Tajikistan, a potential Islamic government in Tajikistan would not be similar to that of Iran because Tajikistan is Sunni.

Moreover, those who tend to exaggerate the Iran-led Islamic fundamentalist challenge to these republics tend to forget the significant changes that have taken place in Iran itself. Iran today [in 1992] is not the Iran of ten, five, or even three years ago. Indeed, it is more concerned with its own economic reconstruction than an aggressive export of Islamic revolution. Iran's behavior since 1989, when the disintegrative forces became strong in the Soviet Union, clearly illustrates this. Indeed, the more radical elements in Iran have complained that the Iranian government has not taken advantage of the new circumstances to promote its Islamic ideology. Even some U.S. commentators admit that there is no evidence that in its contacts with the new states Iran has tried to encourage them to adopt its political model.

In addition to Iran's own domestic dynamics, the strengthening of the pragmatic moderate trend in Iran has also been a function of dramatic changes in the character of the international political system following the Soviet Union's disintegration. Iran is aware of the serious dangers to its interests of a revolutionary policy. The implications of these changes have not been lost on other Islamic groups and countries either, although their rhetoric still remains defiant.

Other reasons also indicate why it is highly unlikely that the newly independent republics would choose to go the road of militant Islam.

First, Muslim groups in these states lack an effective power base and financial resources. With the elimination of the Soviet threat and with their negative experience in Algeria [where in January 1992 a military coup prevented the election of an Islamic party], the Saudis, a principal—if not *the* principal—financial supporter of these groups, are unlikely to provide them with funds.

Second, unlike the situation in Iran, where the clerical establishment was supported by religious endowments and individual donations, these groups lack such resources. The official Muslim establishments were part and parcel of the old Soviet bureaucratic system and have no credibility with the people, nor do they have any inclination to create an Islamic government.

Third, even if some of these republics were to adopt the outward signs of an Islamic government, as in Saudi Arabia and Pakistan, by declaring the Quran or the Shari'a to be the source of law, it is unlikely that they would adopt an outwardly militant, expansionist, and anti-Western posture.

Economic factors and the enormous developmental needs of these countries would also act as a strong deterrent to any militant type of behavior because the Western countries, pro-Western conservative Arab regimes, and the international organizations, which are the only sources of finance and technology, would refuse to help them.

Thus, even if these countries were to rely on Islam as the conceptual and ideological underpinning of their new societies and polities, their Islam would not be of the militant brand.

## The Risk of a Pan-Islamic Bloc

The notion that the ex-Soviet Muslim states could become the nucleus of a pan-Islamic front capable of challenging and threatening U.S. and Western interests is also highly unrealistic.

First, 1,400 years of Islamic history is proof that allegiance to Islam has never been enough for political unity. Not only was Islam—despite its universal message, which transcends race and ethnicity—not able to eliminate, or even reduce, the impact of ethnicity and cultural diversity, it was itself corrupted and fractionalized by their tenacity. The Muslim world now is as divided as ever, if not more so, along ethnic and sectarian lines.

All recent efforts to create a Muslim political grouping or coalition have also foundered on the same grounds. The latest of these was attempted during the Persian Gulf War, when Saddam Hussein's call for a pan-Islamic response to what he tried to portray as an imperialist-Zionist assault on Islam went unheeded. Even the policies with respect to the Persian Gulf War of an avowedly Muslim state and champion of pan-Islamism such as Iran were determined by purely nationalist considerations.

In fact, it could be stated with near certainty that pan-Islamism will never succeed because there can never be agreement on who would lead such a movement. All of those who preach pan-Islamism want it only on their own terms and under their own leadership.

Western fears of Islam are, therefore, exaggerated and a Western policy toward the newly independent republics that is determined too much by the fear of Islam and the growth of pan-Islamism would be misguided. Such a policy could open Western countries to manipulation by these states because they could play on Western fears of Islam. It could also give them a pretext to delay democratic reforms. Moreover, by appearing anti-Islam, the West could undermine its standing with these people.

## The Threat from Iran?

The fear of Iranian influence and its ominous implications for U.S.-Western interests is even more unrealistic and unwarranted than the fear expressed in regard to Islam.

First of all, the basis upon which the fear of the Iranian threat is founded is very weak. Regarding signs of Iran's expansionist ambitions in the ex-Soviet Muslim republics, proponents of this theory have no evidence to go by stronger than to note trips by a number of Iranian officials—including its foreign minister—to these countries and the signing of memorandums of understanding on potential cooperative ventures in such fields as transportation, energy, and trade.

Even if all these agreements were to be implemented—an unlikely prospect for the near future given the lack of financial resources—they would not amount to Iranian political or economic domination of the region. Indeed other countries, notably Turkey, are far ahead of Iran in establishing their presence. For example, there have been more exchanges of officials between Turkey and the ex-Soviet Muslim republics than between them and Iran. In fact, before establishing any contacts with Iran, these countries' leaders first made a point of making a pilgrimage to Ankara in order to underscore the priority they accorded Turkey. . . .

Given this picture, talk of Iranian economic—and by extension, political—domination of the ex-Soviet Muslim republics is unrealistic. Indeed, Iran's efforts to establish economic and political ties with these states derive more from its fears for its own security and territorial integrity than an expansionist impulse. Many of Iran's Turkic-speaking ethnic minorities are represented among the populations of, for instance, Azerbaijan and Turkmenistan.

Irredentist tendencies toward Iran among the Muslim republics [seeking the recovery of "historic" lands], the existence of separatist elements within Iranian minorities, and a resurgence of Turkic nationalism and pan-Turkism are extremely alarming to Iran. In consequence, Iran's emphasis on Islamic solidarity should be seen not as an attempt to create a militant pan-Islamist front, but as an effort to mitigate the surge of pan-Turkist sentiments that could be threatening to its territorial integrity.

In fact, in general Iran is feeling increasingly hemmed in and threatened and many of its foreign policy acts—some extremely unwise—are desperate efforts to reduce this feeling of encirclement. If efforts to exclude Iran from the region or to promote anti-Iranian sentiments continue, however, Iran may be forced to manipulate the Islamic factor in ways feared by the West, even though this would harm Iran more than it would others. Thus in devising its policy toward the region, the West should not exaggerate the Iranian threat. Moreover, the West would be well advised to remember the lessons of the 1980s, when an excessive fear of Iran and Islamic fundamentalism and neglect of Iran's internal changes contributed to the Saddam Hussein phenomenon. . . .

## Ingredients for a Prudent Policy

If the current trends in the U.S. and Western approach to the newly independent Muslim republics entail considerable risk of negative fallout in terms of enhanced risk of conflict and regional instability, on what basis could a more prudent policy be developed?

The first principle is that U.S.-Western policy should be based on positive rather than negative impulses. In other words, rather than basing their policy, as they appear to have done, on the principle of containing Iran and Islam, the United States and the West should develop a policy to promote democracy, pluralism, respect for the rights of religious and linguistic minorities, and improvement in the economic and social conditions of the new states.

Initially, the United States seemed to be adopting this approach when it made good relations with the United States contingent on the new states' respect for certain basic principles. The U.S. position changed, however, out of supposed fear of Iran and the spread of fundamentalist Islam. One consequence of this situation is that the United States has had to compromise on its principles and embrace governments that have changed very little, if at all, since Communist days.

The United States cannot afford a rigid approach to these issues. But just as its exaggerated preoccupation with the Communist threat in the Third World during the cold war years led it into alliances with some very unsavory regimes, contributing to the failure of democracy in many of these countries, now its exaggerated concern with Islam could have the same effect. Indeed, there is some evidence that the leaders of these new states are manipulating the U.S. fear of Islam and dislike for Iran to their advantage.

Moreover, most of these states' present leaders are likely to change in the not too distant future. The absence of an open atmosphere that would permit the formation of progressive successors, coupled with some of the extreme nationalist tendencies noted earlier, would mean that the groups from whose ranks the new leaders were likely to emerge would be ultranationalist fascistic elements or, indeed, Muslim militants. This is no mere speculation. Rather, the Middle East's experience clearly shows that the lack of participatory politics has prevented the formation of progressive leaders and institutions and created a vacuum that Muslim extremists are now trying to fill. In the past, repressive governments used the threat of communism to prevent any debate and convince the West to support them. Now their excuse is the threat of Muslim fundamentalism.

In short, by exaggerating the Islamic threat and thus refraining from encouraging democracy, Washington may indeed contribute to that threat's materialization.

Another principle is to base policy on a correct reading of the geographical, cultural, and historical realities of the ex-Soviet Muslim republics. A policy centered on Turkey that aims at total exclusion of Iran is unrealistic and potentially harmful. A better strategy for the United States and the West generally would be to make clear their opposition to any form of extremism, including Islamic, irrespective of its origin. If it is proved that Iran is actively fomenting extremism, then countermeasures would be not only justified but necessary. But to characterize any Iranian contact a priori as a mortal threat would be counterproductive. . . .

Because it would inevitably be a player in the region, rather than isolating Iran the United States and the West should recognize positive changes in that country and, through a judicious use of carrots and sticks, gradually improve relations with it, and thus strengthen these positive trends and eventually eliminate the so-called Iranian threat.

The ability of the ex-Soviet Muslim states to improve their economic conditions will largely determine their political future. The United States and the West would be well advised, therefore, to help them in this endeavor.

In general the West should expand relations with these states at all levels and in all fields. It should in particular help in the formation and training of a new generation of political leaders and professionals. This, more than anything else, would help the new states move in directions favored by the West. Ultimately their future will be largely determined by the interplay of forces indigenous to them and their neighbors. A Western strategy along the lines sketched above that recognizes the historical and cultural intricacies and ambiguities of these states and is not based solely on the simplistic notion of containing Islam could help move them in directions that would best serve both their interests and those of the West.

*"The country that is often mentioned as a candidate for a Khomeini-style revolution is . . . Egypt."*

# The Islamic Revolution Is Taking Root in Egypt

Mark Juergensmeyer

Witnessing the religious violence in Egypt of 1992–94, some experts have predicted that Egypt will be the next Iran—that it will be the next country to experience a radical Islamic revolution. In the following viewpoint, Mark Juergensmeyer argues that the Islamic revolutions occurring in the Middle East, like religious revolutions before them, combine religion with nationalism—the modern Western concept of the nation-state. In Egypt, he contends, the combination of Islam and nationalism has a strong tradition, as evidenced by the writings of Abd al-Salam Faraj and Sayyid Qutb. According to Juergensmeyer, though Egypt is not likely to experience a radical Islamic revolution as complete and sudden as Iran's, it is possible that Egypt will evolve toward an Islamic system of government. Juergensmeyer is editor of the Comparative Studies in Religion and Society series from the University of California Press.

As you read, consider the following questions:

1. What are the characteristics of religious nationalist movements, according to Juergensmeyer?
2. Why were Nasser and Sadat unpopular with the Islamic nationalists in Egypt, according to the author?
3. What are some aspects of jihad, according to Faraj, cited here by Juergensmeyer?

Excerpted from Mark Juergensmeyer, *The New Cold War? Religious Nationalism Confronts the Secular State*. Berkeley and Los Angeles: University of California Press. Copyright ©1993 by The Regents of the University of California. Reprinted with permission of the publisher.

Although the rise of revolutionary movements that embrace a religious nation-state is new, the movements inherit a long tradition of religious protest and social change. Religion and politics have been intertwined throughout history and around the globe, and a number of rebellions against authority, from the Maccabean revolt in ancient Israel to the Taiping Rebellion in China, the Wahhabiya movement in Arabia, and Puritanism in England, have been religious in character. Some of them, like the movements to be discussed here, were rebellions against secular authorities. The Puritans, with their theocratic revolt against the increasing secularism of seventeenth-century English politics, may be regarded as precursors of modern antisecular radicals.

The new movements are different from their historical predecessors in that they are reactions to, and are attempts to forge a synthesis with, a specific political form that originated in the modern West: the nation-state. In responding to it, religious nationalists evoke ethnic loyalties and religious commitments that are by definition specific. These movements are identified with particular geographic and linguistic regions. To understand the phenomenon, then, we have to see it in its diversity. . . .

## The Islamic Dream of a Global State

One could question whether the sights of these revolutionary movements are aimed solely at the national level. Like the ideological rhetoric of the old Cold War, the political rhetoric of many of the movements seems directed toward a supranational ideal. This is especially true of the Muslim movements. The longing for a global state of religious harmony is an old Islamic dream, and for years the great Islamic empires appeared to be on the verge of making that dream a reality. For this reason, many Muslim activists hesitate to speak of solely national interests and instead express pan-Islamic ideals. Many espouse Muslim nationalism in general; pictured on the wall of one of the Palestinian leaders in Gaza is a map of the world on which is superimposed the Qur'an drawn as if it had hands extending from Morocco to Indonesia. Some Muslim writers go so far as to regard the very idea of nationalism as anti-Islamic. Kalim Siddiqui has described nationalism as "the greatest evil that stalks the modern world," and although he acknowledges that many Muslim movements are indeed nationalist, he sees their nationalism as a short-term goal and looks forward to a Muslim unity "beyond the Muslim nation-states."

Even though this yearning for a single Islamic nation runs deep in Muslim consciousness, most Muslim activists seem happy to settle for an Islamic nationalism that is limited to the particular countries in which they reside. In the modern period, as Ira Lapidus explains, "the capacity of Islam to symbolize social identity has been merged into national feeling." The most obvious example is Iran; the Shi'ite form of Islam that predominates there is rarely found elsewhere. But even in Sunni areas, such as Egypt and Palestine, religious sentiments are fused with national concerns. The religious revolutionaries there fight for an Egyptian or a Palestinian identity as well as a Muslim one. Even the proponents of a worldwide Islamic nation, such as Siddiqui, concede the necessity for "a succession of Islamic Revolutions in all Muslim areas of the world." They expect that these will eventually be united through "'open' or 'soft' frontiers" to replace the boundaries between Islamic states. My guess, however, is that the borders will stay immutable and solid, for the pan-Islamic sentiments of Arabs and other Muslims have always been vexed by intra-Islamic rivalries, many of which were exacerbated in 1991 by the Gulf War.

---

### "When We Take Power . . ."

Dr. Abdel-Hamid Mahmoud speaks with the calm determination of a man who knows his day is coming. He favors the future unconditional tense: "We will prevail . . . ," "When we take power . . ." His disciples at the al-Rahma mosque in Asyut, Egypt, listen respectfully, intervening only to illustrate a point that their teacher, a gaunt thirty-year-old veterinarian and self-taught Koranic scholar, has made. "The system in Egypt is a failure," he intones. "We will replace it with an Islamic system that spreads justice all over the world."

Stephen Hubbell, *The Nation*, September 28, 1992.

---

Even so, Islamic nationalism in one country can encourage the growth of Islamic nationalism in other countries. In the 1980s, the Islamic revolution in Iran served as a model for the emergence of modern Islamic nation-states elsewhere in the world. In the early 1990s, Islamic leaders in Sudan promoted Muslim activism throughout the region. After 1989, when Lieutenant General Omar Hassan Ahmed Bashir established an Islamic regime in Sudan, thousands of young Muslim revolutionaries came to study in Sudanese universities and to train in its military camps. Hassan Abdullah Turabi, the Islamic leader described by Kim Murphy, an American reporter, as the "behind-the-scenes power" in Khartoum, is also mentioned as "one of the key architects" of Islamic movements in Algeria, Tunisia, Egypt, Ethiopia, Nigeria, Chad, and Afghanistan.

In each of these countries, however, the impetus toward an Islamic nationalism was distinctively tied to each country's history and culture, and it is doubtful that Sudanese or any other external agents made a decisive difference. . . .

Muslim political activism is on the rise throughout the world, but it is not orchestrated by a central command, nor are its goals antithetical to national interests. Many Muslim activists are indeed nationalists; some support subnational, local, and ethnic entities; and a few favor a pan-Islamic federation of states. Most, however, are united in their stand against the adoption of Western secular nationalism. Like religious activists everywhere, they criticize secular rule from a religious perspective; they employ religious language, leadership, and organization in their attempts to change it; and they hold up the promise of a new religious order as a shining ideal. . . .

## Egypt's Incipient Religious Revolt

The event that set the standard for religious revolution throughout the Muslim world was the Islamic revolution in Iran. . . . Can the religious revolution that Khomeini created in Iran be exported to other places in the Islamic world? Many observers think that it can, and the country that is often mentioned as a candidate for a Khomeini-style revolution is the largest Muslim country in Northern Africa and the Middle East: Egypt. During an informal conversation among a group of international journalists, one of them told me emphatically that Egypt would be the new Iran. He was speaking about the rise of what is often called militant Islamic fundamentalism and its political impact. The journalist pointed to the great gulf between the secular political elite in the genteel areas of the cities and the Muslim clergy in rural Egypt and in the Cairo slums. A similar situation, he recalled, brought about the downfall of the shah of Iran.

There is no question that the rise of Islamic activism is a serious and potentially explosive aspect of contemporary Egypt. After all, President Anwar Sadat was assassinated by a member of al-Jihad, a radical Muslim group, in 1981. In 1984, Egypt's minister of the interior was assassinated by a member of the same group; and in October 1990 al-Jihad is said also to have been responsible for the brutal killing of the speaker of the Egyptian Assembly, Rifaat el-Mahgoub, who at the time of his death was second in power only to President Hosni Mubarak. One motive for the assassination was the movement's unhappiness over the government's stand against Iraq's Hussein (who, although a secular Arab, was admired by many Muslims for his anti-American and pro-Palestinian stand). Perhaps more importantly, members of al-Jihad were incensed over the role Mahgoub is said to have played in blocking legislation aimed at strengthening the influence of Islamic law in Egypt's courts. In Egypt, as in many other Arab countries, trifling with the spread of Islam is serious business.

However, Egypt is not necessarily going the way of Iran. The radical Islamic movements in Egypt are different in basic ways from their Iranian counterparts. Sunni Muslims have neither the theological nor the organizational connection to politics that Shi'ites do, nor has Egypt had the same pattern of suppression of Islam that Iran has had. The Egyptian movements are much less centralized. Despite the fear of many Westerners that the virus of Khomeinism would spread (and perhaps Khomeini's wish that it had), Muslim activists throughout the Sunni world seem surprisingly ignorant of and uninterested in the Iranian experiment. "They have their political problems," a member of the Muslim Brotherhood in Cairo told me, referring to the Iranians, "and we have ours." Although there is sometimes a tremor of admiration in their voices when they speak of the power of the Iranian revolution, the Egyptians seldom offer that upheaval as a model for their own.

## The History of Egyptian Radicalism

Although some scholars see more of an Iranian influence in Egypt than meets the eye, the more obvious interaction is the other way around: the influence of radical Egyptian Muslim movements on the Iranians. In the late 1940s and early 1950s, the Iranians' Fedayeen-i-Islam was created in imitation of the guerrilla Muslim Brotherhood (Jam'iyat al-Ikhwan al-Muslimin), which was spreading terror at the time throughout Egypt. Egypt's Muslim Brotherhood had been founded in 1928 by Hasan al-Banna, and another radical Muslim movement, the Young Egypt Society (which advocated a kind of Islamic socialism), was founded soon after, in 1933.

The leaders of these early Egyptian movements of Islamic politics were reacting against the transnational modernism that remained as the legacy of the British Empire (and before it, the Ottoman). Western culture, political influence, and economic control were the elements of a modernity that some of the early nationalists wished to reject. For that reason, Egyptian nationalism from the outset grew in both religious and secular directions. The Muslim Brotherhood represented the Islamic form of Egyptian nationalism, and the Wafd Party represented its secular side. When King Faruk (Farooq) and the whole tradition of Egyptian monarchy were overthrown in 1952, it was largely the Wafd vision of a secular Egypt that emerged triumphant.

Yet even after Faruk, Islamic nationalism continued to be a potent force in Egyptian politics. The great leader of the revolution, Jamal 'Abd al-Nasir (whom the Western world knows as Gamal Abdel Nasser), had at one time been associated with the Muslim Brotherhood, as had his successor, Sadat. Despite their willingness to defend the Islamic aspects of Egyptian nationalism, neither Nasser nor Sadat was sufficiently strident in his ideology nor obsequious enough in his response to the Muslim leadership to remain in the favor of Islamic extremists. By the 1960s, the leaders of the Muslim Brotherhood and Nasser were locked in bitter opposition; some of the leaders attempted to overthrow Nasser's regime, and he promptly threw them in prison.

The love-hate relationship between Muslim leaders and secular politicians continued in the 1970s during Sadat's regime. On the one hand, Sadat released the leaders of the Muslim Brotherhood from prison, lifted a ban on the writings of Muslim radicals, and was instrumental in the drafting of the 1971 version of the Egyptian Constitution, which proclaimed, in Article Two, that the goal of the judicial system was eventually to make shari'a (Islamic law) the law of the land. On the other hand, he did little to carry out this goal or the other Islamic reforms he had earlier touted. Sadat's concessions to Coptic Christians were widely denounced, and his wife was portrayed as being promiscuous. Pictures of her dancing with U.S. president Gerald Ford at a formal occasion at the White House were circulated as evidence of her infidelity. The accords with Israel arranged by U.S. president Jimmy Carter were considered further signs of Sadat's moral decay, and he eventually succeeded in "having everyone turn against him," as one Egyptian scholar explained, in part because "he tried too hard to please everyone." His killers were members of al-Jihad.

## The Meaning of Jihad

Although al-Jihad has been at the fringes of the Muslim Brotherhood, and its various splinter organizations have made a deep political impact, its ideology is the antithesis of Sadat's moderate Muslim stand. But despite its violence, its leaders have not been lunatics. One of them, Abd al-Salam Faraj, was the author of a remarkably cogent argument for waging war against the political enemies of Islam. His pamphlet, "Al-Faridah al-Gha'ibah" ("The Neglected Duty"), states more clearly than any other contemporary writing the religious justifications for radical Muslim acts. It was published and first circulated in Cairo in the early 1980s. This document grounds the current activities of Islamic terrorists firmly in Islamic tradition, specifically in the sacred text of the Qur'an and the biographical accounts of the Prophet in the hadith.

Faraj argues that the Qur'an and the hadith are fundamentally about warfare. The concept of jihad, holy war, is meant to be taken literally, not allegorically. According to Faraj, the "duty" that has been profoundly "neglected" is jihad, and it calls for "fighting, which means confrontation and blood." Moreover,

Faraj regards anyone who deviates from the moral and social requirements of Islamic law to be fit targets for jihad; these targets include apostates within the Muslim community as well as the more expected enemies from without. Perhaps the most chilling aspect of his thought is his conclusion that peaceful and legal means for fighting apostasy are inadequate. The true soldier for Islam is allowed to use virtually any means available to achieve a just goal. Deceit, trickery, and violence are specifically mentioned as options available to the desperate soldier. Faraj sets some moral limits to the tactics that may be used—for example, innocent bystanders and women are to be avoided, whenever possible, in assassination attempts—but emphasizes that the duty to engage in such actions when necessary is incumbent on all true Muslims. The reward for doing so is nothing less than an honored place in paradise. Such a place was presumably earned by Faraj himself in 1982 after he was tried and executed for his part in the assassination of Sadat.

## A Tradition of Radical Islam

This way of thinking, although extreme, is not idiosyncratic to Faraj. He stands in a tradition of radical Islamic political writers that reaches back to the beginning of this century and earlier. Among Sunni Muslims worldwide, the most important radical thinker has been Maulana Abu al-Ala Mawdudi, the founder and ideological spokesman for Pakistan's Jamaat-i-Islami (Islamic Association). His ideas were echoed by Egypt's most influential writer in the radical Muslim political tradition, Sayyid Qutb. Qutb was born in 1906 and, like Faraj, was executed for his political activities. Although he was not as explicit as Faraj in indicating the techniques of terror that were acceptable for the Islamic warrior, Qutb laid the groundwork for Faraj's understanding of jihad as an appropriate response to the advocates of those elements of modernity that seemed to be hostile to Islam. Specifically, Qutb railed against those who encouraged the cultural, political, and economic domination of the Egyptian government by the West. Qutb had spent several years in the United States studying educational administration, but this experience only confirmed his impression that American society was essentially racist and that American policy in the Middle East was dictated by Israel and what he regarded as the Jewish lobby in Washington, D.C. Alarmed at the degree to which the new government in Egypt was modeled after Western political institutions and influenced by Western values, Qutb, in the early 1950s, advocated a radical return to Islamic values and Muslim law. In *This Religion of Islam*, Qutb argued that the most basic divisions within humanity are grounded in religion rather than race or nationality, and that religious war is the only form of killing that is morally sanctioned. To Qutb's way of thinking, the ultimate war is between truth and falsehood, and satanic agents of falsehood were to be found well entrenched in the Egyptian government. It is no wonder that the government found such ideas dangerous. Qutb was put in prison for most of the rest of the 1950s and was silenced forever in 1966.

## The Future of the Radical Movement

The radical ideas of Mawdudi, Qutb, and Faraj have circulated widely in Egypt through two significant networks: universities and the Muslim clergy. The two networks intersect in the Muslim educational system, especially in the schools and colleges directly supervised by the clergy. The most important of these are the ones connected with Cairo's Al-Azhar University. They enroll only a small percentage of Egyptian students—perhaps 5 percent or so—at all levels of the educational system. It is a significant number, nonetheless, because of the impact of the Muslim teachers in relating the traditional truths of Islam to modern ideas. As the dean of the Faculty of Education at Al-Azhar University explained to me, the school's mission is to show how modern academic subjects and fields of professional training—including business, medicine, law, and education—can be taught from an Islamic perspective. Not surprisingly, the university is often viewed as a fountainhead of radical Islamic ideas, and a great number of militant Muslim activists receive their training there.

Despite its dreams, the radical Muslim movement has yet to be sufficiently united to threaten President Mubarak with anything like the revolution in Iran. Even though it showed its destructive power in the 1990 assassination of the speaker of the Assembly, al-Jihad remains a small splinter organization. The larger parent movement, the Muslim Brotherhood, has become somewhat more moderate. Though not accepted as a legal party, it has been well represented in the legislature. Members of the Brotherhood, running as independent candidates in the 1987 elections, won 38 seats out of the 448 in the People's Assembly. The platform of the Brotherhood was clearly articulated by its leader, Abu al-Nasr, in an open letter to President Mubarak in February 1987. According to Nasr, the movement has four main positions: pride in its Egyptian identity and tradition, the conviction that the current problems of Egypt are largely spiritual and moral in nature, the expectation that Islamic values will be made the basis for all aspects of Egyptian society, and the desire for Islamic organizations to have the freedom to operate as they wish.

These are, in a sense, reasonable positions, but their very reasonableness is a cause for concern among those who do not wish them to succeed. The movement cannot easily be dismissed as fanatical, and its slate is more likely to be adopted

266

through the routine actions of parliament and by governmental fiat than if it were advocated in a more strident and vicious way. Although the Persian Gulf War in 1991 divided the various Muslim factions in Egypt over questions of stance and strategy, this division only made more clear the public acceptability of the moderate stand. For that reason, if the Islamic revolution succeeds in Egypt, it will most likely be by degrees. A gradual revolution, however, might bring about changes as profound and unsettling to the West as any that a more sudden shift in ideology and power could accomplish.

---

*"The strength, breadth and depth of secular society in Egypt is real."*

---

# The Islamic Revolution Is Not Taking Root in Egypt

Michael Collins Dunn

The assassination of Anwar Sadat in October 1981 marked the beginning of violence associated with the Islamic revival in Egypt. Since 1992, renewed terrorism has killed hundreds of people (including several foreign tourists), prompting the Egyptian government to crack down on the Islamic Group, al-Gamaa al-Islamiyya. In the following viewpoint, Michael Collins Dunn argues that the fundamentalist Islamic Group represents a minority in Egypt that is not likely to gain power. The majority of Muslims oppose the violence of the Islamic Group, according to Dunn, and though there is a broad revival of religion in Egypt, Egyptian society also has a strong secular base that makes an Islamic revolution unlikely. Dunn is senior analyst of International Estimate, Inc., a consulting company in Virginia that provides analysis of the Middle East and Asia, and editor of its biweekly newsletter, the *Estimate*.

As you read, consider the following questions:

1. According to Dunn, what are the growing number of debates between the clerical establishment and the secularists in Egypt a symptom of?
2. How did Sayyid Qutb, cited by Dunn, portray the secular state?
3. What are the possible relationships of the "New Jihad" to al-Gamaa al-Islamiyya, according to Dunn?

From Michael Collins Dunn, "Fundamentalism in Egypt," *Middle East Policy*, vol. 2, no. 3, 1993. Reprinted with permission.

There is no denying that the Egyptian government of President Husni Mubarak is facing a major challenge from radical Islamists, though those commentators who automatically assume that this will translate into a change of government are probably misreading the situation. The basic resilience of Egyptian society, the pervasive national security apparatus available to the government and the repulsion even most Islamic revivalists in Egypt feel towards random violence directed at public targets all work against the efforts of the radicals to topple the state. . . .

Few [cases of Islamic revivalism] are as important to the rest of the world as the events in Egypt. With its strategic location, population of some 60 million, and alignment with the West, Egypt's future is of concern far beyond the immediate region. Not even Algeria, where the level of political violence is much higher than in Egypt, creates so much concern abroad.

In addition, events in Egypt have had their echoes far from the Nile. Sheikh Umar Abd al-Rahman, the blind spiritual leader of *al-Gamaa al-Islamiyya*, the "Islamic Group" which has claimed many but not all of the attacks in Egypt, is accused of complicity in the February 1993 bombing of the World Trade Center in New York and in a plot to bomb the United Nations and two key traffic tunnels in New York. A man who was little known even in Egypt has suddenly become front-page news in America.

## A Transfer of Power?

Yet, as is so often the case in general reportage about Islamic revivalism and politics, for all the words written about Egypt, only occasionally does one garner a clue that the Egyptian situation is more complex than a mere confrontation between "Islamic Fundamentalism" on the one hand and the Mubarak government on the other. Such superficial analyses also often assume that since the Mubarak regime is demonstrably unpopular with many Egyptians, this is likely to translate into a transfer of power to—whom? The shadowy, unnamed leaders of al-Gamaa? Umar Abd al-Rahman in his New York jail? There is no clear leader, no charismatic figure, no Ayatollah Ruhollah Khomeini waiting in the wings at this time.

If the radical challenge to the state were to bring about the removal of the present government, it would almost certainly be because growing disorder prompted the military or security services to intervene, as happened in Algeria. At least in the short term, that would lead to harsher measures against the Islamists, not their triumph.

This does not mean that what is going on in Egypt is unimportant, or to be dismissed as mere urban terrorism. This viewpoint is an attempt to raise some of the issues involved in the conflict between al-Gamaa and other movements on the one hand and the government on the other, but also the deeper issues of the role of Islam in politics in Egypt. . . .

## The Broader Islamic Revival

To many outside observers, and no doubt to some avidly secularist Egyptians, the extremism of al-Gamaa and similar groups is seen as simply one end of the spectrum of religious revivalism, directly related to and following logically from the other examples of religious conservatism making themselves felt throughout Egyptian society. This is a dangerous assumption, since it could lead from the extension of the crackdown on extremism to a crackdown on all Islamic revival, a movement with much broader appeal across Egyptian society.

There is no denying that a broadly based Islamic revival is going on in Egypt. It is evident in the streets: more women are wearing the head-veil, including career women. There are fewer places that serve alcohol outside the major hotels, and those that do are very discreet about it. At Friday prayer, mosque attendance spills over into the adjacent streets. Television preachers are popular, and the radio station carrying the Quran is widely listened to.

But this increase in piety does not always translate into a political agenda. In fact, the Sufi orders, which are anathema to the political Islamists as an "innovation" and unorthodox, have always been strong and seem to be growing in strength as well. The general problems of the country—economic disasters, overpopulation, uninspiring leadership—seem to be spurring a return to religion in all its forms, not merely its radical political form.

Throughout Islamic history there have been calls for renewal, for a return to basics, for a purification of the secularized state. These have been particularly frequent in difficult times, and also at the beginning of each Islamic century: the Islamic year 1400 began in 1979. Sometimes such calls are simply religious, other times they are linked to political demands, and sometimes they have even been messianic in their vision. Bits and pieces of all these appear in today's Egypt.

No one will deny that Egyptians are more devout now than they were back in the Gamal Abdel Nasser era [1952–1970], when "Arab socialism" sought to offer a secular vision of the future. But only those secularists to whom the sight of people praying is some sort of threat are alarmed by the general return to piety. Recently there was a scandal over the death of a man from the city of Minya who had gone to Cairo to visit the tombs of saints and died in police custody. Presumably he was suspected of political radicalism, but in fact most political "fundamentalists" look upon saint veneration as a Sufi, and thus unorthodox, innovation. Not every man on a pious pilgrimage or woman wearing a headscarf is a threat to the state.

This is a crucial distinction. In fact, when religious figures in public life appear to overstep the bounds of the accepted civic religion, there is an uproar. In recent years the government has sometimes yielded to the Islamic revival, withdrawing controversial books. One professor was denied tenure because clerics ruled his writings smacked of atheism.

These events have all provoked public controversy and debates in the press. And although one of the sharpest critics of the extremists and even of moderate Islamic revivalism, the late Farag Foda, was gunned down in 1992 for his efforts, his writings retain a readership. Of all these events, only the killing of Foda was a purely political act and a challenge to the existing society. The others may have made life uncomfortable for the targets of Islamic wrath, but their significance should not be overblown. . . .

When such controversies arise they are debated in the Egyptian press and deplored by the intelligentsia. As a result, the perception grows that there is a rising tide of Islamic radicalism. What is easy to overlook is the vigor of the response. For every such move there is a strong secularist riposte, and while Farag Foda may have been silenced others still support the traditions of Egyptian secularism.

## A History of Religious-Secular Debate

There is a history of just this sort of religious-secular debate in Egypt. The presence of al-Azhar, the 1000-year-old university mosque that is the center of Sunni orthodoxy in Egypt and, in many ways, for much of the Middle East, is an important factor. The Egyptian *ulama* [religious authorities] may be co-opted by the state, but they are more than willing to preach against excessive secularism. Al-Azhar attacked Ali Abd al-Razzaq in the 1920s for suggesting the caliphate was no longer necessary, and it attacked Taha Hussein for what it saw as dangerous secularist ideas about pre-Islamic Arab poetry.

The secularists of course fought back. In the Nasser era Khalid Muhammad Khalid wrote a blistering attack on the official clerical establishment, *Min huna nabda* (From here we start), in which he saw them as a priestly class standing in the way of progress. Ironically, Khalid himself by the 1980s was involved in revivalist Islam.

The point is that there have long been tensions between the clerical establishment and the secularists. These disputes are sometimes rather arcane, other times very relevant to everyday life—debates over birth control, for example. They are not, however, a symptom of the present political radicalism, but rather of the general tendency towards a return to piety.

Egypt has a large educated middle class, particularly in Cairo and Alexandria. While many of the professionals among them do support Islamist groups such as the Muslim Brotherhood, they are not well represented in the violent, radical groups. These draw, rather, from the poorer slums of the capital and from the frustrated youth of the Upper Egyptian cities. These youths have an education—often the first college graduates or even the first generation of literates in their family—but cannot find a job, cannot in fact enter the Egyptian elite.

The Egyptian middle classes were created to some extent by the Nasser era and are not going to go away, however. Those who minimize their importance are probably making a fundamental mistake. Like the security forces, they are a major obstacle to the radicals' achieving the sort of revolutionary Islamic state they envision. . . .

## The Radicals: Who Are They?

Nazih Nuzhi Rashid, whose right leg was blown off in the bombing attack on Interior Minister Hasan al-Alfi in August 1993 and who subsequently died, was a young man in his thirties, but he had nearly two decades of experience in the violent Islamist underground. First arrested in the 1970s as a high-school student for involvement in the abortive attack on the Technical Military Academy, Rashid had had numerous run-ins with the law and was being hunted for robbing a jewelry store when the attack took place.

Any look at the key figures in the radical Egyptian underground turns up such careers as his. Although the names of the group may change, the same faces keep turning up. Through the years some have been executed, others have been jailed for long periods or operate from exile, and still others are on the run.

Years ago, the noted Egyptian sociologist Saad Eddin Ibrahim studied the backgrounds of the members of some of the early groups which plotted against Anwar Sadat, and found what has come to be a standard pattern in such groups elsewhere: most were young men, themselves educated but often from a rural or illiterate background, frequently from Upper Egypt. One of the unanticipated results of widespread education in Egypt has been the production of large numbers of college-educated youth, even in the most remote areas of the country, who have little hope of finding a job that pays well and may have to settle for low-paying bureaucratic sinecures. The flight to the cities—greater Cairo today may hold a quarter of the country's population or more—also means that the social supports of extended family and village are no longer present. The mosque becomes the sole familiar support from one's origins that is still available in the city. The fervor of Islamist preachers is generally more stirring than the more bland sermons of the official, government-issue imams.

Many of these young people no doubt turn to mainstream Islamic groups like the Muslim Brotherhood, despite the domination of that group by aging men; others clearly are attracted to the Sufi orders and more personal, mystical means of escaping the frustrations facing them in their lives. But still others prove to be prime soil for the radical groups to cultivate.

## Religious Extremism vs. Corrupt Government in Egypt

Terrorist violence [in Egypt], which the Western press has blown up to the most lurid proportions, has simply not affected life in Cairo or Alexandria, and it's made the assailants tremendously unpopular. No one I spoke with failed to mention that the perpetrators of an August 1993 bomb attack against a Government official riding in his car were apprehended, beaten up, then handed over to the police—by ordinary Egyptians who reacted spontaneously to the outrage. I happened to be speaking to a Cairo journalist by phone on August 19, the day after Interior Minister Hassan al-Alfi was wounded in a bomb attack just off Tahrir Square. Three Arab passers-by were also killed. Like the bomb that went off in Shubra (a poor section of Cairo) earlier in the summer, these indiscriminate killings further alienate the large majority of Egyptian Muslims. "In the battle between a religious extremism and terrorism seeking to bring down a corrupt and basically repressive Government, the choice for many of us, lamentable though it may be, is to side with army and regime," Gamal al-Ghitani says.

Edward W. Said, *The New York Times Magazine*, November 21, 1993.

The radical groups, for the most part, share an ideology usually attributed to the late Sayyid Qutb, one of the key thinkers of the old Muslim Brotherhood who, in his last years, grew more radical in response to years in prison under Nasser. (He was executed in 1966.) In his later writings Sayyid Qutb portrayed the secular state as *jahili*—essentially comparable to the idolatrous pagan society which preceded Islam. By extension, radical Islamists have argued that it is not only justified but, in the eyes of some, incumbent upon true believers to wage *jihad* against the secular state. Mainstream Islam has always taught that one cannot wage holy war against Muslims and has in recent centuries emphasized that the internal jihad, the struggle with oneself, deserves priority. Mainstream Islam has also emphasized that anyone who asserts the Muslim creed is to be treated as a Muslim. The radicals disregard these tolerant approaches and preach violent revolution against the secular state. They also insist that jihad should itself be considered a pillar of the faith—

273

*al-farida al-ghaiba* or "the neglected religious duty" in the words of the Jihad group's ideological leader Muhammad Abd al-Salam Faraj (executed for the Sadat assassination) and others.

In this respect, these radical revolutionary groups differ greatly from the more moderate political Islamists like the Brotherhood, who seek to transform society from within by restoring the practice of the faith and encouraging the adoption of Islamic law in society. . . .

## Al-Gamaa al-Islamiyya

Al-Gamaa al-Islamiyya, "the Islamic Group," is the name under which the group which claims to have perpetrated some (not all) of the attacks in the past few years has claimed responsibility. The name is close to but not identical to that of the *"Gami at Islamiyya"* or "Islamic societies" which grew up on Egyptian university campuses in the 1970s and 1980s. Among those who have been clearly linked with it are, again, Umar Abd al-Rahman. In the past, Egyptian authorities have said that the Gamaa is run by a "Shura Council" (consultative council) partly in country and partly in Peshawar, Pakistan, where the "Afghan" wing of the movement received their training in arms and explosives. Among the leaders in Peshawar is said to be Ayman al-Zawahri, a physician who spent three years in prison after the Sadat killing. But Ayman al-Zawahri has emerged as the alleged leader of the "New Jihad.". . .

The Gamaa has been blamed for a wide range of assassination attempts, bombings and shootings, including most of the attacks on tourists. It has claimed responsibility in some of these cases, often by fax from Peshawar. (Recently Pakistan has begun cracking down on radical Arab groups based in Peshawar since the end of the Afghan fight against the Russians.)

However, it has strongly denied being responsible for some of the more recent attacks. . . .

This has led to reports, which cannot be confirmed independently, that the always loosely organized Gamaa has split. . . .

The exiled wing of Gamaa, led by Ayman al-Zawahri, has reportedly opposed any attempt at a truce. By one argument, the radical wing began the attacks in Cairo in order to embarrass the more moderate wing and frustrate any efforts at a truce with the government. If so it has succeeded, for the crackdown is the most extensive in recent history, with 15 persons hanged in the summer of 1993 and 12 more under sentence of death at that time.

## The "New Jihad"

Lately some statements have appeared in the name of a group calling itself the "New Jihad," which the government says is led by Ayman al-Zawahri and which may thus represent the off-shoot exile or "Afghan" wing of the Gamaa under a new (or a revived) name. A group now under indictment calling itself the "Vanguards of Conquest" is said to be identified with this New Jihad, and the title "Vanguards of the New Jihad" has started to appear in government statements. . . .

Is it to be considered a rival group of the Gamaa, a radical off-shoot, or just another name change to befuddle the authorities and give an impression of a Medusa of groups when there is only one small one? An allegation against the New Jihad is that it is actively seeking to penetrate the armed forces. This was a characteristic of the original Jihad [founded in 1979 by Abd al-Salam Faraj and Umar Abd al-Rahman]—it took soldiers to assassinate Sadat. . . .

Of course, analyzing the internal splits and differences of an underground group is notoriously difficult, and often one has to depend on statements by the Interior Ministry, which may be disinformation. In any event, the escalation of violence in Cairo may well stem from a split within al-Gamaa, a split linked to the Afghans, both those abroad and those veterans of the Afghan war who have returned to Egypt with their knowledge of bomb-making and organization.

### How Great a Threat?

There are indications that the government has at least some knowledge of who the main agents of violence are. Nazih Nuzhi Rashid, already mentioned, was on a most-wanted list when he attacked General al-Alfi. Admittedly he had escaped capture, but his identity was known. A small, well-organized and dedicated group committed to violence and organized in a cell structure can successfully disrupt social peace even without widespread popular support, as leftist groups like the Red Brigades in Italy or Baader-Meinhof in Germany showed in the 1970s.

When there is a broad sympathy with some of the political agenda of the radicals—popular disgust with political corruption, a yearning for a more Islamic society—such groups may enjoy greater immunity. In Mao Zedong's words, the guerrilla swims like a fish in the sea of the people. There is real doubt that this stage has been reached in Egypt. While the government has unquestionably alienated many people by indiscriminate roundups in traditionalist neighborhoods and has rounded up many Islamist preachers who may know nothing of the political radicals, average Egyptians are still reportedly pursuing and catching bomb-throwers who try to run from the scene of their attack. In most of the attacks which have taken place, there have been arrests.

There is still a tendency for Western analysts to expect events in Egypt, Algeria or some other country to replay the events in

Iran in the late 1970s. Then, all the specialists and intelligence analysts were wrong; predictions that it won't happen elsewhere may be wrong again.

Indeed they may. But Egypt is not Iran. It is not Algeria either. The strength, breadth and depth of secular society in Egypt is real. While disillusionment with the government is also real, it is hardly unprecedented: except for a few moments in the 1960s when Nasser was riding high, Egyptian governments have rarely been popular in the streets.

The successful assassination of Anwar Sadat and the nearly successful one against General Hasan al-Alfi are reminders that the radicals can transform Egyptian life, however. But the removal of the senior leadership, even including President Mubarak, would not mean that power would pass to the small bands of radicals of al-Gamaa or New Jihad. The army and the security services would presumably step in.

What if this occurred—if somehow the armed forces, either in response to an assassination or a deepening collapse of order in Cairo, took power? Remember that Egypt has very little tradition of military coups: the 1952 "Revolution" is really the only one since Colonel Ahmad Urabi's day in the last century. Remember too that the Egyptian army, while generally secular, is not as intensely so as the Algerian army has proven itself. Former Field Marshal Muhammad Abdel Halim Abu Ghazala has been mentioned by many Egyptian intellectuals as a possible compromise that could please moderate Islamists as well as the secularists. . . .

In any event, it is extremely difficult at this time to write a scenario which would bring the radical Islamists to power—or even the moderate Brotherhood, except in some broader coalition. The regime is challenged, and social peace disrupted to a far greater degree than in recent memory. But the regime is showing its teeth, and they are sharp ones. If it does not make the mistake sometimes made by secularists of confusing all Islamic revival with the radicals who are throwing bombs, it is unlikely to galvanize the ordinary men and women who support the mainstream Islamist groups into rebellion. If it does make that mistake, it could fail, but what replaces it is likely to be a military state, not an Islamic one.

*"If communism has often been described as a disease, then Islamic fundamentalism is a plague infecting the entire Islamic world."*

# The West Should Be Wary of the Spread of Islamic Fundamentalism

Amos Perlmutter

In the following viewpoint, Amos Perlmutter warns that Islamic fundamentalists have successfully penetrated all levels of society in several Middle East countries, from charitable organizations to armies, with the aim of creating an Islamic state. He argues that Islamic groups that are hostile to the West are likely to topple friendly Middle East regimes because the Islamic fundamentalists are well organized and better able to provide services to people than the existing regimes. Perlmutter is a professor of political science at the American University in Washington, D.C., and editor of the *Journal of Strategic Studies*.

As you read, consider the following questions:

1. According to Perlmutter, what did the secular regimes that advocated pan-Arabism fail to do?
2. What is the agenda of the Islamic fundamentalists, according to Perlmutter?
3. Why is it wrong to say that the fundamentalists are a creation of Iran, in the author's view?

Amos Perlmutter, "Islamic Threat Is Clear and Present," *Insight on the News*, February 15, 1993. Reprinted by permission of the *Washington Times*.

If communism has often been described as a disease, then Islamic fundamentalism is a plague infecting the entire Islamic world, from Morocco to India. The menace of communism was always linked to the threat and power of Soviet nuclear weapons. It was an ideology and a movement that never really established firm roots in the societies it took over by coups or military occupation. The Marxist-Leninist language was alien to Russia, Eastern Europe and China, not to mention the Third World countries that communism tried to penetrate.

Islam, on the other hand, is an old and powerful instrument being exploited by a new generation of fundamentalist leaders. It poses a real and continuing danger and has the potential to destabilize a variety of fragile regimes in the Middle East.

## Islamic Fundamentalism Replaces Pan-Arabism

The old Arab nationalist ideology of Pan-Arabism was destroyed in the Sinai desert in 1967. Secular, praetorian-dominated regimes under the guise of Pan-Arabism, from Nasserism to Baathism, have replaced the old regimes of notables and pashas, from Egypt to Syria to Iraq. These regimes failed miserably to modernize, and they created a serious rift between regime and society that fundamentalists are now exploiting.

Egypt is an almost textbook example of the process. After the disastrous earthquake there in October 1992, it was the fundamentalist hospitals and subgroups that provided immediate help to the victims while the government's rigid and elephantine bureaucracy ground to a halt. It was a classic example of how the fundamentalists have networks within networks that have penetrated every fiber of the Egyptian social fabric. In Syria and the Gaza, they are doing the same. The penetrations are clandestine but patterned along the fundamentalist social structures of Egypt.

It's a mistake to think of fundamentalism as appealing only to the poorest people. The movement has recruited from the Egyptian middle classes and includes doctors, scientists, engineers, lawyers, writers, journalists and other elites. More significantly, it has penetrated the army, as was brutally demonstrated by the assassination of President Anwar Sadat by fundamentalist officers in 1981. Additionally, fundamentalists have penetrated the civil service, specifically the ministries of National Education and Religious Affairs.

Clearly, the fundamentalists have an agenda. Although there are ideological and theological differences among the various groups, they are united in a goal to topple praetorian military regimes in Egypt, Syria and Algeria. They share the intention to end secular Pan-Arabism in all its forms and replace it with an overarching Islamic concept of government, society, economics and politics in all Muslim states and societies. Their ideological goal is an Islamic state in one form or another.

Tactically, they are divided between smaller, more militant groups that want to resort to violence, assassination and terror to expedite the coming of the Islamic state and larger, more "pragmatic" groups that call for a gradual but nevertheless steady penetration of society and government. These are the groups that Westerners like to think of as "moderates," but they are moderate only in their tactics, not in their goals.

## Iran and Sudan Are Not the Causes

Experts like to explain away the rise of fundamentalism by pointing to Iran or [the Islamic regime of] Sudan as causes. This is unconvincing. Fundamentalism did not suddenly sprout up with the emergence of the ayatollahs in Iran. Fundamentalism in various forms has operated in the Middle East since the late 1920s and early 1930s. The philosophy of Islamic reform espoused by Sheik Abduh, the chief religious figure of Egypt under British occupation, informed the first Ikhwan Al-Muslimin, the notorious Egyptian Muslim Brotherhood.

---

## The Growing Islamization of Egypt

Egyptian officials charge that Iran and Sudan bear a large responsibility for the Egyptian militants. But the Egyptian Islamic movement seems largely homegrown. After all, Egypt is the cradle of Islamic militancy. There are several different schools of militants today in Egypt, all of which have their ideological roots in the Muslim Brotherhood.

While membership in the brotherhood is officially banned, the group is tolerated—a status of which it takes full advantage. It scored well in parliamentary elections in 1987, through an alliance with a legal opposition party. But the group's biggest success has been in winning control of the governing boards of professional associations, including those of lawyers, doctors, engineers, and pharmacists. These elections are far more democratic than political elections, which are heavily rigged, and they reflect the growing Islamization of Egyptian society.

Stanley Reed and Sarah Gauch, *Business Week*, July 12, 1993.

---

The Muslim Brotherhood played a key role in the Egyptian revolution of 1952, but Gamal Nasser soon enough began to suppress the group's leadership, seeing it correctly as a threat to his regime. Egyptian rulers from Nasser to Sadat to Hosni Mubarak have oppressed, banned and then freed fundamentalist leaders, depending on how serious a threat they posed.

Even though the fundamentalists are opposed to modernization, such technology as radio and cassettes actually has enhanced their message by giving them a wider audience. It's true, too, that financial, military and training support from Iran, as well as an influx of graduates from the Afghanistan volunteers, has made a considerable impact on the fundamentalists' terror and military capabilities.

There's a pattern common to all the fundamentalist movements. It's wrong to say that the fundamentalists in Egypt are the creation of Iran or that the fundamentalists in Gaza are a response to Israel's hard-line Likud governments. The Islamic fundamentalists are a viable political subculture in Egypt and Syria. They are the products of local and immediate events. Rooted in society itself, they are a very real representation of the anti-Western, antimodern forces in the Arab and Islamic world.

Fundamentalists almost won the election in Algeria in December 1991 [the elections were ended by a military coup], and they constitute a large part of Parliament in Jordan. In Sudan, they set the tone. In Syria, the oppressive regime of the Alawis still keeps them in check, but that will unquestionably change once Syrian president Hafez al-Assad passes from the scene. In Syria, the fundamentalists remember well the Assad-Baath massacre in 1982 at Hama, where 20,000 Muslims were killed. In Gaza, fundamentalists have to deal with the prospect of a war with the Israeli Defense Forces.

With about 4 million Muslims in Europe, where mosques were built by the Saudis in the hopes of eliminating Muslim radicalism, fundamentalist preachers and neo-Marxist teachers churn out propaganda that is anti-Western, anti-Christian and anti-Saudi.

The fundamentalist wave is real and on the rise. It should not be surprising to see at least one particularly vulnerable Arab regime succumb to its political, social or terrorist pressure soon. The creation of a fundamentalist Muslim state is the ultimate aim—of both the "radicals" and the "moderates."

*"To whatever extent it may ultimately prevail in the [Islamic world], Islamic fundamentalism is a vital and growing force."*

# The West Should Accept the Spread of Islamic Fundamentalism

Moorhead Kennedy

The February 1993 bombing of the World Trade Center in New York City raised alarms for some that the worldwide growth of fundamentalist Islam would unite the Middle East in opposition to the West. In the following viewpoint, Moorhead Kennedy argues that Islamic fundamentalism is growing as a necessary alternative to the Arab nationalism—an imitation of Western nationalism—that failed to spur economic and political development in the Middle East. Kennedy advises that the West accommodate itself with Islamic fundamentalism. Kennedy, a former foreign service officer held hostage in Iran from 1979 to 1981, is president of Moorhead Kennedy Associates, Inc., which trains executives to do business with other cultures.

As you read, consider the following questions:

1. How does Islam differ from Christianity, according to the author?
2. What was Arab nationalism's low point, according to Kennedy? What, in his words, was Islamic fundamentalism's response?
3. What is Islamic fundamentalism's positive side, according to Kennedy?

Moorhead Kennedy, "Why Fear Fundamentalism?" *Los Angeles Times*, March 15, 1993. Reprinted by permission of the author.

"The West does not want independence based on Islamic thoughts for Islamic countries," Iranian President Hashemi Rafsanjani said in 1993. "They are confronting an important movement, and they do not like it." Indeed, finding a kind word about Islamic fundamentalism is not easy. An Op-Ed piece in the *New York Times* characterized this important movement as "rage, religious fury, holy war, and political hypocrisy"—and that was before the February 1993 explosion at the World Trade Center attributed to Muslim fundamentalists.

Quite apart from the profound injustice done to millions of law-abiding Muslims, equating Islamic fundamentalism with terrorism closes minds at a time when the American public badly needs to understand this important world movement.

To whatever extent it may ultimately prevail in the vast area stretching from Morocco to Mindanao in the Philippines, and in several former Soviet republics, Islamic fundamentalism is a vital and growing force. It has great appeal for young people, notably Palestinian and Jordanian university students. A version of it is increasingly visible and influential in our own African-American community. In its various manifestations, Islam will become, before long, the second-largest American religious grouping, after Christianity and ahead of Judaism.

## Understanding Islamic Fundamentalism

Americans will have to come to terms with Islamic fundamentalism. Where should we start?

First, we need to understand that Islam is not only a faith, like Christianity. It is also a political system, a legal system and a way of life. Even the Israelis, normally astute about developments in the Arab world, missed this reality. Even as they closed universities in the occupied territories, they encouraged seminary study, hoping to turn the minds of their subject people away from Arab nationalism toward the peaceful ways of religion.

Instead they got Hamas, championing the liberation of Palestine not for reasons of Arab nationalism, but for Islam. The expulsion of 432 Hamas followers to no-man's-land on the Lebanese border in December 1992 became Israel's most acute diplomatic embarrassment of recent years.

In Hamas, Israel is faced with an uncompromising maximalist approach, that of total liberation of the sacred land of Palestine as demanded by God, who will repay martyrs for this cause with everlasting life. In contrast to a Western-style movement like the Palestine Liberation Organization, which is willing to compromise, Islamic fundamentalism is a formidable opponent. The difference between the PLO's approach and that of the fundamentalists has to do with how each views the West.

Starting from a position, real and perceived, of inferiority, the

Middle East has been trying to come to terms with the West. Its coping device was imitation, perhaps most evident in Western-style nationalism and the evolution of national states, complete with ideologies, parliaments, anthems and flags. Imitative Arab nationalism found its culmination in Gamal Abdel Nasser, its low point in Nasser's humiliating defeat by Israel in 1967.

---

### Western Paranoia About Islam

Since the bombing of the World Trade Center, Americans have begun to absorb European paranoia about Islam, perceived as a force of darkness hovering over a virtuous Christian civilization. It is ironic that the West should increasingly fear Islam when daily the Muslims are reminded of their own weakness. "Islam has bloody borders," Samuel P. Huntington says. But in all conflicts between Muslims and pro-Western forces, the Muslims are losing, and losing badly, whether they be Azeris, Palestinians, Iraqis, Iranians or Bosnian Muslims. With so much disunity, the Islamic world is not about to coalesce into a single force.

Kishore Mahbubani, *Foreign Affairs*, September/October 1993.

---

A great many Arabs concluded that they had been following the wrong model. They could never be successful trying to be what they were not. Similarly, in 1979, in Iran, the westernizing Shah was overthrown. "We no longer have to be imitation Americans," the Islamic revolutionaries cried. "We can be ourselves." The basic question, "Who am I?" is answered by many in Muslim countries through a return to their Islamic roots.

### Islam and the West

Why the deep anger, the rage, directed against the United States? Because our culture, pervasive and appealing, is what the fundamentalists are trying to expel from deep within themselves and their societies. Yet, as they reject our culture, they are forced to recognize its superiority in many important respects. Their continuing dependence on it deepens their anger. They rail against our culture's recreational sex, widespread alcoholism and drug abuse as "Western decadence"; by contrast, they hold themselves to be freshly inspired to decency.

Islamic fundamentalism has its own very positive side. Its medical clinics in the poorest parts of Cairo, for example, evidencing in a practical way the duty of Muslims to care for the poor, are a source of popularity and respect.

Islamic law, the Sharia, or "path to salvation," is the sum of duties required by God of human beings, with respect not only to God, but also to one's fellows. It is the infusion of divine purpose into human relationships that distinguishes Islamic law from the secular jurisprudence of Western countries. The restoration of the Sharia as the operating national legal code is a cardinal feature of Islamic fundamentalism.

At Harvard Law School, I analyzed the differences between the Islamic law of inheritance and that of Massachusetts. Islamic law struck me as far more humane, for example in its recognition of family relationships and its provisions for aging parents.

With its main tenets fixed in the 10th Century, the Sharia is inadequate for many of the needs of modern society. As a social statement of ethical principle, however, the Sharia is hard to surpass.

How, then, can the United States come to terms with this vital and important movement? Let me suggest four initial steps:

- *Work hard on the flash points.* For example, the longer the Arab-Israeli peace process is delayed, the stronger will be the influence of the extremists. Future flash points should be identified and worked on; don't overlook the largely Muslim former Soviet republics.
- *Understand motives.* The key to the battle against terrorism is understanding. Unless we understand the reasons for anger against the United States on the part of an extremist fringe, we cannot effectively anticipate and counter the actions they are likely to take. Failure in this battle extends beyond the loss of life and property; it also poisons the domestic atmosphere with heightened discrimination and threats against the rights of a significant minority.
- *Set a better example.* The more uncaring and corrupt our own society, including the political process, appears to be, the more we strengthen that side of Islamic fundamentalism that most resents us. Domestic reforms make effective propaganda abroad.
- *Take it seriously.* Evidence greater understanding and sympathy for fundamentalism's more praiseworthy goals. Identify what unites our better sides.

Upon my return from hostage captivity in Iran, a senior State Department official remarked, "Who would ever have thought that all this could have happened because of religion?" The same disdainful attitude continues to prevail in Washington. Has anyone there thought to publish a comparison between the better goals of the Islamic fundamentalists and those expressed in President Clinton's inaugural speech?

Rafsanjani is calling upon the West to grow up, to stop being afraid of what we are unwilling to understand, to accord to others rights that we claim for ourselves and our allies and to have the courage to make common cause even with those whose means appear unfamiliar, bizarre or even (possibly) dangerous.

# Periodical Bibliography

The following articles have been selected to supplement the diverse views presented in this chapter.

| | |
|---|---|
| Shirin Akiner | "On Its Own: Islam in Post-Soviet Central Asia," *Harvard International Review*, Spring 1993. Available from PO Box 401, Cambridge, MA 02238. |
| Jeffrey Bartholet | "A Wave of Terror All Their Own," *Newsweek*, August 30, 1993. |
| Patrick Clawson and Daniel Pipes | "Ambitious Iran, Troubled Neighbors," *Foreign Affairs*, special issue: *America and the World*, 1993. |
| John L. Esposito | "The Political Leverage of Islam," *The Christian Century*, April 10, 1991. |
| Michael M.J. Fischer | "Is Islam the Odd-Civilization Out?" *New Perspectives Quarterly*, Spring 1992. |
| Patrick D. Gaffney | "Popular Islam," *The Annals of the American Academy of Political and Social Science*, November 1992. |
| Dilip Hiro | "Islamist Strengths and Weaknesses in Central Asia," *Middle East International*, February 5, 1993. Available from 1700 17th St. NW, #306, Washington, DC 20009. |
| Stephen Hubbell | "True Belief's Grim Patience," *The Nation*, September 28, 1992. |
| Robert D. Kaplan | "Eaten from Within," *The Atlantic Monthly*, November 1994. |
| Kanan Makiya | "Who Am I?" *Dissent*, Spring 1993. |
| Judith Miller | "Faces of Fundamentalism," *Foreign Affairs*, November/December 1994. |
| Edward Mortimer | "New 'Ism' in the East," *World Monitor*, September 1992. |
| Caryle Murphy | "Egypt: An Uneasy Portent of Change," *Current History*, February 1994. |
| Martha Brill Olcott | "Central Asia's Islamic Awakening," *Current History*, April 1994. |
| Stanley Reed | "The Battle for Egypt," *Foreign Affairs*, September/October 1993. |
| Edward W. Said | "The Phony Islamic Threat," *The New York Times Magazine*, November 21, 1993. |
| Lamin Sanneh | "Muslim-Christian Encounters: Governments Under God," *The Christian Century*, December 2, 1992. |

# Glossary

*abd*  Servant or slave.

*adl*  Social justice.

**Allah**  God.

*Allahu Akbar*  "Allah is Most Great."

**ayatollah**  A high-ranking religious leader among **Shia** Muslims.

**Baath**  "Renaissance"; the name of the political party that led the anticolonialist revolution in Saudi Arabia and Iraq, espousing secular, socialist prescriptions and **pan-Arab** ideology.

*bazaaris*  Refers to merchants, who make up a separate economic class in Iranian society.

*chador*  The covering worn by women in Iran, consisting of a dark cloth that covers the head and body and conceals the figure.

*Dar al-Harb*  Literally, "House of War"; the non-Muslim world that is deemed hostile to **Islam**.

*Dar al-Islam*  Literally, "House of Islam"; the Islamic world.

*Dawa*  Literally, "call"; signifies an invitation to join the faith of **Islam** or the spreading of the message of **Islam**.

*dhimmi*  A non-Muslim living in an Islamic community.

*faqih*  A legal expert in Islamic jurisprudence.

*fatwa*  An interpretation of religious law issued by an authoritative scholar or leader.

*fiqh*  Islamic jurisprudence.

*gamaa/jamaa*  (plural: *gamaat/jamaat*) Literally, "society" or "group"; *al-Gamaa al-Islamiyya* is the name adopted by a number of political Islamic groups and movements.

**Hadith**  Traditions or sayings attributed to Muhammad in the writings of his contemporaries and referred to for authoritative precedent in interpreting the **Quran**.

**hajj**  The pilgrimage to Mecca that is one of the pillars of the Islamic faith; all who are able are required to make the pilgrimage at least once in their lifetime.

**Hezbollah**  Literally, "Party of Allah" (*hizb* = party); an Islamic political party in Lebanon that has been accused of terrorism.

*hijab*  A veil that fully covers the hair, or, more broadly, the modest dress that is required of Muslim women by the *sharia*.

*Hijra*  Migration; refers mainly to the migration of Muhammad and his followers from Mecca to Medina.

*huddud*  Literally, "limits"; the limits of acceptable behavior; the specific punishments designated under *sharia* for specific crimes, such as intoxication, theft, adultery, and apostasy (disavowing the faith).

*ijma*  Consensus of opinion among the community or the *ulama*.

*ijtihad*  Independent judgment on religious matters or principles of Islamic jurisprudence that are not specifically outlined in the **Quran**.

**imam**  Religious or political leader particularly among **Shia**.

286

**Islam**   Submission to God and to God's message revealed to Muhammad; the religion of **Muslims**.

*jahili*   Ignorant; the state of the world before Islam.

**jihad**   Struggle; can be any struggle, from a personal striving to fulfill religious responsibilities to a holy war undertaken for the defense of **Islam**.

*khalifah*   (often caliph) Literally, "successor" to Muhammad; the viceregent or political leader of the Muslim state.

*majlis*   Council.

*Majlis-i shura*   Consultative council; parliament.

*masjid*   A mosque, or place of worship for Muslims. *Mosque* is a word of French origin.

**mujahedeen**   (singular: *mujahed*) Persons who wage **jihad**.

*mujtahid*   A person who exercises *ijtihad*.

*mushrik*   A polytheist, or person who does not believe there is only one God.

**Muslim**   A person who submits to God by following **Islam**.

*al-Nahda*   "Renaissance"; the name of an Islamic political party in Tunisia.

*niqab*   Garments worn by Muslim women that include a face covering and gloves.

**pan-Arabism** A movement seeking to unite the Arab nations of the Middle East and North Africa.

*purdah*   A Persian word denoting the modest dress of women and the separation of women from men.

*Qawm*   People or nation.

**Quran**   (often Koran) Literally, "the recitation"; the text of Muhammad's revelations and prophecies; the Holy Book of the Islamic faith.

*al-Sawa al-Islamia*   The "Islamic Awakening"; the term sometimes used to refer to the political Islam phenomenon.

*sharia*   Literally, "the way"; the Islamic legal code as stipulated in the **Quran** and **Hadith**.

**Shia/Shiite**   Literally, "party" or "sect," specifically referring to the "party of Ali"; a Muslim who follows Ali (the cousin and fourth successor of Muhammad), who was deposed as leader of Muhammad's followers.

*shura*   Consultation; the duty of a leader to seek the consultation of religious experts or the people.

**Sunna/Sunni**   Literally, "path"; following the example of Muhammad set out in the **Quran** and **Hadith**; refers to the majority Muslim denomination (as differentiated from **Shia**).

*surah*   Chapter of the **Quran**.

*takfir*   Excommunication; to pronounce someone an infidel.

*tawhid*   Unity; belief in the oneness of **Allah**, signifying monotheism.

*turath*   Cultural heritage.

*ulama*   (singular: *alim*) Religious scholars, leaders, and experts.

*ummah*   Community; specifically the community of Muslims.

*Wahhabi*   A particularly strict (puritanical) Islamic movement that predominates in Saudi Arabia.

# For Further Discussion

## Chapter 1

1. Mary-Jane Deeb describes militant Islamic groups as being committed "to achieving their goals not in the distant future but in the present" and as being willing "to maneuver tactically to achieve their goals." What other characteristics does she ascribe to these groups? How does her characterization contrast with that of Ghassan Salamé?

2. Ghassan Salamé says that the Islamic movements "intend to pressure governments to gradually implement the Islamist program before directly challenging a regime's rule." How does Rabia Bekkar's description of Algeria's Islamic Salvation Front compare with Salamé's description of Islamic movements? How does her attitude toward the Islamic movement contrast with Salamé's?

3. Julie Flint argues that Sudan is being subjected to an Islamic dictatorship through repression and terror. How does Hassan al-Turabi respond to such charges? How does Flint describe al-Turabi's role in the government of Sudan? Which argument do you find more convincing, and why?

## Chapter 2

1. Karima Bennoune argues that because Algeria's Islamic Salvation Front has carried out violence against women while struggling for power, one would expect the brutality to increase once they come to power. How does this assumption contrast with the situation in Iran described by Nesta Ramazani? Based on these two viewpoints, do you think Islam is inherently repressive of women? Explain your answer.

2. Nawal el-Saadawi describes her work with a feminist organization in Egypt. According to Sherifa Zuhur, what is the attitude of younger Egyptian women involved with the Islamic movement toward these feminist organizations? How are el-Saadawi's affiliations and experiences reflected in her viewpoint? Which of the two women's arguments do you find more convincing, and why?

## Chapter 3

1. Bernard Lewis argues that liberal democracy is a concept that arose from specific historical conditions unique to the West, and since Muslim countries do not share this history, it is more difficult for democracy to develop there. What do

John O. Voll and John L. Esposito say about the historical development of democracy in the West? How do they view the conditions for democracy in the Muslim world? Which interpretation of the conditions for democracy seems more credible, in your opinion? Explain.

2. Robin Wright says of Algeria's Islamic Salvation Front, following the military coup that overturned its election victory, "the energetic Islamists offered a legitimate and familiar alternative, if not a very detailed program" for governing Algeria. Would Martin Kramer agree that the Islamic group's program was "not very detailed"? Explain.

3. Asád AbuKhalil argues that the Quran "has very little to say about matters of government." He rejects what he calls "the myth of 'Islamic answers to all of today's problems.'" How does the concept of *ijtihad* defined by Greg Noakes contrast with AbuKhalil's argument?

## Chapter 4

1. Steven Emerson contends that "under the ideology of militant Islamic fundamentalists, . . . the West by its very existence is deemed hostile." What do you think Michael Jansen's response would be to this statement?

2. Mohammad Mohaddessin is a member of an exiled group that seeks to overthrow the current Iranian government. Sayyed Fadlallah is considered the spiritual leader of the Shiite Muslim Hezbollah group in Lebanon. How are their affiliations reflected in their arguments?

## Chapter 5

1. Leon T. Hadar describes "the process of creating a monolithic threat" that is occurring in relations between the West and Islam. Could Daniel Pipes's viewpoint be seen as an example of this process? Explain.

2. Samuel P. Huntington argues that in international relations "states from different civilizations compete for relative military and economic power . . . and competitively promote their particular political and religious values." How does this scenario for international relations compare and contrast to Rachid Gannouchi's two possibilities for future relations between the West and Islam? Which possibility do you think is more likely? Why?

3. R. Scott Appleby describes the governments of the Middle East as "rulers whose power is based exclusively on military might, bereft of authenticating ideologies to bolster their sag-

ging regimes." How does Jonathan S. Paris describe these governments? How does his prescription for U.S. policy differ from Appleby's? In your opinion, which prescription is a better course for the United States? Why?

## Chapter 6

1. Yossef Bodansky cites Iran's buildup of weapons as evidence that it intends to expand its influence and promote Islam in other countries. What does Shireen T. Hunter say is the purpose of Iran's weapons buildup? In your opinion, does what she says effectively counter Bodansky's argument?

2. Mark Juergensmeyer argues that Egypt has a long tradition of nationalism that invokes Islam. How does this contrast with Michael Collins Dunn's description of Egypt's political and societal tradition? In your experience, does the U.S. tradition of nationalism invoke religion? Explain.

# Organizations to Contact

The editors have compiled the following list of organizations concerned with the issues debated in this book. The descriptions are derived from materials provided by the organizations. All have publications or information available for interested readers. The list was compiled on the date of publication of the present volume; names, addresses, and phone numbers may change. Be aware that many organizations take several weeks or longer to respond to inquiries, so allow as much time as possible.

**Alhambra Productions**
467 Saratoga Ave., Suite 460
San Jose, CA 95129
(408) 244-1402

This company produces and distributes educational books, tapes, and videos of contemporary interpretations of Islamic teachings. Among the titles it offers are *Can the West Learn from Islam?* and *Womanhood: An Islamic Perspective.*

**American-Arab Anti-Discrimination Committee**
4201 Connecticut Ave. NW, Suite 500
Washington, DC 20008
(202) 244-2990

This organization fights anti-Arab stereotyping in the media and discrimination and hate crimes against Arab-Americans. It publishes a series of issue papers and a number of books, including the 1991 *Report on Anti-Arab Hate Crimes.*

**American Muslim Council (AMC)**
1212 New York Ave. NW, Suite 525
Washington, DC 20005
(202) 789-2262

This nonprofit organization was established to identify and oppose discrimination against Muslims and other minorities and to raise the level of social and political awareness and involvement of Muslims in the United States. It publishes the monthly newsletter *AMC Report* and numerous pamphlets and monographs.

**AMIDEAST**
1100 17th St. NW
Washington, DC 20036
(202) 785-0022

AMIDEAST promotes understanding and cooperation between Americans and the people of the Middle East and North Africa through education and development programs. It publishes a number of books for all age groups, including *Islam: A Primer.*

**Arab World and Islamic Resources and School Services (AWAIR)**
2095 Rose St., Suite 4
Berkeley, CA 94709
(510) 704-0517

AWAIR provides materials and services for educators teaching about the Arab World and about Islam at the precollege level. It publishes many books and videos, including *The Arab World Notebook, Middle Eastern Muslim Women Speak*, and *Islam*.

**Council on American-Islamic Relations (CAIR)**
1511 K St. NW, Suite 807
Washington, DC 20005
(202) 638-6340

CAIR is a nonprofit membership organization dedicated to presenting an Islamic perspective on public policy issues and to challenging the misrepresentation of Islam and Muslims. It fights discrimination against Muslims in America and lobbies political leaders on issues related to Islam and Muslims. Its publications include the quarterly newsletter *CAIR News* as well as periodic *Action Alerts*.

**International Institute of Islamic Thought/Association of Muslim Social Scientists**
555 Grove St.
Herndon, VA 22070
(703) 471-1133

This nonprofit academic research facility promotes and coordinates research and related activities in Islamic philosophy, the humanities, and social sciences. It publishes numerous books in both Arabic and English as well as the quarterly *American Journal of Islamic Social Science* and the *Muslim World Book Review*.

**Islamic Circle of North America (ICNA)**
166-26 89th Ave.
Jamaica, NY 11432
(718) 658-1199

ICNA works to propagate Islam as a way of life and to establish an Islamic system in North America. It maintains a charitable relief organization and publishes numerous pamphlets in its Islamic Da'wah series as well as the monthly magazine the *Message*.

**Islamic Information Center of America (IICA)**
Box 4052
Des Plaines, IL 60016
(708) 541-8141

IICA is a nonprofit organization that provides information about Islam to Muslims, the general public, and the media. It publishes and distributes a number of pamphlets and a monthly newsletter, the *Invitation*.

**Islamic Texts Society**
Mockingbird Valley
Louisville, KY 40207
(502) 897-3641

This organization publishes and sells English translations of works of importance to the faith and culture of Islam, with the aim of promoting a greater understanding of Islam. Among the titles it offers is *Understanding Islam and the Muslims*.

**Middle East Council**
**Foreign Policy Research Institute**
3615 Chestnut St.
Philadelphia, PA 19104
(215) 382-0685

This nonprofit organization is dedicated to promoting American interests and values in the Middle East through education, research, and publishing on American foreign policy. It publishes a bimonthly bulletin, *Peacefacts*, as well as numerous books.

**Middle East Institute**
1761 N St. NW
Washington, DC 20036-2882
(202) 785-1141

The institute's charter mission is to promote better understanding of Middle Eastern cultures, languages, religions, and politics. It publishes numerous books, papers, audiotapes, and videos as well as the quarterly *Middle East Journal*. It also maintains an Educational Outreach Department to give teachers and students of all grade levels advice on resources.

**Middle East Outreach Council**
University of Chicago
5828 University Ave.
Chicago, IL 60637
(312) 702-8298

This nonprofit, nonpolitical organization seeks to increase public knowledge about the lands, cultures, and peoples of the Middle East through workshops, seminars, and educational materials. It publishes the *Middle East Outreach Council Newsletter* three times a year.

**Middle East Policy Council**
1730 M St. NW, Suite 512
Washington, DC 20036
(202) 296-6767

The purpose of this nonprofit organization is to contribute to an understanding of current issues in U.S. relations with countries of the Middle East. It publishes the quarterly journal *Middle East Policy* as well as special reports and books.

## Middle East Research and Information Project (MERIP)

1500 Massachusetts Ave. NW, Suite 119
Washington, DC 20005
(202) 223-3677
fax: (202) 223 3604

MERIP's mission is to educate the public about the contemporary Middle East, with particular emphasis on U.S. policy, human rights, and social justice issues. It publishes the bimonthly *Middle East Report*.

## Middle East Studies Association

University of Arizona
1232 N. Cherry Ave.
Tucson, AZ 85721
(602) 321-7752

This professional academic association of scholars on the Middle East focuses particularly on the rise of Islam. It publishes the quarterly *International Journal of Middle East Studies* and runs a project for the evaluation of textbooks for coverage of the Middle East.

## Muslim Public Affairs Council (MPAC)

3010 Wilshire Blvd., Suite 217
Los Angeles, CA 90010
(213) 383-3443

MPAC is a nonprofit, public service agency that strives to disseminate accurate information about Muslims and achieve cooperation between various communities on the basis of shared values such as peace, justice, freedom, and dignity. It publishes and distributes a number of reports on issues of concern to the Muslim community, such as U.S. foreign relations and human rights policy. It is scheduled to begin publishing a newsletter under the title *Impact*.

## National Council on Islamic Affairs/
## American-Arab Relations Committee

230 East 44th St., Suite 3F
New York, NY 10017
(212) 972-0460

This group organizes demonstrations and lobbies to improve American-Arab relations, particularly on the issues of Bosnia and Palestine. It publishes a bimonthly newsletter, *Islam in America*.

## The New School

PO Box 10520
Oakland, CA 94610-9991
(510) 465-9709

This nonprofit educational organization is "committed to learning for people of all backgrounds and ages in their development as thoughtful, compassionate, productive members of society." It publishes the monthly newsletter *Synapse*.

**United Association for Studies and Research**
PO Box 1210
Annandale, VA 22003-1210
(703) 750-9011

This nonprofit organization examines the causes of conflict in the Middle East and North Africa, the political trends that shape the region's future, and the relationship of the region to more technologically advanced nations. It publishes *Islam Under Siege* and *The Middle East: Politics and Development*, two series of occasional papers on current topics.

**Washington Institute for Near East Policy**
1828 L St. NW
Washington, DC 20036
(202) 452-0650

The institute is an independent, nonprofit research organization that provides information and analysis on the Middle East and U.S. policy in the region. It publishes numerous books, periodic monographs, and reports on regional politics, security, and economics, including *Hezbollah's Vision of the West, Hamas: The Fundamentalist Challenge to the PLO, Democracy and Arab Political Culture, Iran's Challenge to the West, Radical Middle East States and U.S. Policy,* and *Democracy in the Middle East: Defining the Challenge.*

# Bibliography of Books

| | |
|---|---|
| Ervand Abrahamian | *Khomeinism.* Berkeley and Los Angeles: University of California Press, 1993. |
| Lila Abu-Lughod | *Writing Women's Worlds: Bedouin Stories.* Berkeley and Los Angeles: University of California Press, 1992. |
| Akbar S. Ahmed | *Postmodernism and Islam: Predicament and Promise.* New York: Routledge, 1992. |
| Leila Ahmed | *Women and Gender in Islam: Historical Roots of a Modern Debate.* New Haven: Yale University Press, 1992. |
| R. Scott Appleby | *Religious Fundamentalisms and Global Conflict.* New York: Foreign Policy Association, 1994. |
| Nazih Ayubi | *Political Islam: Religion and Politics in the Arab World.* New York: Routledge, 1990. |
| Aziz al-Azmeh | *Islams and Modernities.* New York: Verso, 1993. |
| Donna Lee Bowen and Evelyn A. Early | *Everyday Life in the Muslim Middle East.* Blooming-ton: Indiana University Press, 1993. |
| Richard W. Bulliet | *Islam: The View from the Edge.* New York: Columbia University Press, 1994. |
| François Burgat | *The Islamic Movement in North Africa.* Austin: University of Texas Press, 1993. |
| John P. Entelis and Phillip C. Naylor | *State and Society in Algeria.* Boulder, CO: Westview Press, 1992. |
| John L. Esposito | *The Islamic Threat: Myth or Reality?* New York: Oxford University Press, 1992. |
| Michael M.J. Fischer and Mehdi Abedi | *Debating Muslims: Cultural Dialogues in Postmodernity and Tradition.* Madison: University of Wisconsin Press, 1990. |
| Carolyn Fluehr-Lobban | *Islamic Society in Practice.* Gainesville: University Press of Florida, 1994. |
| Jan Goodwin | *Price of Honor: Muslim Women Lift the Veil of Silence of the Islamic World.* Boston: Little, Brown, 1994. |
| Yvonne Y. Haddad, John O. Voll, and John L. Esposito | *The Contemporary Islamic Revival: A Critical Survey and Bibliography.* Westport, CT: Greenwood Press, 1991. |

Suzanne Haneef — *What Everyone Should Know About Islam and Muslims*. Des Plaines, IL: Library of Islam, 1993.

Dilip Hiro — *Holy Wars: The Rise of Islamic Fundamentalism*. New York: Routledge, 1989.

Shireen T. Hunter — *Iran and the World: Continuity in a Revolutionary Decade*. Bloomington: Indiana University Press, 1990.

Raphael Israeli — *Muslim Fundamentalism in Israel*. London: Brassey's, 1993.

Deniz Kandiyoti — *Women, Islam and the State*. Philadelphia: Temple University Press, 1990.

Nikki R. Keddie and Beth Baron — *Women in Middle Eastern History: Shifting Boundaries in Sex and Gender*. New Haven: Yale University Press, 1992.

John Kelsay and James Turner Johnson — *Just War and Jihad: Historical and Theoretical Perspectives on War and Peace in Western and Islamic Traditions*. Contributions to the Study of Religion, no. 28. Westport, CT: Greenwood Press, 1991.

Geoffrey Kemp — *Forever Enemies? America and the Islamic Republic of Iran*. Washington: Carnegie Endowment for International Peace, 1993.

Gilles Kepel — *Muslim Extremism in Egypt: The Prophet and Pharaoh*. Berkeley and Los Angeles: University of California Press, 1993.

Gilles Kepel — *The Revenge of God: The Resurgence of Islam, Christianity, and Judaism in the Modern World*. University Park: Pennsylvania State University Press, 1994.

Martin Kramer — *Political Islam*. Beverly Hills, CA: Sage Publications, 1980.

Bruce B. Lawrence — *Defenders of God: The Fundamentalist Revolt Against the Modern Age*. London: I.B. Tauris, 1990.

Bernard Lewis — *Islam and the West*. New York: Oxford University Press, 1993.

Kanan Makiya — *Cruelty and Silence: War, Tyranny, Uprising, and the Arab World*. New York: Norton, 1993.

Martin E. Marty and R. Scott Appleby — *The Fundamentalism Project*. 3 vols. Chicago: University of Chicago Press, 1991-93.

Martin E. Marty and R. Scott Appleby — *The Glory and the Power: The Fundamentalist Challenge to the Modern World*. Boston: Beacon Press, 1992.

| | |
|---|---|
| Ann Elizabeth Mayer | *Islam and Human Rights: Tradition and Politics.* Boulder, CO: Westview Press, 1991. |
| Fatima Mernissi | *Islam and Democracy: Fear of the Modern World.* Reading, MA: Addison-Wesley, 1992. |
| Fatima Mernissi | *The Veil and the Male Elite: A Feminist Interpretation of Women's Rights in Islam.* Reading, MA: Addison-Wesley, 1991. |
| Valentine M. Moghadam | *Modernizing Women: Gender and Social Change in the Middle East.* Boulder, CO: Lynne Rienner, 1993. |
| Jamal J. Nasir | *The Status of Women Under Islamic Law.* London: Graham and Trotman, 1990. |
| Daniel Pipes | *In the Path of God: Islam and Political Power.* New York: Basic Books, 1983. |
| James Piscatori | *Islamic Fundamentalisms and the Gulf Crisis.* Chicago: American Academy of Arts and Sciences, 1991. |
| David Pryce-Jones | *At War with Modernity: Islam's Challenge to the West.* London: Alliance Publishers for the Institute for European Defence and Strategic Studies, 1992. |
| Martin Riesebrodt | *Pious Passion: The Emergence of Modern Fundamentalism in the United States and Iran.* Berkeley and Los Angeles: University of California Press, 1993. |
| Salman Rushdie | *The Satanic Verses.* New York: Viking, 1989. |
| Edward W. Said | *Culture and Imperialism.* New York: Knopf, 1993. |
| Timothy D. Sisk | *Islam and Democracy: Religion, Politics, and Power in the Middle East.* Washington: United States Institute of Peace, 1992. |
| Emmanuel Sivan | *Radical Islam: Medieval Theology and Modern Politics.* New Haven: Yale University Press, 1990. |
| Bassam Tibi | *Islam and the Cultural Accommodation of Social Change.* Boulder, CO: Westview Press, 1990. |
| Judith E. Tucker | *Arab Women: Old Boundaries, New Frontiers.* Bloomington: Indiana University Press, 1993. |
| E. van Donzel | *The Encyclopaedia of Islam.* New York: Brill, 1993. |
| John O. Voll | *Islam, Continuity and Change in the Modern World.* Boulder, CO: Westview Press, 1982. |

| | |
|---|---|
| John O. Voll | *Sudan: State and Society in Crisis*. Bloomington: Indiana University Press, 1991. |
| Robin Wright | *Flashpoints: Promise and Peril in a New World Order*. New York: Knopf, 1991. |
| Fareeha Zafar | *Finding Our Way: Women in Pakistan*. London: Zed, 1994. |
| Sami Zubaida | *Islam, the People and the State: Political Ideas and Movements in the Middle East*. London: I.B. Tauris, 1993. |
| Sherifa Zuhur | *Revealing Reveiling: Islamist Gender Ideology in Contemporary Egypt*. Albany: State University of New York Press, 1992. |

# Index

and United States, 202, 248, 282, 284
women's roles, 72, 75
Rahman, Omar Abd al-, 33, 159-60,
269, 274, 275
Ramadan, 150
Ramazani, Nesta, 72
rape, 65, 91
Reed, Stanley, 279
religion
and basic human divisions, 265
causes conflicts, 83, 208-10
changing roles of, 83, 148-49, 203
and discrimination, 209
as force for change, 122-23
fundamentalist movements, 208
and history of rebellions, 260
Islamic understanding of, 179
keeps world ignorant, 148
and morally sanctioned killing, 266
as oppressive, 83
revival of, 208
as revolutionary, 83, 209
separation of church and state, 159
as social phenomenon, 83
*Risalat* (prophethood), 113, 115-16
Rodman, Peter W., 233
Rushdie, Salmon, 32, 191
and apostasy, 52, 174
death sentence for, 130-31, 173-74
*Satanic Verses*, 32

Saadawi, Nawal el-, 80
Sadat, Anwar el-
assassination of, 27, 29, 130, 262,
264, 265, 275
and Muslim Brotherhood, 263-64,
279
political programs of, 81, 85, 264
Said, Edward W., 130, 273
Salamé, Ghassan, 25
*Satanic Verses* (Rushdie), 32
Saudi Arabia
dependence on West, 137-38, 142,
201, 236
exploits fear of Islam, 201-202
government in, 145
human rights in, 33
and Iran, 200
Mecca, 173, 200
secularism
Islamic government needs, 139-46
con, 147-53
Islam opposes, 25-31, 35, 46-47, 49,
262, 273, 278-79
as target of Islamic terrorists, 35
Serbia, and Muslims, 165-66, 216-17
Shah Mohammad Reza Pahlavi
Family Protection Law, 74

overthrow of, 27, 72, 142, 283
and United States, 28, 48, 142, 193,
234
women's rights under, 74, 75
*shari'a* (Islamic law)
and abuse of civil rights, 51
in Algerian law, 21, 23
as basis for government, 134-35, 226
definition of, 179, 283
and Egyptian law, 29, 87
and gender roles, 80
in Mauritanian legislation, 29
and non-Muslims, 50-51, 57, 134
offers protection to people, 48-49
in Pakistani legislation, 29
and penal code, 225
and punishment, 51-52
secular laws should replace, 146
in Sudan, 46, 48-49
and Universal Declaration of
Human Rights, 134
variations of, 51
and women's roles, 68, 91
Sharjah, blasphemy sentences in, 33,
35
*shura* (consultation)
and democracy, 105, 110, 114, 151
and FIS, 22
and fundamentalists, 135
in Iran, 184
in Qur'an, 109, 116-17, 142, 145
*Sisters' Literary and Artistic
Proclamation*, 77
Socialist Forces Front, 124
Somalia, U.S. intervention in, 165
Soviet Union, collapse of, 121-22,
144, 244, 251
Stockton, Ronald R., 49
Strait of Hormuz, Iran's control of,
248-49
Sudan
changing political status, 52-53
civil war in, 56-60, 166
coup in, 18, 29, 244
democracy in, 51, 56
foreign relations of, 53-54
government in, 135, 228, 261
stifles opposition, 56-59
human rights abuses in, 53, 56-59,
226
and Iran, 53, 244-45
Islam helps development in, 46-54
military in, 57, 60
National Islamic Front (NIF) in, 46,
55-57, 235
revolution in, 55, 58, 180-81, 245,
261
security forces in, 57

309